THE TOWNS OF TOMPKINS COUNTY

Atwater's

To King Ferry

To Genoa

CAYUGA COUNTY

Lake Ridge

North Lansing

West Groton Road

West Groton

Lake Ridge Point

Milliken Road

341B

Lansing Station

Lake Ridge Road

LANSING

Salmon Creek

Locke Creek

Auburn Road

Benson Corners

To Interlaken

SENECA COUNTY

Ludlowville

84

Peruville Road

Trumansburg Village

TAUGHANNOCK FALLS STATE PARK

Taughannock Point

Myers Point

Myers

South Lansing

34

West Dryden Road

Trumansburg Creek

Halseyville

Willow Creek

89

Willow Point

Triphammer Road

Taughannock Falls

Warren Road

227

ULYSSES

Jacksonville

Salmon Creek

Waterburg

Trumansburg Road

Lansing Village

TOMPKINS COUNTY AIRPORT

ORNITHOLOGY LABORATORY

13

Fall Creek

Perry City Road

Park Pond

Halseyville Road

McKinneys

TOMPKINS COMMUNITY HOSPITAL

Hayts Road

Cayuga Heights Village

366

Hayt Corner

96

STEWART PARK

Varna

To Mecklenburg

Millers Corners

Applegate Corners

79

ALLAN H. TREMAN STATE MARINE PARK

Mecklenburg Road

Beebe Lake

Forest Home

CORNELL UNIVERSITY

Cascadilla Creek

ENFIELD

Enfield

City of Ithaca

*

Hibbard Corner Ellis Hollow

ITHACA

Bostwick Road

Enfield Creek

*

ITHACA COLLEGE

Bostwick Corners

327

ROBERT H. TREMAN STATE PARK

Buttermilk Falls

BUTTERMILK FALLS STATE PARK

Coddington Road

Slaterville Road

Bese

Lake Treman

SCHUYLER COUNTY

Trumbull Corners

Millard Hill Road

West Danby Road

Danby Road

Miller Road East

Connecticut Hill Road

Trumbull Cors. Rd.

Covered Bridge

Nina

Buttermilk Creek

Miller Road West

CONNECTICUT HILL WILDLIFE MANAGEMENT AREA

Sebring Road

Elmira Road

Newfield

13

Newfield Depot Road

Stratton

Cayuga Inlet

96B

Danby

Jennings Pond

DANBY

To Elmira

NEWFIELD

West Danby

34

96

South Danby

To C

ARNOT FOREST

DANBY STATE FOREST

South Danby Road

CHEMUNG COUNTY

To Spencer

Tompkins County in 1990

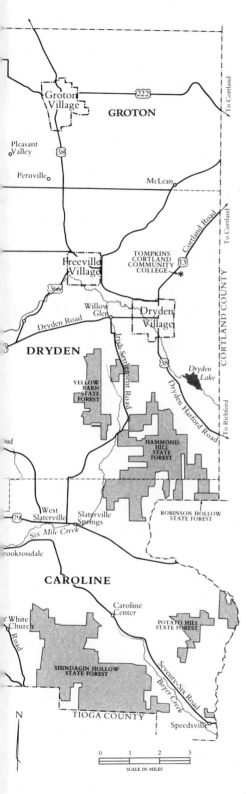

The Towns of Tompkins County

From Podunk to the Magnetic Springs

EDITED BY

Jane Marsh Dieckmann

CONTRIBUTORS

Molly Adams

Louise Bement

Bruce Brittain

Rachel Dickinson

Jane Marsh Dieckmann

Margaret Hobbie

S. K. List

Linda McCandless

John Marcham

Pamela Monk

John Munschauer

Carol U. Sisler

Susan Thompson

DeWitt Historical Society of Tompkins County

Ithaca, New York

Published 1998

Library of Congress Cataloging-in-Publication Data

The towns of Tompkins County : from Podunk to the Magnetic Springs / edited by Jane Marsh Dieckmann : contributors, Molly Adams . . . [et al.].
      p.   cm.
Includes bibliographical references and index.
ISBN 0-942690-39-7 (alk. paper)
    1. Tompkins County (N.Y.)—History, Local. 2. Tompkins County (N.Y.)—History. I. Dieckmann, Jane M. II. Adams, Molly, 1936–   . III. DeWitt Historical Society of Tompkins County.
F127.T7T69   1998
974.7'71—dc21   98-12822

Unless otherwise indicated, the illustrations have come from the collections of the DeWitt Historical Society.

Contents

Preface

The DeWitt Historical Society is pleased to add this book to more than three dozen publications designed to help residents of and visitors to Tompkins County, New York, understand how this community came to be—to inform and entertain readers about earlier years, to help them appreciate the present, and to assist them to plan wisely for the future.

Work on this history of the nine towns of Tompkins County began in May 1990, two years after the DeWitt Historical Society published *Ithaca's Neighborhoods*, about the diverse enclaves that make up the only city of Tompkins County.

From the start *The Towns of Tompkins County* has been planned as a companion to *Ithaca's Neighborhoods*. Individual writers were assigned to trace the growth of each town, plus the Village of Cayuga Heights and two distinct communities—Forest Home and Renwick Heights—within the most populous town, that of Ithaca.

Margaret Hobbie, county historian and director of the DeWitt at the time, was key to the launching of this project. Jane Marsh Dieckmann has been its guiding force ever since, cajoling writers and corraling and editing manuscripts, photos, and maps. She has also provided the index for the book.

She and the rest of us on the society's Publications Committee thank the many writers and researchers who contributed time and energy to the task, to the staff of the DeWitt and its volunteer reference room personnel, Tompkins County Historian Gretchen Sachse, and fellow committee members, especially Russell Bourne, an experienced historian and writer and a relative newcomer to our community. Individual writers thank others who assisted in notes to their chapters. A special note of appreciation goes to Richard Rosenbaum, who designed the book, and to Thomas Chefalo of the county Planning Office, who created the maps for the individual towns.

The cost of publication has been borne anonymously by a Tompkins County family.

We hope this book will encourage individuals and groups to take an interest in the history of their own families, neighborhoods, and towns, as well as to draw on and preserve resources around them. Readers are also encouraged to use the rich resources of the DeWitt Historical Society at the Tompkins County Museum in Ithaca.

John Marcham

July 1997

THE TOWNS OF TOMPKINS COUNTY

Tompkins County: An Overview

Jane Marsh Dieckmann

Tompkins County, located in the southern portion of New York State's
Finger Lakes region, is best known as an area of extraordinary natural beauty and
a center of education. With its gleaming lake, spectacular gorges and waterfalls,
rolling hills, and cultivated fields, the setting has long been admired by travelers
and residents. And the county's diverse institutions of learning and varied communities have brought to this place a wealth of creative people and ideas.

The first settlers were, like most pioneers, occupied with the clearing of land,
farming, and small industries. Early in the nineteenth century, with the setting
up of stagecoach routes and railroad lines, the opening of the Erie Canal, and the
establishment of steamboat traffic on the lake, the county became a bustling
commercial area, and many settlements along these routes prospered. By the
mid-1830s, with nearly one hundred industries, the Village of Ithaca had established itself as commercial center of the county, with the potential, many
thought, to become the business hub of the entire upstate region. Great projects
were hatched for canal links and profitable railroad lines, but these grand hopes
were never realized, partly due to straightened financial times but mainly because of the discouraging difficulty of the terrain. The railroad companies, which
saw two building booms in the nineteenth century, ultimately were defeated by
the hills and deep gorges. Even so, Ithaca has remained the county's commercial
and political center.

During the nineteenth century small industries all over the county provided
local services. They developed specialized businesses, which included farm machinery, typewriters, pipe organs, steam traction engines, carriages, steel bridges,
and the Ithaca Calendar Clock. Farming remained as the county's major industry,
and dairying became the principal farm enterprise in the northeastern part of the
county.

The opening of Cornell University in 1868 marked the beginning of the
county's most important business: education. The university grew and was
joined in 1890 by Ithaca College, increasing the numbers of county residents
involved. The coming of the automobile and improved roads allowed people to
commute to jobs, leading to residential development of outlying areas and greater
concentration of employment in the town of Ithaca. Today Cornell University is

I

1. Ithaca, June 1951. This aerial photograph shows the central position of the City of Ithaca at the head of Cayuga Lake. In the background is the Town of Lansing. The old Ithaca fairgrounds, site of numerous county events over the years, are in the foreground. The oval area, the running track for horse races, is the site of two large grocery stores today. Because it is lowland and near the Inlet, the region is often flooded.

the county's largest employer, with over eight times more people on its payroll than its nearest competitor. Of the county's 28 major employers, 11 are in the educational sector.

Although small in area and population (recorded as 97,018 in 1990 and projected to be 222,999 by 2020), the county boasts a modern airport and hospital, a large public library system, and strong health services. The home of three state parks and the highest waterfall east of the Rockies, it also is a center for tourism and outdoor recreation.

Tompkins County covers 491 square miles and includes the City of Ithaca and nine towns: Caroline, Danby, Dryden, Enfield, Groton, Ithaca, Lansing, Newfield, and Ulysses.[1] Within these towns are six incorporated villages—Cayuga Heights, Dryden, Freeville, Groton, Lansing, and Trumansburg—and many small communities. Of the towns Ithaca is the smallest, with 28 square miles, Dryden the largest with 96.

Land Formation and Resources

The area we know as Tompkins County was once part of a great, shallow bay, formed about a half-billion years ago and inhabited by sea plants and animals.

Over tens of millions of years the sea dried up and the muds hardened, forming the dark, flat-layered shale that is our most common rock. A time of rainfall followed, streams cut through the hardened mud, water gathered into rivers and flowed to the sea. About a million years ago a massive sea of ice began to spread southward from Canada and, following the course of the earlier rivers, chiseled its way through the region. Cayuga Lake was changed from a shallow river valley into a deep trench (today it measures 474 feet its deepest point). Eventually the ice melted, and a large freshwater lake covered the region. About ten thousand years ago the lake drained, leaving scars on the hillsides. Today waterfalls, in narrow, steep-sided gorges, mark a creek's passage through the ancient shales.[2]

The waterways were of prime importance in the early days of the county. Six principal streams come together at the head of Cayuga Lake—Fall, Cascadilla, Six Mile, Buttermilk, Inlet, and Enfield (or Five Mile) creeks. Two other major creeks empty into the lake close to the northern borders of the county, Salmon on the east side, Taughannock on the west. Most run through deep gorges before entering the lake; waterfalls and cascades are commonplace. For the early settlers and indeed for most nineteenth-century manufacturing, these creeks provided essential water and waterpower. Each town in the county writes its history around this waterpower.

The land and its resources have also shaped the life and activities of the people. In the northern section of the county and on the flats were areas of rich and fertile soil, easily adapted to farming; in other sections heavy forests provided timber while the rocky hills, though not good for farming, provided a wealth of good building stone.

Early Settlements and Land Distribution

The first settlers around the head of Cayuga Lake, arriving probably a thousand years ago, called themselves Ho-de-no-sau-nee. In about 1600 five Indian nations of the Finger Lakes region—Mohawk, Oneida, Onondaga, Cayuga, Seneca— formed the Iroquois Confederacy, and in the eighteenth century, when joined by the Tuscarora nation, they became known as the League of Six Nations. From the sixteenth century onward Europeans visited the region—traders, soldiers, missionaries. Finally European Americans arrived, looking for land upon which to settle.

According to Indian legend the Creator told the forefathers of the Iroquois that they would find a great and beautiful land he intended for them, with fertile valleys beside blue waters held in by rocky shores. When they asked how they would know the place, the Great Spirit stretched forth his hand and answered, "Ye shall know Your LANDS, for I have pressed my hand upon the land and in my FINGER PRINTS, rest forever your blue waters."[3]

The Indians established settlements throughout the area that became Tompkins County. Their major village was in the Inlet Valley, west of the foot of Buttermilk Falls; it was named Coreorgonel, which means "where we keep the pipe of peace." There long bark houses were set in a semicircle within a stockade, and the settlers grew crops and planted orchards on the surrounding flatland.

2. First Fall on Six Mile Creek, 1870s. Mills, like this one on the north side of the creek, were part of the landscape at the time. The bridge in the background is at approximately the same place as the present span on Giles Street near the Van Natta dam. Though within city limits today, this area was part of the Town of Ithaca until the early 1900s. Photograph by Joseph C. Burritt.

Because most Indians of the Iroquois Confederacy sided with the British during the Revolutionary War, and some assisted in attacks against the American settlements, General George Washington ordered that they be driven from their villages. In June 1779 Major General John Sullivan launched a campaign of devastation, and by autumn his troops had destroyed fifty Iroquois towns (among them Coreorgonal), burning dwellings and laying waste to crops and orchards. Very few Indians remained in the area after these raids, and in 1789 the Cayugas surrendered their land to the state.

The formerly Iroquois territory acquired by the new U.S. government offered vast lands for settlement by white men and women. Men had been encouraged to sign up to fight by the promise of land after the war was over. A portion of the

Iroquois lands east of Seneca Lake, amounting to more than 1.5 million acres, was designated the Military Tract, and a survey was started in 1790. It was initially decided that twenty-five townships of 100 lots of 600 acres each would be needed; three more townships soon were added. The townships were given classical names mostly; a few were named for great English writers. Private soldiers and noncommissioned officers received 500 acres of land from the state and 100 from the federal government. Officers were entitled to larger amounts, up to 6,000 acres for a major general. The area assigned to each soldier was determined by lot. Only a few soldiers settled on their land, most selling for a small price and some selling the same lot several times. The state set up land commission offices in Auburn to straighten out the confusion over titles. Because the original 1790 survey by state surveyor Simeon DeWitt was rather sketchy, each settler had to have his lot surveyed individually at the cost of 48 shillings.[4]

All but the three southernmost towns of Tompkins County were originally part of the Military Tract. Township no. 22, encompassing the northwestern corner of the county and the Ithaca area, was named Ulysses; the townships of Hector (no. 21) and Dryden (no. 23), as well as parts of Milton (no. 17) and Locke (no. 18) were included. The present towns of Newfield, Danby, and Caroline were among twelve townships that comprised the Watkins and Flint patent, issued by the state to New York lawyer John W. Watkins and Royal W. Flint in 1794 for an estimated 363,000 acres, at a price of 3s 4d per acre. Another parcel of land in the county was conveyed to Robert and Samuel W. Johnson of Stratford, Connecticut, in 1795.[5]

The lands that became Tompkins County had already been part of widely varying jurisdictions. The original New York county of Albany was formed in 1683 and with subsequent enactments came to comprise all the territory within the province of New York (and what is now the state of Vermont as well). Over the next one hundred years parcels of land were taken off to form new counties, which were divided in turn to make additional counties. As more settlers arrived, their numbers increased the need for new jurisdictions. This dividing and shifting of land played a major role in the creation of our county.

The Formation of Tompkins County

Tompkins County came into existence officially through an act of the New York State legislature on April 7, 1817, created from portions of Cayuga and Seneca counties. From Seneca County came Hector and Ulysses (along with Covert, though for only two years). From Cayuga County came Dryden and the southern portions of Genoa (originally Milton) and Locke, which became Lansing and Division (Groton shortly thereafter), respectively. A second law annexing the towns of Caroline, Danby, and Cayuta from Tioga County was passed on March 22, 1822; the name Cayuta was changed to Newfield one week later, and the law went into effect on March 22, 1823. Hector and a section of Newfield became part of Schuyler County on January 1, 1855, while Catharine in Chemung County annexed a small strip from Newfield in 1856.

Tompkins, the state's fiftieth county, is among its youngest; only twelve were organized more recently. The same April 1817 legislative act designated the hamlet of Ithaca in the Military Township of Ulysses, with a population of about 400, as the county seat. On March 16, 1821, almost four years after the establishment of the county, the towns of Ithaca and Enfield were taken off from Ulysses; Ithaca became an incorporated village on April 2 of the same year.

The county was named for Daniel D. Tompkins (1774–1825), who in March 1817 had been inaugurated as the nation's sixth vice president. He had already served ten years as governor of New York State. Appointed commander of the militia of the Third District during the War of 1812, he was able—despite the strong antiwar sentiments of his legislature and most residents—to muster, organize, and equip an army of 50,000 men and to raise funds for the war effort. As he was leaving the governorship, Tompkins recommended that a day be set for abolition of slavery in the state. The legislature immediately enacted a law declaring that "every negro, . . . born before the 4th day of July, 1799, shall, from and after the 4th day of July, 1827, be free."[6]

The People

The Indians of the region, the Cayugas, cleared the land and engaged mostly in farming and hunting. Aside from the principal settlement of Coreorgonal, inhabited mostly by the Tutelos, they had a small fishing village called Ne-ah-Dak-ne-at (which means "at the end of the lake") where Stewart Park is today. In Ithaca they cleared land at the head of Linn Street and near the present-day Tuning Fork at the foot of the State Street hill. Other Indian settlements were located in Newfield where the Saponeys had a village (called Poney, later Pony, Hollow), in the hills of Danby where they spent their summers, in Lansing on Salmon Creek, and on the lake shore at Esty's. Two villages in the northern part of the Town of Ulysses, one at the mouth of Taughannock Creek and another near Waterburg, miraculously escaped destruction by Sullivan's soldiers.[7]

After the Indian settlers had been driven from their villages, white families began to move in. Lured by reports of the land's richness in soil and timber, they came from the Hudson Valley (mainly from a Dutch section of Ulster County), Connecticut and other areas in New England, Pennsylvania and New Jersey, Maryland and Virginia. They came by horse and wagon, often clearing the roadway as they traveled. Mostly farmers, some were carpenters, shoemakers, tanners, and coopers. All went to work to clear the land, in order to grow food and raise livestock.

Farming was hard work, and much of the county, especially the southern portions, was hilly and rocky, with poor soil. In addition state taxes were high and had to be paid in cash. Many early farmers moved on. Laura Case, the wife of one such farmer, wrote back to family in Caroline in 1832:

Traveling from St. Louis to Pekin [Illinois] we did not ascend one hill equal to Mr. Taft's nor did I see one rock in the road except when we crossed the small streams. . . . To see thousands of acres without a tree, covered with grass and as free from a stump or a rock as your floor and almost as level as what you have never seen but I have seen it.[8]

All over the county other farmers stayed and tilled the land, some starting farms still cultivated today by their descendants.[9]

Most white settlers from the South brought their slaves with them, but an equal portion of the county's early black population consisted of free men and women. The earliest census on record, taken in 1820, counts a total population of 20,679; of the blacks listed, 55 were free men and women and 50 were slaves (of whom 32 resided in the Town of Caroline). The first slave in the county, Richard Loomis, came with Robert McDowell, one of the first men to settle in downtown Ithaca. Peter Webb, a slave of John James Speed of Caroline, purchased his freedom in 1818. When the state granted freedom in 1827, a grand celebration was held at the Methodist Episcopal church on Aurora Street in downtown Ithaca.

During the nineteenth century black people, who faced not only slavery but serious discrimination, lived in scattered areas around the county. Most were grouped in small communities in the Village of Ithaca, however, and attended church there. Strict segregation existed in the Methodist Episcopal church as elsewhere (in Caroline there were seats for them only in the balcony of the Rev. Mandeville's Dutch Reformed church), and soon the blacks sought to establish their own congregation. They chose the African Methodist Episcopal Zion denomination. St. James was chartered in 1833 and built on Wheat Street (Cleveland Avenue today) in 1836. It is the oldest existing church in Ithaca.[10]

Before the Civil War the church played an important role in the Underground Railroad. In this carefully organized and secret network of stations established between states in the South and free states bordering on Canada, Ithaca was a stopping-off place from which several routes went north, including one along the road to Trumansburg, passing by the Hayts Chapel. St. James provided a safe haven for slaves escaping to freedom, for many of its pastors were themselves escaped slaves and eager to be stationmasters. In the 1840s, and especially after the passage of the Fugitive Slave Act in 1850, traffic through Ithaca was heavy, and many runaways found shelter and aid. George A. Johnson, a prominent black barber with a shop on State Street, was known to call on his friend Ben Johnson, local attorney and third village president, for help that included clothing, food, money, and often safe hiding on the lake steamer going north.[11]

Life for the blacks was difficult. They had received no education and little training; few had any property. They worked in low-level jobs as laborers, domestic servants, gardeners, waiters. Some were employed in E. S. Esty's tannery, others were craftsmen and worked making bricks and in the building trade. Many domestic servants became close to the families for whom they worked. Dinah Ten Broeck, for example, born in Kingston, New York, around 1813, became the property of the Bogardus family when very small and moved with them to Lansing when she was about three. She stayed on the Bogardus farm, never again seeing her mother or any member of her family. Though freed in 1827, she spent her life raising the Bogardus children and grandchildren. She had no schooling

3. Dinah Ten Broeck (c. 1813–1903)

and worked for the family until her death in 1903. A memorial appeared in the *Ithaca Journal*; it spoke of her love of flowers, music, every lovely and beautiful thing. "Her family loved her, referred to her judgment, and she, in turn, lived for them, forgetful of self and happy in their interests, which were her own." Her grave is in Pleasant Grove Cemetery in the Village of Cayuga Heights, where she shares a monument and burial plot with the Bogardus family.[12]

In the cemetery adjacent to Hayts Chapel are numerous graves of other black county residents. In Ithaca two memorials pay tribute to writer Alex Haley (1921–1992), whose family study *Roots* pointed the way for countless individuals to undertake serious genealogical research and won for its author a special Pulitzer Prize. Haley was born in Ithaca, son of a father studying in the agriculture college at Cornell and a mother enrolled in the Ithaca Conservatory of Music. In 1992 the Haley memorial swimming pool across from the Greater Ithaca Activities Center was opened, and next to his birthplace on Cascadilla Street is the Alex Haley Memorial, dedicated in 1993.[13]

Today most blacks live in the Southside and Northside neighborhoods of Ithaca, which has one of the highest percentages of blacks among New York cities. In the nineteenth century blacks were about 4 percent of the county's population. According to the 1990 census, which included students, their numbers came to only about 3.3 percent, whereas people from Asia and the Pacific islands made up almost 5.5 percent.

The first white and black settlers came mostly from the new United States. Immigrants from Europe trickled in during the nineteenth century, with a wave arriving around the turn of the century. In 1900 about one-tenth of the county's population was foreign-born; by 1930 the proportion had decreased to about one in eighteen. The first to come in numbers were the Irish, who began arriving in the early 1830s. They worked as domestic help and unskilled laborers, in railroad building and contracting work. In 1836 they formed the county's first Roman Catholic parish and were served by visiting priests until 1848. With other Catholics they built their first church in 1851, on the site of the present parish house of Immaculate Conception Church, and dedicated it as St. Luke's.

The Irish in Ithaca held their first annual Friendly Sons of St. Patrick banquet in 1863 (in 1870 a snowfall on March 16 and 17 was so deep that the event had to be postponed for a week). By that time many Irish were employed in the construction of the new buildings at Cornell. A few families lived in Trumansburg, where the men worked on the railroads and in the stone quarries. In the early years of the twentieth century they lived mostly in the Washington Park area of downtown Ithaca and sent their children to Immaculate Conception parochial school, which had opened in 1884. The Irish community in Dryden still holds an annual St. Patrick's Day dinner and dance.

Just a few Jews lived in the county in 1850; more had arrived by the 1880s. They lived mostly in the Northside neighborhood of Ithaca and in 1906 formed their first congregation, which met in the home of Isadore Rocker. The only synogogue in the county, Temple Beth-El, was built in 1928 on the corner of Court and Tioga streets in Ithaca.

Large numbers of Italians came into the region between 1900 and 1930. Most were employed in blue-collar jobs, heavy construction, and road building. Italian workers were responsible for laying most of the brick pavement of State Street as well as for much of the masonry and elegant iron grillwork in the city. In 1905 a group of single Italian men, ranging in age from their teens to forties, settled on the old Conover farm just south of the city, leased by an Italian immigrant labor agent, Frank Speno. Crowded together in shacks and small houses in an area called the Klondike, the men worked on the railroad and for Morse Chain. Other Italians lived along the Inlet, in the Southside, and alongside Hungarians and Jews on the north side of Ithaca. In the county today people of Italian descent are involved in all the professions, especially restaurants and such long-standing family enterprises as Fontana's Shoe Sales and Repair on Eddy Street in Collegetown, started in 1907 by Cesare Fontana, since 1981 owned and operated by great grandson Steve. Much of the preservation of local heritage has been supported by one individual of Italian origin, Joseph Ciaschi. Thanks to his efforts, distinguished landmarks in Ithaca, among them the Boardman House, Lehigh Valley station, Farmers and Shippers hotel, and Clinton Block, have been saved from demolition and given a new lease on life.

The first Greeks came to the county in 1898, led by John Chacona, who was attracted to Ithaca by its Greek name and promptly opened a candy store. Most came from a tiny mountain village north of Sparta, Tzintzina, and settled in to run candy stores, fruit and grocery stores, and restaurants. For years Chacona had

4. Greek party, 1956. Toula Gordon, John
Dentes, John Poulos, and Paulette Chelekis
Manos are in costume for a Greek Indepen-
dence Day program in Ithaca.

his business next to the Ithaca Hotel; known popularly as the "Sugar Bowl," it
specialized in fine confectionery, ice cream, and sodas. About 1907 the Chacona
family was joined by cousins, the Manos brothers, who worked first as clerks and
then established their own confectionary on Stewart Avenue. Sometime between
1910 and 1919 John Chacona put up the Chacona Block, with Greek motifs on its
facade, at the top of College Avenue in Collegetown. In 1926 Constantine Manos
opened Pop's Place in the building, a confectioner's and ice cream store with a
mosaic tile floor, which he ran until 1926. The Manos diner on Elmira Road, run
by William Manos, opened in 1963.[14]

By 1940 there were 62 Greeks and by 1971, 111. Despite their small numbers
the Greeks in Ithaca have been highly visible and have formed a close community
with the church at its center. In the early 1950s a priest was coming from En-
dicott to conduct Greek Orthodox services on Saturday morning. Between 1957
and 1966 the congregation worshiped at the Cosmopolitan Club on Bryant Avenue on East Hill. In 1966 they acquired the former Congregational church at
Seneca and Geneva streets and named it St. Catherine. Although it serves a
population of fewer than 200 adults, it is the focus of their social activities. The
Greeks have kept many ties to the culture and religion of the homeland, particularly the customs and traditions of Tzintzina.

Many immigrants settled in the county's center, but other groups looked elsewhere. Between 1890 and 1935 some Finns came, mostly from lumber and mining camps in Michigan and Minnesota, and settled in the southwest corner of

Danby. Others moved into Newfield around 1910 and organized a Lutheran church in 1913. They were devoted to farming and rose to the challenge of growing good crops in the difficult, rocky soil of these towns. Many became poultry farmers. Attracted by newspaper advertisements, Czech settlers also began to arrive in Newfield in 1905 and like the Finns turned to making poor land productive. In 1918 they built Bohemian Hall as a meeting place for as many as 130 members. Sunday schools provided lessons in the native language, and everyone knew dances from the old country.

The county's institutions of higher education have attracted many foreign teachers and students. These academic opportunities, as well as refuge from war, have helped to swell the Asian population. In 1900 there were two Chinese people living in the county. By 1990 the number had grown to more than five thousand Asians.[15]

Land and Water

The contours of the land—the flats and rolling meadowlands, forested hills, deep-stream gorges with waterfalls, the lake that pokes into the county's northwest corner—have of course shaped the history of the county. The land was cleared and farmed; early settlers harnessed the power of swift streams by building dams and mills, using them to grind grain for food and cut lumber for building. They burned the trees to make potash, which they exported. The streams could not be used much for transport of goods, but the lake could, and very soon steamboats and barges were carrying products in and out of Ithaca.

Although the terrain created problems—getting produce to market, operating modern heavy machinery—farming was widespread. According to the 1855 state census, farmers made up slightly under one-sixth of the total population of 5,038 (the next largest category, laborers, numbered 502). Through the nineteenth century, farms were generally small. In 1880 the county's farms produced $1.848 million in crops, and dairy farms produced butter and cheese as well as milk. Groton and Dryden led the other towns. One hundred years later crop production came close to $40 million; about one-quarter of farms in the county were dairy farms, producing only milk. Crops too have changed; in the early 1920s tobacco was significant, but today it is not even listed in the census.

The land held other resources. Salt was discovered early, and manufacturing plants were in operation in the nineteenth century (see the Ithaca and Lansing chapters). The War of 1812 closed the nation's access to Canadian gypsum, used for fertilizer, which led to exploitation of Ithaca's rich deposits. At that time on a single day as many as eight hundred wagons might be carrying shipments of gypsum south over the Ithaca-Owego Road. Until the mid-1950s gypsum was used in the manufacture of cement.

Since 1900 the shift has been away from agriculture and toward an urban-industrial society, especially in the Town of Ithaca. Farmers were the largest population group in 1855, but in the 1990s farming accounts for only 3.5 percent of total employment. The Cornell campus and Plantations occupy the largest

5. Farm scene, 1907. Mrs. Will Graves, a resident of Dryden, is raking hay. Photograph by Verne Morton.

6. Road building, September 13, 1909. Roads all over the county were under construction during the first decades of the twentieth century. The site is Forest Home Drive beside Beebe Lake, among the many areas connected with Cornell University known for beautiful walks and scenic vistas.

7. Flooding in Ithaca. During the 1935 flood water from Cascadilla Creek swept up over the bridge posts next door to 405 North Aurora Street. The photograph, dated July 7, is from the Charles Blood Collection.

land area in the town, with only small acreages given over to crop cultivation and experimentation.

The county's waterways, which have played a major role in the development of every community, have also brought widespread damage and destruction. The biggest flood in the county's history came in 1935. On Saturday, July 6, the area was in the grip of a five-day heatwave; the temperature was 96.4° at noon, with a forecast of thunder showers and cooling weather. Several thunderstorms arrived, but Sunday morning dawned hot and muggy. It started to rain hard, and by afternoon all the streams were rising. Four inches of rain fell by nightfall, and the city's storm sewers could no longer handle the water. Then came a cloudburst, pounding rain that dumped another 5.46 inches. Water from the Inlet began to extend across the flats, rising as high as four feet in some parts. The lake crept almost as far south as Buttermilk Creek.

The center of Trumansburg was swept away, and the business district of Myers heavily hit. In the Town of Dryden, Freeville was under water, the area nearest Virgil Creek devastated. Bridges in Newfield were damaged so severely that people had to detour through Danby to reach Ithaca. In the Inlet Valley the DL&W railroad tracks were left hanging in midair over the raging creek. The havoc in some areas of the Buttermilk Falls and Treman state parks was irreparable.

Travel was suspended as whole sections of roads and railroad beds were washed away, along with the bridges. Twelve lives were lost, and damage within a few hours mounted to more than $5 million. Local and state police, county officials, Civilian Conservation Corps workers, and volunteers in trucks and boats pitched in to rescue those stranded and in danger, some of them in trees and on rooftops. During one forty-eight-hour period 651 people received care in Cornell's Barton Hall alone. Although outside aid came from the Red Cross and the WPA, most of the clean-up was done by the communities themselves.[16]

Government and Services

Local Governments

Well before Tompkins County was established, in 1801 the New York State legislature had passed several acts that set up regulations for local government. These acts designated a judiciary system and outlined the powers and duties of town officers—a supervisor, clerk, three to five assessors, one or more collectors, two overseers of the poor, three highway commissioners. Constables, fence viewers, and pound masters were to be elected as towns saw fit. When the Town of Ithaca was formed in 1821, these various offices were filled by election. In addition two constables were appointed, as were three commissioners and three inspectors of schools, three trustees of gospel and school lot, and one pound master.

Town governments were set up according to these regulations. Early in the twentieth century the overseer of the poor became the town welfare officer, and in 1885 it became mandatory to appoint a town health officer. Today these services fall to the county government.

Towns today elect the following officials: supervisor, clerk, four town council members, two justices, and a highway superintendent. Other officials are appointed as needed. The Town of Lansing, for example, has a town engineer, park superintendent, and recreation director, whereas Enfield has none of these.

The Town of Ithaca is set up somewhat differently. Although located within the town, the City of Ithaca has an independent government, elected officials, and taxation system. The incorporated Village of Cayuga Heights, with its own elected officials and services, nonetheless is part of the Town of Ithaca, pays taxes within the town, and has representation on the town board.

The Town of Ithaca has a supervisor and six board members, of whom one is deputy supervisor. All are elected, as are two town justices. The offices of clerk and highway commissioner—both appointed by the board (but elected in the other towns)—go back to the earliest days of the county. Other departments have been added in the twentieth century. The first town planning board was appointed in 1937, but the zoning board of appeals did not come along until 1954, when the town adopted a zoning ordinance. In 1974 the first full-time professional town engineer was hired. He was Larry Fabbroni who, trained in engineering and in planning, became the planning officer as well; he also took charge of the zoning department. He remained head of three departments, hiring one assistant for zoning and several for planning, until 1986 when he left to take a position in the city government. In June of that year zoning was made a separate department and in the fall planning was split off from engineering.

The town board also appoints committees and boards, which in recent years have covered finance, conservation, codes and ordinances, agriculture, public works, and a special committee for the 175th Historical/Anniversary Celebration in 1996. In 1993 the town adopted a comprehensive plan for land use into the twenty-first century, with the principal aim of preserving farmland and open spaces.

Of the town's 39 employees, 20 operate out of cramped quarters in the Town Hall, a small Queen Anne house on East Seneca Street purchased by the town in 1974. Other offices are at the highway barn on Seven Mile Drive, and the town justices have their quarters in the Old County Courthouse on East Court Street.[17]

County Government

With the growth of the hamlet of Ithaca as a trading and manufacturing center and the establishment of communities in the rural surroundings, the early settlers of the area requested a new county. Their appeal was granted and passed by the legislature on April 7, 1817. The act provided that the courthouse and jail for the new county should be built by voluntary subscription executed by bonds in the amount of $7,000, to be guaranteed by May 1—that is, within a month. Failing this guarantee, the area would revert to the counties of Cayuga and Seneca. Provisions of the act were met promptly by twenty freeholders of the new county, thereby giving county supervisors the authority to proceed. Land for the site—the corner where the present courthouse stands—was given by Simeon DeWitt; the deed, the first recorded in the county clerk's office, was filed on May 2, 1817.

In 1818 a building for a courthouse and jail was ready for occupancy. The new county's governing body was the board of supervisors, elected to represent districts of the village (later the city) and the towns of the county. In 1909 the county clerk became a salaried worker, receiving $2,400 per year. Through the years the county board has developed as a powerful and influential local body.

In 1969 the county was reapportioned, and the board of supervisors adopted a charter and code for county government. The major body was renamed the Tompkins County Board of Representatives, with no fewer than 15 members, no more than 20, elected in general elections for a four-year term. In the 1990s the board numbered 15—1 from each of the five city wards, 3 from the Town of Ithaca, and 7 from districts carved from the other towns. Also elected were clerk, sheriff, and district attorney.

The board elects its chairperson for a one-year term; he or she in turn appoints individuals to head and serve on various committeees, including budget and administration, personnel, planning and public works, social and health services, public safety and corrections, and intergovernmental relations.

County Services

Changes in governmental services have been enormous. The earliest services were establishment of a court to hear pleas and supervision of schools; in 1827 the supervisors voted to build a poorhouse, located in the Town of Ulysses, with rooms for seventy-five persons.[18]

The original courthouse of 1818 was replaced in 1854 by what is now called the Old Tompkins County Courthouse on Court Street (the present courthouse was built in 1932), a Gothic Revival building of brick (later covered by gray stucco) with a handsome, Victorian-ceilinged courtroom on the second floor. On the first floor were rooms for the supervisors, grand jury, sheriff, and district attorney. When the present courthouse opened, the older building began to house a succession of county offices and public agencies; in 1939 the DeWitt Historical Society took over the entire second floor and most of the basement, staying until 1973. By the 1970s the building had fallen into disrepair. Complete renovation, as a Bicentennial project, began in fall 1975 and the building was reopened in 1976, providing county offices and courtrooms.[19]

Back in 1893 the *Ithaca Journal* ran a series of six front-page articles proposing a new building in downtown Ithaca (on the site of the present post office and parking garage) to house city and county offices. According to the plan, and architectural drawings confirm it, the building was to go up in three stages, with additions to be made as services expanded over the years. It was never built, of course, and its projections for space requirements proved way off the mark. Naturally, no allowance was made for the Department of Motor Vehicles, for example, which grew to occupy a good portion of the courthouse basement and since 1981 its own separate building in Hancock Plaza. Totally unforseen as well was the growth of government concern with social welfare. The 1893 building plan allotted one room to the city's superintendent of the poor. In 1949 the city's role in welfare matters was absorbed by the county, whose Department of Social Services used more than five floors of office space in three buildings during the 1970s and 1980s and in the 1990s takes up most of the old Biggs building on West Hill.[20]

As this brief account of building plans shows, the story of county services is one of growth and consolidation. The first board of health in the village was set up in 1831, mainly to attend to unsanitary privies and overflowing cesspools. The city became owner-operator of a public water supply in 1904, and in 1946 the Tompkins County Health Department was inaugurated to serve the whole county. A county mental health clinic and board were set up in 1965. What was originally a village hospital in Ithaca became the Ithaca City Hospital in 1912, then the Ithaca Memorial Hospital in 1926. In 1946, with the creation of the county health department, the hospital took over the Biggs Memorial Hospital (opened in 1935 for the care of tuberculosis patients), becoming the Tompkins County Hospital in the late 1950s. When a new hospital building opened in May 1980, the Biggs property was turned over to the county for a health facility. The hospital reverted to private hands on January 1, 1981, and was renamed Cayuga Medical Center in September 1995. In much the same way, Ithaca had a library even before it became a village. In 1863 Ezra Cornell put up an elegant library, which also provided space for public meetings. In 1969 the Tompkins County

8. Old Courthouse on Court Street, 1982. At this time the brick building in the background served as the county jail. Since 1944 the courthouse has housed county offices.

Public Library was constructed to replace the Cornell Public Library, razed in 1960.

Other services have come under county jurisdiction: the airport in 1956, Tompkins Cortland Community College in 1968. Mental health services were centralized with the 1991 opening of a new six-story building at 201 East Green Street. In 1987 a new county administrative complex opened on Warren Road in the Town of Lansing, housing the sheriff's department and a county jail. The red

9. Cornell Public Library, c. 1880. Dedicated in 1866, the library served the county until its demolition in 1960 as part of the city's urban renewal program. Photograph by Joseph C. Burritt.

brick building on East Court Street, put up in 1933 as a county jail, was renovated according to historic preservation guidelines and put to use as county offices in 1994.[20]

Many services are shared among the towns and their communities. The Ithaca post office, which serves Ithaca (city and town), Danby, Enfield, and parts of Lansing, opened its main building on Warren Road in the early 1990s. Just south of the post office is the airport that serves the county.[21] The City of Ithaca's fire department serves the Town of Ithaca's communities except Cayuga Heights, which has its own service. All fire companies routinely respond to calls from other communities as needed. The Southern Cayuga Lake Intermunicipal Water Commission, known as Bolton Point, just over the Ithaca town line in the Village of Lansing, supplies water to the towns of Dryden, Ithaca, and Lansing, and the villages of Cayuga Heights and Lansing. In September 1996 Bolton Point celebrated its twentieth anniversary (and burned the mortgage). At that time there was talk of the City of Ithaca joining the service, the state's first such cooperative arrangement among more than two municipalities.

Schools

The public school system, although not directly under county jurisdiction, has also seen broad consolidation. In 1812 a state law, backed by Governor Daniel D. Tompkins, created a public school system throughout the state and provided for a public school within walking distance of every child. Each community thus had at least one school, usually providing instruction for all ages in one room. Through most of the century many small, one-room, mostly rural schools were scattered throughout the county; the 1855 state census lists 161. Some of the larger communities had private academies. In 1874 the state legislature passed the Public School Act, consolidating the schools of different towns into districts. The academies joined the school system, and most towns formed their own districts. The Ithaca Academy building became the Ithaca High School, which opened in 1875 with 150 students and 5 faculty members. Kindergarten programs came into the schools in 1903.

The idea of the neighborhood or community school survived. Not until the advent of modern roads and large, modern buildings did schools come to be consolidated further. Before the construction of the modern Elmira Road, for example, young boys and girls attended the Inlet Valley School while older students went to the high school in the center of Ithaca. Most of them walked.

Consolidation came to the outlying areas first. Trumansburg formed its own district in 1928, Dryden in 1936, Newfield in 1939, Lansing in 1948. In the 1950s Ithaca formed its consolidated school district, reorganizing 44 local schools (some with local names, all with union numbers) into 14 elementary, 1 junior high, and 1 senior high.[22] This reorganization included the towns of Caroline, Danby, and Enfield as well. The small schools closed and new elementary schools were built and opened, Enfield's in 1959, Caroline's in 1960, Danby's in 1962. In the late 1950s private bus companies joined with the Ithaca district to transport students to and from the schools. When the new Ithaca High School was opened in 1960, its previous home (the DeWitt Building) was converted to a second junior high for the district. In the 1960s more elementary schools replaced older schools, among them Cayuga Heights, Northeast, and Glenwood. Two new junior high schools, neither within city limits, were opened in 1971, along with two alternative schools, East Hill and Markles Flats. In the 1980s the Danby and Glenwood schools were closed, along with Cayuga Heights (reopened in 1988). A middle school system was initiated at the time, and in 1984 ninth graders moved to the high school.

Although districts in Caroline, Danby, Enfield, and the Town of Ithaca were absorbed by the Ithaca city schools, the Dryden, Groton, Lansing, Newfield, and Trumansburg districts have remained independent. In fact, the central system now sees a trend toward decentralization. Of the eight remaining elementary schools in the Ithaca City School district, four are outside city limits (Caroline, Enfield, Cayuga Heights, and Northeast), as are the two middle schools, the Special Children's Center, the Head Start program (for many years in St. Paul's Church downtown and now in the Town of Danby), and Tompkins-Seneca BOCES.

Redundant school buildings were adapted to different uses. Some small schoolhouses became private homes. The schoolhouse on the corner of Pleasant Grove

10. Forest Home School, early 1960s. The school, seen from Judd Falls Road, is letting out for recess. The building today is home to the Cornell Plantations. Photograph courtesy of Forest Home Archives.

and Hanshaw roads in Cayuga Heights, once surrounded by fields of sheep, was converted into a dentist's office, while the Forest Home schoolhouse became headquarters for the Cornell Plantations. The Inlet Valley school houses the privately run Waldorf School of the Finger Lakes, which moved there in 1987. Some larger buildings were sold and turned into retail and apartment spaces, others were recycled by the school system.

The story of Tompkins County and its towns tells of diverse people coming from far and wide to settle and live together, mainly in a sharing and cooperative way. Each town developed in a distinctive manner, determined by its particular resources and terrain. In a time that looks toward the twenty-first century, the area is a special place, blessed with unusual resources of ingenuity, diligence, and adaptation in its people and with landscapes of breathtaking and constantly changing natural beauty. May this heritage and these surroundings remain healthy and vigorous in the years to come.

1   Town of Ithaca

The County's Central Town

Jane Marsh Dieckmann

The Town of Ithaca lies at the heart of Tompkins County. Its situation is central, both geographically and politically. The county's only city and the county seat (Ithaca), its only suburban village (Cayuga Heights), and its two major educational institutions (Cornell University and Ithaca College), are located within the town's borders. Most places of county government and services, many of which originally started in the Village of Ithaca, have remained in the city and the town.

The Town of Ithaca has occupied this significant place from the beginning. The earliest travelers and settlers, attracted by the land and resources, and by the area's scenic beauty, gravitated to the head of Cayuga Lake. Most major creeks of the county flow into the lake in the Town of Ithaca, and the chief routes of transportation have always passed through the major community—Ithaca. This city at the center is bounded on the north by the lake and surrounded on three sides by the town. The city is the subject of another book; this chapter deals principally with the town's outlying areas.[1]

The Town of Ithaca came into being officially on March 16, 1821, at the newly erected courthouse in the village, and originally was made up of thirty-one lots of the Military Tract, covering thirty-six square miles. In the earliest accounts it was described as three hills and the flats. Sandy loam in the valley and on the hillsides brought abundant crops of grains and fruits once the land was cleared. Waterpower from the numerous rapid streams led to early establishment of factories and mills. And salt deposits, found later in the nineteenth century, led to the establishment of the Remington Salt Company in 1901 on the east shore of the lake, at Remington Point. Until 1920 the company operated brine wells and a processing plant. The salt was shipped out by boat and rail.

The population of the town has grown steadily. It nearly doubled between 1960 and 1990, with 92 percent of that growth outside Cayuga Heights; a significant factor was the development in the early 1960s of the modern Ithaca College campus, south of the city line on South Hill. In 1990 55.4 percent (or almost 10,000) of the town's population of 17,797 lived on East Hill, 31.3 percent (about 5,500) on South Hill; West Hill and the Inlet Valley with more than 2,000 residents accounted for almost 13 percent.

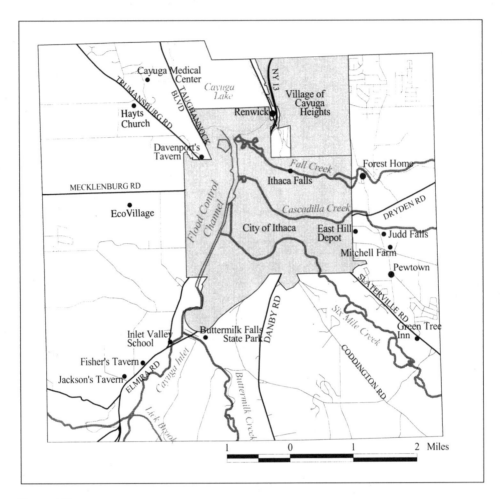

Town of Ithaca

The City of Ithaca has extended its boundaries into the town, mostly to the east and north. It annexed several parcels in 1888, when village became city. The 1853 map shows the State and Mitchell intersection still in the town, whereas the 1893 Sanborn insurance map shows the city line farther to the east at Hazen Street (Linden Avenue). The present eastern boundary appears on maps only in 1919. In 1903 Cornell Heights was annexed, and in 1957 a narrow strip extending the Elmira Road commercial district to the overpass at Buttermilk Falls became city land.

West Hill

Important transportation routes passed through West Hill from the beginning. The original Indian trail along the west side of the lake was used by the early

11. Hayts Chapel, with cemetery and adjoining schoolhouse, shown in 1908.

white settlers. One takes this route, Trumansburg Road today, to reach some important services—the hospital, medical administration buildings and offices, two private schools located in the former Odd Fellows building, Lakeside Nursing Home.

But think back to those early days when settlers walked along the stony path and stagecoaches lurched over the road between Ithaca and Trumansburg. One important stop on the road was Nathaniel Davenport's tavern, where food and lodging were available. Davenport had come from New Jersey and settled on Military Lot no. 87 in 1791. Abner Treman, founder of Trumansburg, is said to have stopped there during the winter of 1793–1794. The place he visited burned, as did its successor; the third house on the site, built in 1820 and known as the Old Stone Heap, is among the oldest surviving buildings in the county.

Further to the north, at Hayts Corners, stands Hayts Chapel, home to a small congregation of, according to the West Hill Congregational Church Book of 1848, "professing Christians of different Evangelical denominations." In May 1847 this breakaway group, mostly from the First Presbyterian Church of Ithaca, started their own worship service and sabbath school in the "Red School House on the West Hill." They asked for letters of dismissal from the downtown church in October. In 1850 Deacon Charles Hayt donated land, a corner of his farm, and the group financed the building of its own chapel and cemetery. Although the church book states only the belief that "we can better advance the Kingdom and Glory of God, by forming ourselves with others of like feeling into a seperate Organisation," these dissenters were outspoken abolitionists.[2] (The schoolhouse was the site of antislavery meetings in the 1840s, one such meeting being noted in the antiabolitionist newspaper *Flag of the Nation* of October 5, 1848.) They clearly opposed the teaching of the Reverend Dr. William Wisner, a compelling minister who had arrived in Ithaca in 1816 and built a large congregation at the Presbyterian church. Wisner was a strong Northern proslavery man. According to Ithaca barber George A. Johnson, "in season and out, he upheld and supported American slavery, and termed it a divine institution, that it was divinely instituted by Almighty God."[3] With the passage of the Fugitive Slave Act in 1850, the little chapel, "erected to God, and dedicated to human freedom," was open to worshipers who sympathized with the slaves and continued to help them on their way to Canada and freedom. The cemetery, originally adjacent to the chapel, is now across the Hayts Road to the north; rules and regulations of the West Hill Cemetery Association, published in 1898, listed offices with information about election and duties. Many black residents of the area, and particularly those active in the freedom movement of the nineteenth century, are buried there.

West Hill is the site of a modern development project, one in keeping with the town's 1993 comprehensive plan to regulate expansion. A housing cooperative of 150 planned units called EcoVillage was approved south of the Mecklenburg Road, construction began on the first unit of thirty homes, and the first residents moved in the fall of 1996. The living units are to occupy only 20 acres of a 176-acre parcel, with the remainder of the land devoted to farming and open spaces.

Inlet Valley

The valley is probably the first area settled in the county. The Indians located their principal village Coreorgonel there. This is rich lowland and though prone to flooding has always attracted farmers. Through the nineteenth and early twentieth centuries the major road through the valley, probably the original Indian trail and first paved about 1910, followed the present Spencer Road along the side of the hill as far as Buttermilk Falls. The DL&W locomotives ran just above the road, scaring the horses in the early days as they roared by. At the falls the road took a right angle west, then a sharp left turn across a bridge spanning Buttermilk Creek; it proceeded across the Lehigh Valley railroad tracks and meandered to the intersection of the Spencer and Newfield roads. City children rode their bicycles or walked to Buttermilk Falls to go swimming until 1936, when the state put in the present, straighter highway, Route 13.

The flat commercial strip we know today originally had only a few houses; most settlement was southwest of the falls. The old brick house at Buttermilk Falls was built in 1824 by William Van Orman, who had settled early in the valley and served as assessor for Ulysses township in 1795; he used bricks he had made himself. It later became a tavern and then passed to the Rumseys, who kept a dairy farm. After their big barn burned in 1918, in a fire started by sparks from the railroad, the family grew crops. There was sand and gravel on the land, and the farmer's son, Edward M. Rumsey, with his son Hugh, exploited it, furnishing sand and gravel first for the construction of the Treman, King hardware store in

Ithaca. Robert H. Treman, who owned part of the land, gave it to the state for a park. The Rumseys started out with a wheelbarrow, a shovel, and a screen to separate the sand from the gravel; they paid one man 20 cents an hour to help out. In June 1922 they formed a partnership called E. M. Rumsey and Son. By 1924, with the original deposits exhausted (later the parking area for the new park), they turned to blasting gravel out of the hillside. In subsequent years they supplied sand and gravel for buildings on the Cornell campus, city streets, schools, and many commercial buildings. The firm merged in 1953 with Ithaca Sand and Gravel Corporation, and the Buttermilk Falls plant closed in 1957.

As to the original tavern, Edward M. Rumsey and his wife started out in one room of the house. In 1948 their son, company vice president and engineer at the plant, Edward L. Rumsey, and his wife, Margaret, moved into the house. In 1983, four years after the death of her husband, Margie Rumsey opened the Buttermilk Falls Bed & Breakfast in the house. Four of her grandchildren have assisted her in the business.

In the early 1920s, beyond the Lehigh Valley railroad tracks, was the Allen homestead. Joseph Allen was a farmer and kept livestock; his daughter took over and ran a small dairy farm. In 1951 Nora J. Dodd, who had been on the staff of the Tompkins County Memorial Hospital, purchased the house, hired five registered nurses, and opened the Dodd Nursing Home. For twenty years she operated the thirty-bed facility but had to close when she could not update the old farmhouse to meet new state requirements. The house was converted into a restaurant. South of the old Allen house was Lick Brook Farm, owned by Allen's son Fred and so called because of a deer lick made by boring holes in a log and filling them with salt. On the knoll was a shed used for storing tobacco; the area later became McGuire Gardens, a family-owned garden store and nursery that closed in 1995.

In the mid-nineteenth century near the present Seven Mile Drive was a toll-gate with Jackson's Tavern next to it. Nearby was Fisher's Tavern, and further down the road on the Inlet Valley Farms property was the Master's Place, also a toll collection point. Nearby, according to Hilda Babcock, was a "large carriage shed with a dance hall over it. The place was called Tadpole and shunned by 'nice people.' Apparently one could get a drink at every mile from Ithaca to Newfield."[4]

One grand house still stands in the Inlet Valley. Fully restored after a fire ripped through the attic and second floor in 1987, it is the home of Turback's Restaurant. Called Sunnygables, among other names, the house was built in 1852 for Thomas Jefferson Williams, whose grandfather had come to the county in 1812. Designed in Carpenter Gothic style, it was made from local trees selected by Williams and cut at a sawmill on Lick Brook. In 1875 the whole house was decorated by a Russian named Zabulski, who did much of the handpainting himself, and a bathroom was installed by John N. Jamieson (of the Ithaca plumbing firm Jamieson & McKinney) at a cost of $266, the first in the town.

In 1919 Sunnygables and 360 acres of farmland were purchased by H. E. Babcock, for many years general manager at the Grange League Federation (later Agway), and the farm prospered for many years.[5] The house became a restaurant called The Gables in the early 1960s. Michael Turback purchased the property in

12. Sunnygables, 1963.

1968; his restaurant, with Victorian and 1890s' American decor, specializes in local foods and New York State wines.

The outstanding natural feature of the valley is the Buttermilk Falls State Park. Of its 733 acres, 164 including the major glen were a gift to the state in 1924 by Robert Treman and his wife. The park has unusual rock formations, two glens, and ten waterfalls; within a mile the creek falls more than five hundred feet, ending in a final cascade where the churning waters look like a milky foam, whence the name. At the lower end the natural pool resembles an old waterhole and has both swimming and wading areas. In the upper part is Treman Lake, created by a 36-foot dam. For many years the water from the creek supplied the city; from an old wooden dam near Pulpit Falls a water main led along South Hill and into the city.

South Hill

The upper portion of the state park lies on South Hill, just north of the town line. In the nineteenth century this area was devoted mostly to farming. The DL&W railroad ran to the east of Coddington Road, often within sight of the farmers. The first farm of the area, located at the corner of Hudson Street Extension and Coddington Road, was called Depot for the original railroad; here the trains divided to go into the village. To the west, on the east side of Danby Road, was

13. The glen at Buttermilk Falls, c. 1870. Photograph by Joseph C. Burritt.

Quinby's Tavern. Still standing today on the corner of Coddington and Danby roads is an 1837 farmhouse, purchased by Ithaca College in the early 1960s.

The largest change on South Hill came when Ithaca College moved out of the city to build its modern campus there, between 1960 and 1965. The college's facilities play a significant role in Ithaca's cultural and recreational life; especially notable are concerts at the college, many of which involve musicians from the wider community.[6]

East Hill

A very early settlement was situated where the modern Snyder Hill Road and Honness Lane come into Pine Tree Road. With thoughts of relocating, William Pew, his wife Hannah, their five sons, and one daughter set out by sleigh in 1800 to visit relatives in the Canadas. The party stopped on the Ellis Hollow Road, where the tavern keeper tried to sell them some land. They moved on to Ludlow-ville, but son John's wife delayed further travel by giving birth. The tavern keeper heard the news, chased after them, and offered the land again. William Pew purchased a 450-acre parcel between the Slaterville Road and Cascadilla Creek, and in 1811–1812 he deeded parcels to three of his sons and his son-in-law. His aim was to develop a larger community with the name of Pewtown.

The family left its mark. For many years son Richard operated the Green Tree Tavern on the Catskill Turnpike; he also built the John Mitchell brick house that stood for years on land later occupied by East Hill Plaza. Daughter Elizabeth and her German husband Matthias Honness had twelve children; Honness Lane is named for them. Son John, designated in local Methodist history a religious leader in the region, owned the largest share of the land, part of which he helped to lay out as East Lawn Cemetery in 1885. The elder William Pew died in 1818 at age 66 and is buried there. Beside him lies Hannah Lacey Pew, of Irish descent, known as a person of wonderful vigor of mind and body; she lived to be 102.[7]

Also buried in the cemetery are members of the Mitchell family, who came from New Jersey in 1802. James Mitchell purchased six hundred acres of Military Lot no. 96, built a log cabin, and settled down with his family to farm. Sometime between 1840 and 1850 a brick farmhouse was built. In 1883 Samuel Barnes of Westchester County married Minnie Mitchell and took over the farm, which passed through generations of farmers to S. William Barnes Jr. By the 1960s the farm had dwindled to forty acres devoted to grain crops and eighteen head of cattle. In 1968 Barnes sold the farm to Cornell University, which opened the land to development including East Hill Plaza, a senior-citizen housing complex, and a motel. Barnes lived in the farmhouse until his death in 1977.[8] In 1990 McDonald's attempted to open a fast food restaurant in the plaza. The proposal met with much local protest and was stopped by a decision of the town planning board. In January 1991 Scott Hamilton, owner of Ide's Bowling opened in October 1953, converted six thousand square feet to the west of the plaza into commercial space, named Judd Falls Plaza.

North and west of East Hill Plaza was land used by the railroad. The East Ithaca depot, with turnouts for coal and freight trains, was opened in 1876, after the abandoning of grand plans for a route through Ithaca to the east. The Elmira, Cortland & Northern, organized from existing lines in 1884, offered train service for the university and the eastern side of the town. In its prime the line ran two express trains daily between Elmira and Syracuse (via Cortland), making the run in four and one-half hours. Despite its claims of elegant coaches and picturesque scenery, the line soon was dubbed the "Empty, Crooked, and Nasty." The Lehigh Valley assumed control in 1896. From 1893 the depot was used for almost forty years as the terminus for a trolley service between downtown and East Ithaca which went up Oak Avenue on a spur from the trolley's main line and then on Maple Avenue. After the trolley service (which provided train connections) ended in 1930, passenger train service began to fade away; it finally closed in 1949. The branch remained in existence, carrying coal to the Cornell heating plant until 1972. The depot was abandoned but was moved several years later to its present

14. East Ithaca depot. Shown here before the turn of the century, the station saw frequent train service and served a varying clientele.

location north of the plaza and converted into a restaurant-bar, which opened in 1977.

Close to the present intersection of Route 366 and Judd Falls Road (renamed Pine Tree Road in 1997), manufacturer Reuben Judd owned a water-powered woolen mill from 1832 to 1858. Nearby were King's lead pipe factory and a factory for making chairs. To the north was the hamlet of Free Hollow, one of the county's earliest manufacturing centers.

Until the turn of the century the northern boundary of the Cornell campus, and of the city, was the Fall Creek gorge. Settlement of the area beyond, mostly open fields, did not start until the Triphammer Bridge was constructed in 1897; by May 1900 streetcars were traveling the famous loop, crossing Fall Creek again on a new lower bridge at present-day Stewart Avenue. The suspension bridge, an engineering marvel, was put across the gorge in the same year. Cornell Heights was annexed by the city in 1903, leading the way to the development of a completely residential area to the north: Cayuga Heights.[9]

Village of Cayuga Heights
Its Development by Newman and Blood

Carol U. Sisler

Jared Treman Newman and Charles Hazen Blood were friends, law partners, and from 1900 to 1938 real estate developers.[1] Having been involved with Edward G. Wyckoff in a three-way partnership to develop a portion of Cornell Heights in 1901, they purchased farmland from Franklin Cornell, divided it into building lots and connected them with dirt roads, installed gas, electric, and water lines, advertised the property, and badgered their friends and associates into buying in and building on what they named Cayuga Heights. Blood referred to the project as a "hobby" on his Cornell alumni form, but Newman dedicated the last years of his life to it, desperately striving to settle his debts. He failed. When he died in 1937 at age 82, his debts far exceeded his assets. When Blood died in 1938, his estate was land-poor but solvent.

What drew the two together? Although both graduated from Cornell University, Newman was eleven years older, the son of an Enfield farmer, a grandson of Abner Treman, one of two children. Blood was the only child of a prominent haberdasher who was a general in the National Guard of New York State. He lived with his parents at what is now 414 East Buffalo Street. The same year Blood graduated from Cornell, 1888, Newman's wife bought a brick house at 440 East Buffalo. Both families were active members of the First Presbyterian Church, but it was probably the neighborly connection that led to partnership in 1894. Blood's father probably thought Newman would be a good influence on his son; Newman, who hung out his shingle in 1880, may well have hoped the Bloods would bring him more business. Although the law partnership dissolved in 1903, the two men, like a pair of Clydesdale horses harnessed together, pulled the heavy financial load of the development of Cayuga Heights, either unable or unwilling to separate themselves, for nearly forty years.

The purchase of the Cornell lands on October 26, 1901, gave Newman and Blood ownership of all the territory from roughly Triphammer Road to the east, the Lake Road to the west, Upland Road to the north, and Kline Road to the south. Although the Renwick lands (see Renwick Heights section below) were slashed by numerous creeks flowing to the lake, the upper lands were meadow and pasture, cleared of trees for agricultural purposes. Now, when one overlooks the Heights from the Johnson Art Museum, all one sees is trees with rooftops occasionally visible through the verdant cover. While many deeds require neighbors not to plant trees or shrubs that would obstruct the view of the lake, Newman planted most of the trees along the roads to improve the appearance of the lots. Newman engaged Harold A. Caparn, a landscape architect from New York City, to advise him about the location of roads and division of lots. The mature white pines that border The Parkway were planted according to Caparn's plan.

Before the lots became attractive to purchasers, two necessities had to be

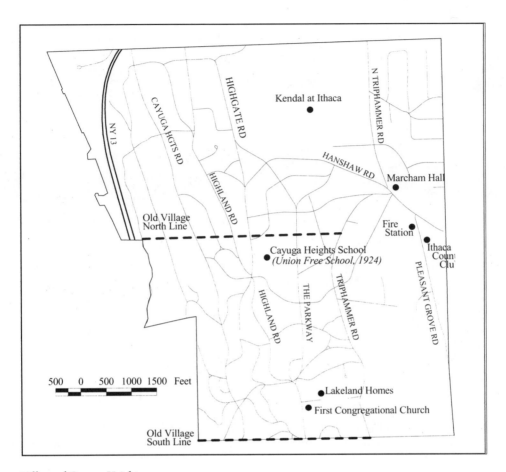

Village of Cayuga Heights

provided—the extension of Cayuga Heights Road northward and the extension of water supply from the city's lines. Both were eventually secured after considerable negotiation with city and county authorities.

On July 2, 1906, an agreement was reached among Newman and Blood, the Ithaca and Cayuga Heights Railway Company, Ithaca Electric Company, the Telephone and Telegraph Company, and the Ithaca Telephone Company allowing the parties to place wires on the railway poles from Thurston Avenue to a point on Highland Road near Pleasant Grove creek.

Besides Cayuga Heights Road, the other roads to be extended into the Heights were the continuation of Highland Road, the opening of The Parkway, and the connection of Wyckoff Avenue to Renwick Drive. Between The Parkway and Highland Road is the entrance to a small lane that provided access to the private domain of Jared T. Newman. In 1903 he built a summer house for his family on land he called The Sentinels for the huge elms that grew in the open meadow. The house was a rambling, shingle-style structure designed by Clinton L. Vivian.

15. Here comes the trolley! This picture, taken c. 1916, shows the intersection of Highland, Hanshaw, and Upland roads. The house is 402 Hanshaw Road.

From the wrap-around verandah, one could see northward to Sheldrake Point and southward to the Newfield hills.

In 1909, however, Newman began construction of a commanding year-round residence designed by Ornan Waltz and Arthur H. Gibb, with Spanish or Mission-style elements. South of Newman's house, on the lower part of Highland Road, his brother-in-law Henry S. Williams had just completed his prairie-style house, also designed by Waltz and Gibb.

East of him another brother-in-law, John Tanner, built a similar quasi-Spanish-style house in 1915–1916. On the middle lot, in 1911, Sherman Peer built the only Gustav Stickley–designed house in Ithaca. These three impressive residences greeted people as they inspected what was happening in the development beyond Cornell Heights.

Driving around Cayuga Heights, one can distinguish the early houses even though many are hidden by overgrown shrubbery. They are generally unpainted or painted stucco with red tile or slate roofs. In some instances the original roof system has been replaced with asbestos shingles. Some have half timbering, and all occupy very large lots. Sometimes, the lot having been subdivided, a more contemporary house adjoins the older residence. Almost all of the early houses are located north of the Kline Road, Highland, and Parkway intersection to Upland Road or along Cayuga Heights Road to Upland. By 1911 twenty-one residences plus the Ithaca Country Club drew city water. Newman and Blood shared the cost of the pipe, which was $6,888.

In 1911 the area was organized as a community; residents who lived along the north side of the city boundary and west of Triphammer Road formed an association. Thirteen people attended the first meeting; major concerns were roads, clearing of snow, and control of tent caterpillars.

Ownership of the lots in Cayuga Heights is confusing. Some of the deeds were in the name of Jared T. Newman and his wife, Jane E. W. Williams, and Charles H. Blood and Louise M. Blood. Other deeds were in the names of the Newmans or the Bloods separately. Some deeds were in the name of the Cayuga Heights Park

16. Grand residences, c. 1916. These homes, marking the entrance to Cayuga Heights, are, *left*, Sherman Peer's at 401 Highland Road; *middle*, Jared Newman's at 409 Highland Road; and *right*, John Tanner's at 104 The Parkway. Peer was Newman's close friend and Tanner his brother-in-law. Photograph courtesy of Cornell University Library.

Association (under Bloods) or the Cayuga Heights Land Company (under Newmans). Some of the lots were in the old Village of Cayuga Heights, whose boundaries some define as where the sidewalk ends, for instance on Highland Road. The other lots were in the Town of Ithaca.

Several restrictions were included in the deeds to maintain a residential atmosphere that would attract potential purchasers with Newman's and Blood's social standing. A 1914 deed stated that no building will be erected within twenty-five feet of the road, that no piggery shall be maintained, that no barn, stable, or other objectionable building shall be erected within one hundred feet of the highway. House plans had to be approved by the developers. These restrictions on the property continued for ten years.

Cayuga Heights had a banner year in 1915–1916. The village was incorporated, its boundary lines having been surveyed by Carl A. Crandall. Elections were held on June 24, 1915, with the following result: C. T. Stagg, president; G. W. Herrick and W. A. Stocking Jr., trustees; W. J. Bells, collection; J. H. Tanner, treasurer.[2] The population numbered 137.

Meeting five days later, the board decided that the maintenance of dirt roads, including snowplowing would be handled by the village. It undertook negotiations with the city to secure fire protection for the village. The city agreed, so long as hydrants were convenient to the properties. The tax rate was $3 per thousand.

Frustrated by opposition to his proposal for the county to extend Highland Road to Hanshaw, Newman made a deal with Roger B. Williams Jr., president of the Ithaca Traction Company. The company would build eight hundred feet of road—including track for the trolley and a small, neat waiting station to be lighted in the evening at what was known as Cayuga Circle—in exchange for two lots in the Heights (now part of the school grounds facing Hanshaw Road). The agreement was proposed on January 3, 1917 and was finally signed on October 18. The traction company agreed that the lots would be owned by Williams.

Finally Blood built his own residence in Cayuga Heights, at 508 Highland Road, and Newman and Blood separated their land holdings. Blood formed the Cayuga Heights Park Association to develop the land which fell between the west side of Highland Road and the east side of Cayuga Heights Road beyond Upland Road, the area known today as Cayuga Park Circle.

White Park

Newman moved full steam ahead to open the White Park section of his lands, named for Andrew D. White, whom Newman considered his intellectual father. He consulted the Urquharts and the Garretts, two of the first purchasers on what became Oak Hill Road, about the name for their street, writing, "I rather think I like Oak Hill Road better than Oakland or Oakwood Drive. I like The Trail equally well but I must confess that every one else seems to think it is not an appropriate name for a street in a civilized community."[3] During World War I construction virtually halted, and inflation drove building costs to prohibitive levels. Also, Newman came to the staggering realization that his debts amounted to $175,000; he was close to bankruptcy.

As postwar inflation declined, he embarked on an active campaign to sell the White Park lots in the spring of 1921. He advertised in the *Cornell Alumni News*, inviting alumni to walk the grounds on Spring Day. In the *Ithaca Journal* he advertised in a chatty descriptive column "White Park Notes," signed with his initials, and he offered wholesale prices (two-thirds of the regular price) for purchasers during the month of June. He produced an attractive brochure and enclosed an intention-to-purchase card. In all he offered thirty lots for sale, as well as the seven in the woods east of Triphammer Road. His campaign was reasonably successful; the mortgages he took on the lots were transferred to his in-laws and others, reducing his indebtedness by $75,000.

As the White Park lots were being sold, Newman decided to sell the big house, to move the summer house northward, and to winterize it for use as his home. A salable lot created between the two was eventually purchased by S. C. Hollister. Newman would not sell the house to a fraternity as long as the Tanners lived nearby. After numerous sales pitches to faculty members and businessmen, he succeeded in selling it in August 1922 to Fred W. Albree for $45,000, $20,000 below the original asking price.

Highgate

In May 1922 Newman announced plans to develop the Troy farm, located north of Hanshaw Road beyond the land of the Cayuga Heights Park Association. He named it for a residential area of north London, and its roads were to have English names. Although the section would be outside the village, he hoped it would soon be incorporated.

In July 1922 the village voted to pave Highland Road from Wyckoff to Upland. In the same year Blood dissolved the Cayuga Heights Park Association.

Newman and Blood were well aware that new tracts of land threatened the sale of unsold lots in the old tracts. People were being given too much choice. Furthermore, some lot owners were making enviable profits on resale. But the two men were determined not to involve real estate agents, because they did not want to pay the commission.

Newman was besieged by small irritations that, as owner, only he could resolve. In August 1923 the city demanded that a leaky water main be repaired, or water to the village would be shut off. The photographer John P. Troy in August 1924 suffered damage to his car on White Park from an iron pipe that protruded sufficiently to strike the base of the engine block. Would he be compensated for the damages? Newman replied that he would. Trying to maintain an orderly appearance in the Heights, Newman had to nag property owners to cut down weeds on their lots and mow the grass. Village president Walter L. Williams asked Newman to trim the shrubs planted on the little circle at the division of Highland Road and The Parkway because automobilists could not see one another. At the same time Newman gave Sunset Park to the village. On August 6, 1927, he also passed on control of the circle.

Sunset Park

Sunset Park was a section of the development which Newman called the Western Slope. It was constructed from the contour and materials on the slope of a sandbank and landscaped by H. M. Blanche. Newman wanted a bench constructed there which would be inscribed with what he felt were the supreme personal values—Beauty, Goodness, Truth. After several rewritings, the bronze tablet read "Here may you too find the love of Beauty, Goodness, Truth."

North of the park Judge Charles Stagg built a handsome residence designed by LeRoy P. Burnham. Burnham introduced distinguished residential facades which combine stucco, half timbering, and brick or stone. Morris and Allison Bishop built south of the park at 903 Wyckoff Road. Constructed in 1930, their house was designed by Conway L. Todd, a graduate architect at Cornell. Newman named the continuation of Sunset Park Sunset Drive and the short connecting street to Cayuga Heights Road Corson Place in honor of his friend Hiram P. Corson. A key to the growth of Cayuga Heights was the location of a school within easy walking distance of the residences. In 1920 Newman gave the original school lot on Upland Road to the village; the schoolhouse was built in 1924. Identified as Union Free School District no. 6, the school contained six rooms and was ruled by Martha Hitchcock as principal until 1948. Retiring at 75, Miss Hitchcock was remembered as a strong-willed, diminutive woman who combed her hair on top of her head to add to her height.

On January 16, 1929, Newman calmed fears that a gas station would be plunked in the middle of the Heights, on the triangle of land formed by the intersection of Wyckoff and Kline Road with Cayuga Heights Road, by giving the parcel to the village. His son Charles had advocated a gas station on the plot because there was no place to buy gas on the Heights.

Klinewoods

After their marriage on July 5, 1928, Charles and Marion Newman asked LeRoy Burnham to design a small house for the lot his father had given them at 110 The Parkway. The newlyweds informed Jared Newman that they could not afford to pay servants and so could not live in the style of their parents and their friends; Marion would manage the house herself, with only occasional day help.

Newman was so impressed with Charles's house and the social and economic realities affecting young couples that in 1932 he created the Klinewoods section of Cayuga Heights, an area for smaller houses. Furthermore, he planned to develop a shopping center containing a gas station and small stores. Although he did not develop the Community Corners, it was an outgrowth of his concept.

Newman and Blood soon completed the outline of the Village of Cayuga Heights: the Berkshire addition of fourteen lots was opened in November 1928. In July 1930 Comstock Road was completed to Klinewoods Road. Newman named it for John and Anna Botsford Comstock, who were old friends. The Parkway was extended to Klinewoods at this time, and to Hanshaw by October 1931. Forest Drive was started in September 1932. Hampton Terrace was developed by Blood in 1932–1933 when the backers of the Westminster Choir, a choral school briefly associated with Ithaca College and the Presbyterian church, failed to locate on the site selected for it.

After six months of failing health Newman died on May 11, 1937. His gross estate was about $90,000 including $44,000 in real estate and $40,000 in stocks and bonds. His debts were $152,000. From September 23 to 28, 1937, a grand auction was held by the Gerth Company under a striped tent, at the intersection of Midway and Triphammer roads. The tuxedo-clad auctioneer sold sixty-two lots for $37,000, at an average price per lot of about $600. They were located in the Midway, Comstock, and Highgate sections.

Blood, the other partner in the development of Cayuga Heights, died nine months after Newman on February 15, 1938. Together the two men had laid the groundwork for a beautiful residential area in Tompkins County.

Village of Cayuga Heights
1940 to the Present

John Munschauer

In 1940 the incorporated Village of Cayuga Heights extended only as far north as the Cayuga Heights School, yet the eye saw a community continuing another half-mile or more before houses became scarce. Only the tax collector saw the village line. A city planner might notice that the streets were laid out a little less like a maze "over the border," but north or south, in the old village or new village as the two areas became known, navigation can be frustrating. Villagers like to walk. They don't get far before some lost stranger or delivery person stops them, seeking help.

The old village, with its solid homes on winding, tree-lined streets, had a special charm, but by World War II anyone wanting to build a home there would have had a difficult time finding a lot. Not all its land was developed. Close by the City of Ithaca, between Highland and Triphammer roads, a nine-hole golf course kept developers at bay until 1919 when the country club moved its course across Triphammer Road. The abandoned land was gradually sold off to individuals and fraternities, most failing to build or resell until after World War II.[1] One section lay vacant as late as 1959, when the First Congregational Church went up on the site of old course's ninth hole.[2]

In 1947 a local developer, Sal Indelicato Jr., who with his father had been building apartments along Triphammer Road, bought one of the largest pieces from a fraternity and built Lakeland Homes. This complex of seven buildings, each with four apartments,[3] quickly became Ithaca's version of the postwar housing projects described by William H. Whyte Jr. in the *Organization Man*, a sociological analysis of young executives. Here lived "up and comers," ambitious young professors and business executives on the make. It was a community of families with babies everywhere. It was a sociable community, its serious discussions taking place in a communal laundry room, its chitchat at cocktail parties. It was a community of struggling achievers: lights shone from windows at 1 and 2 A.M. as residents prepared reports and proposals, struggling to get a promotion, to get out of Lakeland, to get a house.

Whyte's phenomenon was short-lived, at least in Ithaca. By the 1950s affordable houses became available for the Lakelanders, many built in the new village and extended it still further north. Families moved out of Lakeland and other apartments in the area; students moved in—a transition that accelerated when landlords discovered they could rent to students by the person instead of by the apartment.

By 1953 development in the new village crowded the Lansing line. Residents, finding their problems much like those in the old village, petitioned to join. In accepting them in 1954, the village grew from 0.44 square miles to 1.82.[4] The line between old and new may have disappeared, but problems did not. The City of

Ithaca, which had been providing sewer service to the old village, refused to extend it to the new.[5] Septic tanks were proving ineffective, causing the county health department to set new and costly standards, adding another concern to the village's already vexing problems with water, fire protection, and police.

Back then, according to Frederick Marcham, a professor of history at Cornell who was elected a village trustee in 1954, trustees met informally at various homes to do business and enjoy a social evening of snacks and sometimes beer. The system suited a community with a workforce of four men or so who collected garbage "and did a little to keep major roads free from snow," plus a policeman who "sauntered in for duty sometime in the morning."[6]

Water and sewage, however, were issues that couldn't be settled over snacks and beer. The city, serving itself and the village from a precarious water system on Six Mile Creek, was an uncertain supplier. To continue to provide water and sewer service, let alone extend sewers to the newly enlarged village, the city would have had to undertake a major renovation of its systems. It was willing to do so on two conditions: the village must be annexed to the city, and it must pay $110, 000 for the privilege.

Village trustees were, according to Marcham, inclined to go along with the city. Independence meant starting from scratch to build a water and sewer system as well as a first-rate fire and police department. In effect the village would have to be transformed from a dependent of the City of Ithaca to a self-sufficient, politically autonomous community. Ahead for the trustees would be thankless hours of late-night meetings and problems without number relating to sewers, water, payrolls, pension plans, taxes, zoning, citizen complaints, and more. Who can blame the trustees for not wanting to get involved? Yet Marcham felt it was important to make the sacrifice. If he could help it, the trustees were not going to hand the village over to the city.[7]

He was a softspoken, scholarly gentleman with a British accent, and it was hard to imagine his entering the fray against the city, much less coming out the victor. But you have to know that he was once a pugilist who learned to use gentlemanly words, waiting for his opponent to drop his guard so he could land a right hook.

In an interview with Professor Marcham when he was 92, and in his pamphlet "Memories of Cayuga Heights" (written in 1988), this quiet man's punches came through: he thought the city proposal wrong because the city's management of its own affairs was not good; the likelihood that a Cayuga Heights resident would influence city policies was nil; and then there was that $110,000. Whether he objected or not, the village itself would have to give its voice. In one of his more malicious moments he suggested the villagers be assembled and the mayor of Ithaca be invited to speak to them. He knew the mayor of the time could not speak in public; he had little to say and spoke hesitatingly and uncertainly.

The city having had its say, villagers expressed their feelings: "If we become part of the city, saloons will be serving cocktails right in our neighborhoods" (applause for the spunky elderly lady). Someone mentioned zoning to prevent this sort of thing (no applause). The meeting dragged on, each villager had a say twice over, but the spunky lady had said it all. No pollster was needed to predict the outcome.

17. Frederick G. Marcham, 1982. Resident of
the Village of Cayuga Heights from 1932 until
his death in 1992, Marcham was mayor from
1956 to 1988. Photograph by Sol Goldberg
courtesy of John Marcham.

Marcham had led and won the fight to keep the village independent. Villagers
rewarded him by dumping the problems of independence in his lap. They elected
him mayor in 1956, a post he held for thirty-two years. We can capture his spirit
and the way he saw things at the time from his "Memories":

"The Villagers of Cayuga Heights had much work to do in the new pattern they
had chosen." They had to create a fire department; many came forward as voluntary firemen. Sewage disposal had to be dealt with, and this meant

> appointing consultants, working with the Federal Government and the state, buy-
> ing land for a plant, and the almost endless task of dealing with property owners
> through whose land public sewers would run. A new and enlarged Village called for
> a well manned police department, a program for managing roads and more trucks
> and more men to deal with garbage collection and snow-plowing. A big, new
> business.
>
> The Village Board, through its monthly meetings and its Committees, set forth
> policy in these matters, but, without question, the Village Engineer, Carl Crandall,
> kept in motion from day to day the work of translating policy into action. . . . For
> the Village Board, for the Villagers and for me, the crowning event of the sewage
> disposal program was the first shovel of dirt from a Village street that began excava-
> tion for a sewer line.[8]

The village had its sewer, then a police department and a fire department; water
still came from the city which, Marcham recollected, drew its water from the Six
Mile Creek area and other minor sources and, almost year to year, had difficulty
in providing service, particularly in the late summer. "We, in our group of muni-

18. Dorothy Cornell's home. Called Marcham Hall today, this former residence built in 1928 houses the Cayuga Heights Village Hall and Police Station.

cipalities," Marcham wrote, "knew that we could not draw upon the City's system for any important growth of population, and we decided to plan for a new system and began asking the City if it wished to join with us. The City said no."

The key figure in organizing the program, Marcham continued, was Walter Schwan of the Town of Ithaca. Schwan knew the intermunicipal plan would get no Federal or State aid. The village decided on the Bolton Point project for taking water from Cayuga Lake. As the program developed, public works officials of the City of Ithaca objected to it and said so in the Ithaca press, and to representatives in Albany, that no permit for the water plant should be issued. City officials could not present their case in such a way that their water system would accommodate everyone. The state granted the village its permit.[9] In 1976 the completed Bolton Point water treatment plant began delivering water to customers.

In all this Marcham had a vision of what the village should be: "a residential village, a quiet village, a village that accepted a few service stores to meet the needs of villagers, a village with its own functioning fire department, a sewage disposal system, and with a full, around-the-clock police department."[10] He retired from the office of mayor in 1988 after seeing his vision fulfilled. He died on December 16, 1992. Just as the story of Cayuga Heights in the first half of the century is the story of Newman and Blood, so the second half is the story of Fred Marcham.

As Marcham predicted, meetings now run into late evening as trustees pore over budgets, debate zoning laws, and conduct the business of a full-service village. Still, citizens have stepped forward, willing to run for office. Professionals

19. Hitchcock Hall, the original building of the Cayuga Heights School, December 17, 1958. Photograph by Ralph Baker, *Ithaca Journal.*

stretched their already busy careers and took part-time jobs to run the village: Marcham as mayor, Gordon Wheeler as treasurer, and Jack Rogers first as clerk, then as village engineer when Carl Crandall retired. Rogers served for thirty-eight years, retiring in 1994 as village engineer, by then a full-time position.

The Cayuga Heights Fire Company is largely staffed by citizen volunteers. The police force of necessity is paid and consists of a chief, five full-time officers, and up to eight part-time employees. All is for a village of 3,457 residents (according to the 1990 census), which speaks to the villagers' commitment to law and order. More important than the size of the force, however, is the emphasis on police training. William Tucker Dean, village justice for many years, has remarked that, unlike in communities where mishandled police evidence makes it hard to get convictions, in Cayuga Heights when a police officer makes an arrest, the charges stick.[11] Try speeding through the village along Triphammer Road if you want to test this statement.

Thus what Marcham cherished has been preserved—with the possible exception of the Cayuga Heights School, more accurately the Union Free School, which also served Renwick Heights and McKinneys along the lake.[12] In a 1924 Tudor-style building in a parklike setting, the school belonged to the community and the community embraced it, taking an active interest in its educational program and staff. Ithaca has had its share of Nobel laureates, but none was more revered in the village than "Bess" Farnham, "Trix" Nungezer, and the school's other great teachers. In 1956, however, yielding to state regulations and financial pressure, the village gave up control of its school, turning it over to the Ithaca City School District. The old building was altered, then replaced in 1968; the school closed in 1980 in response to declining enrollment, only to reopen in 1988, this time as a part of a social experiment. Buses brought in pupils from other neighborhoods to add cultural diversity to the educational program. Gone from the village and elsewhere were schools built around a sense of community.

The twentieth century drew to a close for Cayuga Heights with a large parcel of open land succumbing to bulldozers, carpenters, and plumbers engaged in building a community that itself would add a new chapter to village history. Just as a golf course had held off development at the southern end of the village, so to the north did the 109 acres of Cornell's Savage Farm, once useful for agricultural experiments, but no longer so by the 1980s. At the same time Dale Corson, Ruth DeWire, and other mostly Cornell retirees were looking into building a retirement community in the Ithaca area. The pieces came together: the Kendal Corporation, developer of retirement communities in Pennsylvania and elsewhere, was approached and became interested; the Savage Farm, ideal for such a community, became available. At a ceremony in spring 1994, ground was broken for Kendal at Ithaca. On December 26, 1995, Enid Cruse, a retired army nurse, moved into a two-bedroom cottage to become Kendal's first resident. By June 20, 1996, when delegates, Kendal residents, and hundreds of friends gathered for an official dedication, all of Kendal's 44 apartments and 90 of its 166 cottages were occupied, and more residents were on the way. In addition to the living units, a health facility can accommodate 35 skilled-care patients and 12 people who need assisted living.

Cayuga Heights ends the century an upper-middle-class community, a village of educators, physicians, lawyers, businesspeople, and other professionals. It boasts being the home of famous scientists, scholars, and authors. Supported to the south by some of the brightest students in the country whose youth and exuberance complement the population, and to the north by elders who add the wisdom of age, Cayuga Heights is ready to enter the next century with a powerhouse of talent. If its citizens remain involved in local affairs in the next century as they have in the twentieth, the future of the village will be bright.

Forest Home

Bruce Brittain

The picturesque hamlet of Forest Home is situated on Fall Creek, in the northeastern part of the Town of Ithaca. Originally developed as a center for water-powered mills and industry, this small community has since evolved into a distinct residential neighborhood. Today, the woods and meadows of the Cornell Plantations and golf course completely surround Forest Home, separating it from

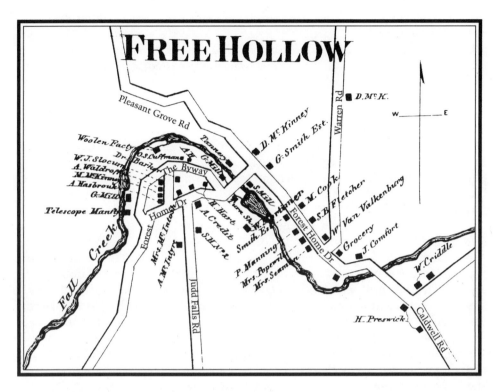

Free Hollow (Forest Home). Source: *New Topographical Atlas of Tompkins County, New York,* 1866. The names of modern roads have been added.

the general suburban sprawl of the greater Ithaca area, and helping it retain its character and identity.

An Indian trail once passed near Forest Home, and several stone artifacts have been found in the community, but the quantities do not suggest a permanent Native American settlement. The first European settlers, Joseph and Martha Sydney, arrived in 1794 and built a mill and bridge in the general vicinity of the current downstream bridge. The availability of waterpower attracted others, and through 1850 the community developed as an industrial center, with many mills and businesses bordering the creek. The name of this new settlement changed from Sydney's Bridge to Phoenix Mills, and eventually to Free Hollow, the name it kept for most of its industrial period.

In addition to grist- and sawmills, typical of early creek-side settlements, Free Hollow had specialized woodworking, cooper, turning, and cabinet shops. The cabinet shop also produced coffins and was operated by the local undertaker, William Criddle. Cloth and paper were important industries, too, with paper, woolen, knitting, and mitten mills located along the creek. The mitten mill was eventually converted to a house where, until recently, needles from the knitting machines were still being found in cracks in the wooden flooring. Other enterprises included a foundry, telescope shop, hemp factory, slaughterhouse, tannery, and leather shop, as well as cider and gunpowder mills. The drying house attached to the gunpowder mill exploded on September 20, 1849, sending pieces up to a half-mile from the site.

The second half of the nineteenth century was one of relative stability for Free Hollow. The mills continued to operate and were periodically rebuilt and updated, but no new mills were constructed. Likewise, the population remained relatively stable, with only three new houses being built during this period. When Free Hollow acquired a post office in 1876, the community name was changed to Forest Home.

The turn of the century signaled the end of the mill era in Forest Home. Improvements in transportation and the increased use of steam and electric power facilitated large, centralized manufacturing and processing, and the small, local mills could no longer compete. The woolen mill closed in 1892; the Empire Grist Mill burned in 1887 and was not rebuilt. The Red Grist Mill continued in production until nearly 1900, and Bool's woodworking mill, the last to operate in Forest Home, closed in 1926.

Although the mills themselves are now gone, traces of this era can still be seen throughout the community—not only the many fine Greek Revival houses but also bits of stone mill foundation, remnants of sluiceways, and the end of an old log dam. The two mill remnants most easily seen today are both located adjacent to the downstream bridge. The concrete impoundment dam for the Bool woodworking mill is located just above this bridge, the stone foundation of the Empire Grist Mill just below. Another significant mill remnant is the vertical shaft cut into the gorge wall where the Red Grist Mill once stood. It can best be seen from the footpath on the side of Fall Creek opposite The Byway.

Of particular historic interest are the two single-lane riveted steel-truss bridges that carry Forest Home Drive across Fall Creek. Built by the Groton Bridge Company nearby (see Chapter 6), they are rare examples of a once-common bridge design. The downstream bridge (1904) is the oldest Warren pony truss in Tompkins County, and the upstream bridge (1909) is the oldest and one of only two remaining steel through-truss bridges in the county.

As the mill era in Forest Home was drawing to a close, a new phase of growth for the community was just beginning. Under the directorship of Liberty Hyde Bailey, Cornell University's new College of Agriculture was growing rapidly, increasing approximately tenfold in just ten years and bringing over a hundred new faculty members and their families to the area. Many of these new families chose to settle in Forest Home, and approximately thirty-five new houses were built between 1900 and 1915, doubling the size of the hamlet.

This rapid growth had profound effects. The old one-room Greek Revival schoolhouse on Judd Falls Road quickly became overcrowded, and so a new two-room elementary school with gymnasium was constructed in 1921. The Forest Home School District was absorbed into the Ithaca City School District in 1956, and the new Forest Home School closed in 1964. (Both former school buildings survive, the first serving as a three-car garage, the second as headquarters for the Cornell Plantations.)

In 1915, with its increased population, the community built the Forest Home Chapel, designed by the dean of Cornell's College of Architecture. Religious

20. Forest Home, c. 1890. This overview was taken from the top of Pleasant Grove Road. Photograph courtesy of Cornell University Library.

services had previously been held in the one-room schoolhouse until a school trustee, who believed in the separation of church and state, locked the doors, putting an end to the practice.

The arrival of so many new residents also caused some social friction within the community. The Sewing Circle, an established women's social organization, chose to restrict its membership to the mill-related residents. In response, the wives of the new Cornell professors and students founded the Embroidery Club, whose membership was restricted to Cornell-affiliated women. With time, however, a sense of community prevailed; the Embroidery Club remains active today and welcomes all adult female residents of Forest Home.

The years since 1915 have seen continued slow residential development, largely as a result of the continuing growth of Cornell University. Approximately fifty new houses have been built, again substantially increasing the size of the community. The years preceding World War II also saw the dissolution of most remaining commercial establishments in Forest Home. Northrup's general store closed, Stevens's gas station went out of business, and Jack Smith's service station was converted first to an ice cream parlor and then to residential use. The tea-room that had been operated by Flora Rose and Martha Van Rensselaer for the instruction of Cornell home economics students was sold and converted first to a

21. Forest Home residence, 1996. Like many others in the community, this house on Forest Home Drive dates from the early 1800s. Photograph by and courtesy of Bruce Brittain.

furniture store and eventually to office space. It is the last remaining commercial establishment in the community. One by one the working farms have been developed for residential purposes or become part of the Cornell Plantations or golf course. Several fine old barns remain in and around the community, however. Houses from all three of Forest Home's major periods of growth are located throughout the hamlet, and the various architectural styles chronicle the community's successful transformation from an early industrial center to a cohesive residential neighborhood.

The Forest Home Improvement Association, founded in 1920, serves as the community's civic association. Early projects included various beautification efforts, assigning street addresses to the houses, and establishing a community water system and street lighting network. More recent projects have included gaining recognition of the community as a New York State Historic District, and the designation of Forest Home Drive as a New York State Scenic Road. The neighborhood also constructed an addition to the chapel, entirely with volunteer labor, and publishes periodic newsletters and an annual directory. The Forest Home Improvement Association is dedicated to preserving and enhancing the scenic beauty, historic heritage, and community spirit that have defined the neighborhood for so many years.

Forest Home has had its share of trauma and tragedy. There have been deaths and drownings, floods and fires, scandal and suicide. Perhaps the most widely known example involved Montgomery Cornell, 19-year-old nephew of Ezra Cornell, and Lucy Criddle, 16-year-old daughter of the local undertaker. On the morning of June 16, 1861, Lucy was found shot dead in Montgomery's buggy, and Montgomery was discovered drowned in the gorge behind The Byway. The *Ithaca Journal and Advertiser* called this a double suicide, and "one of the most extraordinary and heart-rending tragedies it has ever become our duty to report."

One major problem that Forest Home has faced in more recent years is the ever-increasing through traffic that winds its way along the community's modest roads and across the two single-lane bridges, threatening the hamlet's serenity, safety, and integrity. Petitions requesting an alternative route around the community date back to 1910, when Forest Home Drive first became a state highway. They continue today, as the traffic has grown progressively worse.

The hamlet of Forest Home enjoys a strong identity and sense of community. Its beautiful natural setting along Fall Creek, its charming historic architecture and two single-lane bridges, and the neighborliness of its people, all serve to attract and hold residents. In spite of the traffic, it is a great place to live.

Renwick Heights

Pamela Monk

The Renwick Heights neighborhood, a small residential suburb of Ithaca, is a historical fragment, part of what was known as the Renwick Tract for more than a century and a half and today includes Stewart Park.[1] Renwick Heights is nestled at the foot of East Hill, directly below the Village of Cayuga Heights and north of Ithaca Falls. It currently comprises Renwick Drive, Renwick Place, Renwick Heights Road, and the last two houses on Wyckoff. The last official concern tying the neighborhood together was a joint payment for trash pickup, but that has gone by the boards with the advent of door-to-door recycling and individual trash tags. All that remains is an occasional block party or dish-to-pass, arranged by neighbors just to keep in touch.

William Heidt documented the early history of the Renwicks in *The Blue-Eyed Lassie and the Renwicks in Ithaca.* In July 1790 a Revolutionary War veteran drew lot no. 88 of the Military Tract as a bounty for his service. He sold the wilderness acreage to a James Renwick of New York City in December of the same year. James Renwick died without a will in 1802, leaving his son William and a granddaughter, Sara Kemp, as heirs. The courts divided the land, one-half going to Kemp, the other to William and his family. William died, and after

22. Renwick Park, c. 1915. The park had been taken over by the Wharton movie company with the pier converted to a studio. Originally a dance and picnic area, the pavilion later served as a restaurant. The motor car is on East Shore Drive, not yet paved.

various court actions his widow Jean Jeffrey Renwick and seven surviving children inherited the half of Renwick Tract that belonged to their father.

The last of these children, Robert Jeffrey Renwick, moved to Ithaca in 1820; known as Major Renwick, he managed the property and served for a while as Ithaca postmaster. He died in 1875, and his widow, Eleanor Renwick, lived at 102 East Falls Street with her daughter until her death in 1902. A son, James Jeffrey, lived at 120 East Falls until his death in 1928.

In 1894, a financier named Horace E. Hand, and an electrical engineer named Herman Bergholtz obtained title to much of the Renwick Tract. Their plan was to extend a railway from what is now Lincoln Street to the lake. At the lakeshore, they constructed a park, which Henry Abt described in his book *Ithaca*, published in 1926:

> In this amusement park, with lawns, woods and paths laid out by a landscape artist of the firm that planned Central Park in New York City, there was a small landing where small boats were rented, a zoological garden, a theater for vaudeville performances, and a pavilion where "Patsy" Conway's band gave concerts during the

summer months. Thousands of visitors came, often excursions from some distance to enjoy its summer attractions.[2]

By 1914 the park had been leased to the Wharton Studios of movie fame, until the Whartons abandoned Ithaca for a more favorable climate. A. K. Fletcher, a longtime Ithaca resident, has written a memoir of Fall Creek in that era. He recalls movie sets and cameras, noting that the black people of Ithaca had it made because they obtained more "extra work than anyone else."[3] After the departure of the Wharton Studios, the city purchased Renwick Park in 1921, during the tenure of Mayor Edwin C. Stewart. He died before his term was up, leaving the city $150,000 for renovations to the park, which was renamed Stewart Park in his honor. Bergholtz was hired to help restore the area.

The undeveloped land between the northern edge of Fall Creek and Stewart Park was the site of old Percy Field, where baseball was first played in Ithaca in the 1870s. Ithaca High School and Boynton Middle School are now located there. The line demarcating the town from the city stretches through the campus, placing the high school in the City of Ithaca and the middle school in the town.

Residential development of Renwick Heights began in the early 1900s. The neighborhood never became consolidated with the city or with the Village of Cayuga Heights.

2 Town of Caroline

Molly Adams

The Town of Caroline, located in the southeast corner of Tompkins County, was part of the Watkins and Flint Purchase. The earliest settlers bought land from an agent in Owego and were residents of the Town of Owego in Tioga County. Still a part of Tioga County, Caroline became a town in 1811; it was not added to Tompkins County until 1823. The town's history is difficult to grasp because Caroline encompassed many settlements that changed names frequently. No village came to dominate, and the area is now largely residential, with five recognizable population centers: Caroline, at the northeast corner; Speedsville, at the southeast corner; Caroline Center, in the middle; Slaterville Springs, on the former Catskill Turnpike; and Brooktondale, on Six Mile Creek. The sometime vitality of such places as Boiceville, The City, Caroline Depot, Rawson Hollow, Central Chapel, and Besemer is now visible only to an architectural historian or a student of local history.

From Forests to Farms: 1794 to 1866

The first settlers followed Indian trails from Owego to a valley at the headwaters of Six Mile Creek, where the hamlet of Caroline exists today. In 1794 the Widow Earsley bought one hundred acres, then established her extended family the next year, a week after Captain David Rich arrived from Vermont. The Earsley and Rich farms were separated by a road that became the Catskill Turnpike in 1804; there was a tollgate at Rich's tavern, and the turnpike became a potent force in town affairs. Families from the Berkshires quickly joined the Richs and the Earsleys to form the "Yankee Settlement." A merchant named Speed opened a post office here in 1806 but moved in 1812, taking name and office with him.[1] In 1819, the post office replacing Speed's was named Caroline, even though the area was called Tobeytown after a well-known local family.

Early settlers, in addition to clearing the land, looked for water to power lumber- and gristmills. Mills provided jobs and commerce to support other trades. Near Tobeytown, in an area called The 600, an "up and down" sawmill existed as early as 1808. White pine and hemlock trees, often 5 feet in diameter and 150 feet

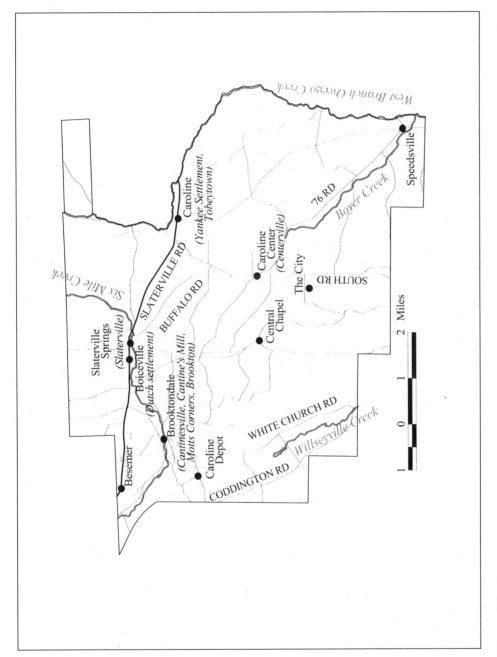

Town of Caroline

tall, were cut there by workers who lived in boarding houses nearby. This mill site is the easternmost of twenty-three in Caroline which have at one time or another drawn power from Six Mile Creek.

In 1789 General John Cantine, who came to central New York to settle land disputes, chose property in Caroline because of Six Mile Creek.[2] His holdings were cleverly arranged along the creek and included the area where Slaterville and Brooktondale developed as well as the land between. His son, John Jr., built a log cabin in 1798 in the Brooktondale area. In 1800 General Cantine brought Benoni Mulks from Ulster County to build a gristmill near the cabin. In 1804 John Jr. put up the first frame house in Cantinesville (or Cantine's Mill); he was active in clearing land and developing agriculture to provide work for the mill. The first Masonic Lodge in Caroline met at Cantine's house from 1808 until 1828, when he sold out and moved to Ithaca.

In 1800 William Roe built several mills on Six Mile Creek below the Indian crossing, the most westerly of the twenty-three sites. The Roe cemetery survives today, as well as a Federal-style house and several barns. The first bridge across the creek was built above the mill in 1825. Benoni Mulks bought land to the east, at the western edge of today's Slaterville, and built a cabin in 1800.[3] With family and friends from Ulster County, he cleared land and built mills from Slaterville to Ellis Hollow Road, where there was a tollgate. This area was at first called the Dutch Settlement, because residents conducted their daily affairs in Dutch.[4]

Meanwhile Augustin Boyer, a hardware merchant from Baltimore, bought 1,044 acres near the present Caroline Center. This land was later divided into several farms.[5] Boyer could see that Owego, on the Susquehanna River, was important both as a source of goods for Caroline and because Ithaca merchants sent their products south through Caroline for shipping from Owego. With help from neighbors, Boyer immediately set about building a road from what is now Speedsville to the Catskill Turnpike at Boiceville, thereby connecting Owego with Ithaca. On July 4, 1808, he named the road "76" in honor of the spirit of independence.[6]

The junction of two such important roads brought business and status to Richard Bush's tavern, built in Boiceville in 1801 and selected as the site of the first town meeting in 1811 as well as the muster for the War of 1812. John Mulks, Benoni's son, built a millrace, pond, gristmill, sawmill, and distillery just west of Benoni's property in about 1815. The bustling center was called Boiceville after Abraham Boice built a tavern there in 1816.[7] North of the turnpike, the Bull farm kept horses for the stages and offered pasture for passing cattle. Bush's tavern closed when the handsome, Greek Revival Bull Tavern opened across the street; it was an important stagecoach stop from 1818 to 1848. The name Krums Corners was later attached to this intersection after Michael Krum became owner of the Bull Tavern.

The first church in Caroline was the Dutch Reformed, which organized in 1812 and put up a large building west of Boiceville in 1820.[8] The minister for twenty-five years was Rev. Garrett Mandeville. Persuaded by his wife's cousin, Simeon DeWitt, to visit Ithaca, he came from Ulster County and served in Ithaca and Trumansburg until 1812, when he bought a farm in Caroline. A post office for

23. Peter and Phyllis Webb,
c. 1850. The 1820 census
showed thirty-two colored
residents in Caroline. Peter
Webb bought his freedom
from John James Speed Sr. in
1818 for $384, and his son,
Frederick Webb, bought Dr.
Joseph Speed's homestead on
Level Green Road in 1850.

Boiceville, opened in 1823, was named Slaterville after Levi Slater, the first town clerk. The village developed to the east with a Methodist church, stores, mills, and taverns to serve the farmers and turnpike traffic.

Members of the Speed family arrived from Virginia between 1805 and 1811, accompanied by associates and slaves. They were influential, possibly wealthy, people. Dr. Joseph Speed settled at Spring Farm on Level Green Road in Caroline in 1805. He was a trustee and the first librarian of the Caroline Literary Association, a private circulating library formed in 1818. Originally a slave owner, he became convinced of the evils of slavery and supported the recolonization of slaves in Africa.

John James Speed Sr., Dr. Speed's cousin, moved with his post office from Tobeytown to an area south of Centerville in 1812 and built houses, mills, and stores. Although the post office would have been called Speedsville, this settlement was referred to as The City, or City Lot. At one time, the Reverend Mandeville lived at The City "keeping a boarding school . . . for about 20 boys" who were preparing for college.[9] Speed left for Ithaca in 1832. John James Speed Jr., who succeeded his father as postmaster and was elected to the State Assembly in 1832, lived in Centerville, which grew up around the intersection of Speed (now Buffalo) Road and 76 Road. This village had a public school in 1820, a Methodist church in 1825, stores and shops, and a stagecoach stop at Rounseville's inn. A fine school called The Academy was built at the corner of Taft Road in 1839.[10]

In 1819 a settler named Laban Jenks, who owned a store and other businesses, built a stagecoach stop and tavern (now known as the Legg House) in a village called The Corners (or Jenksville), at the eastern end of 76 Road. The Universalists, Presbyterians, and Methodists joined forces to build a church there in 1828. This village was a center of commerce because of its connection to Owego. Its residents, tired of getting their mail at The City or Centerville, negotiated with J. J. Speed Jr. The post office was moved, and The Corners became Speedsville in 1835.[11]

Central Chapel and Rawson Hollow were early settlements that have disappeared. Lyman Rawson built a cabin in 1802 on West Owego Creek north of Speedsville and kept a tavern there until he finished the Rawson Hollow Inn, where he did business until he died in 1826.[12] Rawson Hollow had the usual mills and shops by 1807 and a Presbyterian Society in 1813. It was a busy area because traffic moved north from Speedsville to an area on the Catskill Turnpike known as Padlock (now vanished). The second school (on the site of the first) survives as a residence, next to the old inn. West of Caroline Center, in an area called Central Chapel, William Ennest and Joseph Brearley had fine homes early in the century. Other families settled on Bald Hill, above Central Chapel. The Widow VanDeMark came to Bald Hill with ten children in 1813; her descendants were active in the development of Brooktondale.

In 1813, when New York gave money to all townships to establish schools, Caroline had nine schools; by 1820 there were nineteen, some shared with Dryden and Danby. In 1814 the population of Caroline was 905. By 1825, with 2,128 residents, Caroline had many sizable settlements. Stages were active on the Catskill Turnpike, despite the opening of the Erie Canal; and the population increased to 2,623 by 1830. In 1834 the Ithaca & Owego Railroad was completed through the Willseyville Valley, and more communities developed. Pugsley's Depot on the Belle School Road, one of the original stations, had a post office from 1850 to 1860, until it moved to Caroline Depot. People settled along White Church Road (first Leggett and later Cooper Road) and near Caroline Depot. Mail formerly carried by stage came by rail to be distributed to the villages. In addition to telegraph services at the depot, the hamlet had two stores, a feedmill, and several residences.

Although the Catskill stage was discontinued in 1850, traffic continued to move along the turnpike road. Slaterville added a doctor, an undertaker (who also manufactured wagons and carriages), a blacksmith, two stores, and a hotel. A second school was built at the east end of the village after the one on Mulks's farm was torn down by rowdy boys.

In 1830 Cantinesville (now Brooktondale) was transformed when William Mott II bought John Cantine's property, which by then included a gristmill and a sawmill. Mott converted the gristmill, which was on the north side of the creek, to a plastermill and built a new gristmill on the opposite (south) bank of the creek. Mott deposed the postmaster at Terryville (on Coddington Road) and moved the post office to his store at 559 Brooktondale Road. The town, called

Mott's Hollow or Mottville, became Motts Corners with the opening of the post office in 1836. Taking full advantage of the available waterpower, Mott eventually owned six mills and several stores and had a furniture factory that made fine tables. He built a Greek Revival house south of the new mill and later built the Shurter House, where Jacob Shurter ran a hotel and store. He also built houses for families who cleared and farmed his land and produced lumber for him. The ox teams that he stabled east of the Cantine mansion hauled lumber to Ithaca and brought back loads of land plaster stone (gypsum). In winter the teams went to Pennsylvania for sleighloads of blacksmith's coal.[13] Other businesses in Motts Corners included a tannery, a foundry, and a brickyard. The gun shop made gun barrels during the Civil War.[14] In 1863 the Baptists built a handsome church at the base of Perry Hill (now Elm Street).

Centerville became Caroline Center with the opening of a new post office in 1839. By 1866 the village had twenty-five buildings, including two churches, two schools, a tannery, the hotel, a "shoe shop," several stores, a blacksmith shop, and a harnessmaker's. The Morrell family from Lansing raised sheep on five hundred acres of former Boyer land south of the village.

St. John's Episcopal Church was moved from Richford to Speedsville in 1842. In 1850 a temperance hall was built as a meetingplace for groups such as the Masons. The Methodists built a new church in 1851, leaving the old one to be shared by Presbyterians and Universalists. Seth Akins, a carpenter who made coffins and cheese boxes, built a covered bridge over Owego Creek in 1856. By 1866 a fashionable square "commons" had developed on land donated to honor Laban Jenks; it was surrounded by the stagecoach stop, stores, a school, churches and cemetery, and businesses. A creamery was built in 1868, and the school was remodeled in 1872.

By 1865 the Town of Caroline had declined from a peak population of 2,644 to 2,257. Motts Corners, Slaterville, Caroline Center, and Speedsville were significant enough to deserve village maps in the 1866 Atlas. Motts Corners was the largest of these settlements, with a population of three hundred.

From the Civil War to 1900

The end of the Civil War inspired optimism despite a widespread interest in moving west. The "Murdock" line of the Utica, Ithaca, & Elmira Railroad extended train service from East Ithaca south to Pugsley's Depot, making two lines in the Willseyville Valley. Workers began to lay track near Motts Corners as early as 1872. Many developments in Caroline followed on the heels of this railroad activity. Industry in Motts Corners benefited from access to a more convenient railroad; the railroad gained customers for the coal it carried, as well as revenue from farms and industrial goods.

Ezra Cornell's son Frank owned the Upper Mill at Motts Corners from 1870 to 1881 (the mill that Mott had built burned in 1862 and was rebuilt by George White in 1865). Later the Vorhis family called it the Excelsior Mill. The woolen mill became a shingle- and sawmill and later housed stores selling hardware,

24. Wooden Trestle at Motts Corners, 1875. Built between October and December 1875, this structure was 90 feet high and 1,600 feet long and required 750,000 feet of 12-inch-square timbers. When it was removed in 1889, the wooden timbers covered a 10-acre lot. People who lived east of the trestle regretted the loss of the windbreak. Photograph courtesy of Arthur Volbrecht.

farm machinery, and feed until it burned down in 1916. The present store, on the site of a plastermill, seems to have started about 1890, under Frank Vorhis. As late as 1866 few buildings existed on the south bank of Six Mile Creek, for the village had grown up on the north bank, near the first mill. There was open space below Mott's imposing Greek Revival house on the hill. In 1869 the Congregationalists, combining the Methodist and the Dutch Reformed churches, put up a church on land formerly owned by Mott. This congregation had three women ministers: Annis Bertha Ford Eastman (1889–1891), Juanita Breckenridge Bates (1892–1893), and Emily C. Woodruff (1899–1903). A two-room school was built near the church in 1870, and several substantial residences soon followed. The name of the town was changed to Brookton in 1883, because of confusion with a Mottville near Syracuse.

Social activities revolved around the church, the Good Templars, and the Grange. The Brookton Skating Rink opened next to the school in 1884, with rental skates, music, and instructors. It sponsored concerts and supper dances. Professor Leopold Leo, Ithaca's dancing master, brought an orchestra from Ithaca in 1886.[15] In 1889 a "spidery" steel bridge replaced the "burly" wooden trestle that had spanned the valley. In 1893 riders could board the Elmira, Cortland &

25. Great Iron Bridge at Brookton, 1907. The *Cortland Standard* (May 28, 1889) noted that 810,000 pounds of iron were "installed in less than four weeks of working time." Workers prepared sections throughout the week, then cut away wood and installed metal span by span on Sundays when the train wasn't running. Eight hundred feet long, it was half the length of the wooden trestle; extra support for the track was provided by fill on the station end. *Patria* (1917), starring Irene Castle, includes a scene at the bridge. Photograph courtesy of Arthur Volbrecht.

Northern at Brookton or at Besemer for a visit to the Chicago World's Fair; those who wished could return via Niagara Falls.[16]

Besemer developed after 1875 when Josiah Besemer and his son Willis built a station where the new train track crossed the Catskill Turnpike. The post office here was called Besemer's Depot in 1876, then Besemer from 1883 to 1915. Willis Besemer served as the only station agent for fifty-nine years and nine months. His sister Georgia assisted with the mail, the feed business on the second floor, and the station. She also delivered visitors to Slaterville Springs.

In Slaterville Dr. W. C. Gallagher, an energetic entrepreneur, hoped many visitors would come by train. In 1871 he proclaimed his discovery of "an excellent quality of magnetic water."[17] The village population grew to 275 by 1879. Trains from New York City to Besemer's Station or to Caroline Depot brought as many as two hundred summer guests to enjoy country air and medicinal water from the famous Magnetic Springs. The town became Slaterville Springs in 1890, partly to differentiate it from Slatersville in Rhode Island but certainly to capitalize on the local commodity. Victorian-style architecture in Slaterville—St. Thomas's Episcopal Church (1894), Dr. Gallagher's museum, the school, and several fine houses—attest to its prosperity in this period. Visitors supported the stores, two resort hotels, wagon shops, and churches.

Boiceville had dwindled by 1879 to a blacksmith shop, a school, a sawmill, and several residences. The Dutch Reformed parsonage was moved to Caroline Depot

26. District School no. 2, Caroline and Dryden, c. 1910. In 1869 school trustees paid $600 for the lot next to Dr. Gallagher's property. The school was built that summer, the first of many Victorian buildings in Slaterville. By the time of this picture, extra windows had been added on both floors. The building is now the Caroline Town Hall. Photograph courtesy of Caroline History Room.

about 1889. Dr. Gallagher bought the church for $75, dismantled, and used it to construct the building at the corner of Route 79 and Buffalo Road, where the Masons met. The church bell went to the Federated Church in Brookton. The school survives as a residence next to the cemetery.

Caroline Depot was busy with train and mail traffic. It had a stockyard for cattle, and farmers shipped eggs, potatoes, milk, and hay. In the 1890s the railroad brought a special car so students could climb Bald Hill to gather "botanical specimens," mostly arbutus.[18] White Church had a post office from 1876 to 1902, probably in the depot.

Caroline Center, evidently prosperous, was featured in an 1868 county directory that boasted about Cornell University and Ithaca's prospects. The village had eighty-five residents, mostly farmers whose acreage is noted, and businessmen who supported farm occupations. Agricultural societies were being formed to improve farming methods and the quality of livestock. New soil analyses showed that the soil and surface of Caroline were suited for grazing, but many farmers were already dairying. In 1872 the Beaver Dam Creamery was built near Caroline Center; it made no fewer than 26,425 pounds of butter and 31,993 pounds of cheese in the year 1877. Farmers built substantial homes in the City Lot area. Over the hill, near the homes of Ennest and Brearley, a sawmill was active; and

27. Caroline Center Church, c. 1900. The Methodist Episcopal Church in Caroline Center, built in 1825, was taken down piece by piece and rebuilt and enlarged on an adjoining lot in 1866. To the left of the church is the school known as The Academy. Photograph courtesy of Caroline History Room.

Central Chapel built a church, which had a ladies' aid society and a cemetery. The Cemetery Association was active from 1899 to 1925.

Speedsville, with its triweekly stage to Owego, also flourished after the Civil War. In 1879, with a population of two hundred, it had two general stores, a milliner and a tailor, two blacksmiths, a wagon shop, a gristmill, a sawmill, a cheese-box factory, a hotel, three churches, a Masonic Lodge, and a Good Templar Lodge. Bricks were made here, as well as cheese vats, milkcans, and coolers. There was a homeopathic physician and a carriage maker; the Cornet Band gave concerts in the park. A creamery and cheese factory started in 1879 and another in 1894.

In Caroline, formerly Tobeytown, R. G. H. Speed built a cheese factory in 1868.[19] He entered Cornell University with the first class in that same year; the business, meant to finance his education, continued for forty years. The mills, a blacksmith shop, a small grocery store, and a few houses made up the hamlet. A small Methodist church was built through local effort in 1894. In 1887 seven lots of six hundred acres each were transferred from Canaan in Dryden to this part of Caroline.

From 1900 to World War II

By 1900 Caroline's population had fallen to 1,938 (from 2,257 in 1865). It continued to decline to a low of 1,542 in 1920, as more people, unable to make a

28. Rural Free Delivery leaving from the Brookton post office on September 1, 1902. Fred Lounsbery, postmaster, is seen in the post office doorway; the carriers are, *left to right,* Charlie Stanley, John Caveney, Walter VanDeMark, and DeForest McWhorter. Frank Mulks waits in the store doorway. Many rural post offices closed in 1902. When the Speedsville post office closed, mail was delivered there from Berkshire. Photograph courtesy of Mary Caveney Alexander.

living, left their farms. The shrinking population affected both businesses and churches, which closed when collections were too meager to pay a minister.[20] Rural Free Delivery was a new development; although a welcome convenience to many, it removed post office traffic from places such as Caroline, White Church, and Central Chapel. Farm traffic supported White Church and the train stopped for high school students as late as 1932. The school remained on Belle School Road.

In 1903 Charlie Jones set up the Caroline Farmers Telephone Company in Slaterville. From the beginning there were not enough telephones to satisfy demand. As late as 1925, clusters of homes north of Caroline, east of Slaterville Springs, and south of Brookton had almost no service. After an outbreak of typhoid fever in Ithaca in 1903, the Board of Health investigated properties along Six Mile Creek in Brookton and Slaterville and reported on the number of manure piles, tanning vats, hoghouses, and privies that polluted the waters flowing to Ithaca. The accompanying photographs also showed the effect of seasonal flooding on the gravely banks of the creek after a century of clearing and overuse. A

29. Dam for the upper mill at Brookton, c. 1910. The dam had been built with sturdy boards in 1897 by Frank Vorhis Sr. At its peak the mill employed nine men full time, who sometimes worked day and night to produce buckwheat flour. Photograph courtesy of Caroline History Room.

disastrous flood in 1905 undermined buildings and destroyed many businesses. The upper mill in Brookton lasted a long time because its dam was well built and regularly maintained.

As more residents bought cars, roads needed to be improved. The state began applying a "water-bound macadam" surface to the Catskill Turnpike, starting at the Ithaca line in 1904 and proceeding westward in sections; it did not reach the Tioga County line until 1930.[21] Stone walls as well as field stones were crushed for the highway foundation. John "Good Roads" Mandeville went to Scotland to study the macadam process before designing the road through Brookton in 1912. The 76 Road was also surfaced, but the town kept a list of watering troughs for horses as late as 1915.

From 1908 to 1925 an itinerant worker named George Jansen, who dug gardens, painted rooms or houses, washed dishes, or "kept house" when an owner went on

30. The Catskill Turnpike at Boiceville. This section of the road, shown in a postcard sent on November 20, 1912, received a macadam surface in 1910. The houses on the left are still standing. The house on the right, on the site of the Boiceville Tavern, burned about 1932. As New York State Route 79, this road remains a major route in and out of Tompkins County. Photograph courtesy of Caroline History Room.

a trip, recorded events in Brookton along with the daily weather. He noted the death of Emily Mills, who had continued her father's store for thirty years, extending credit to many needy individuals. He commented on people and businesses as well as the Saturday night dances and the availability of "Bald Hill Hooch."[22] In 1908 Dr. Benjamin Lockwood came to provide medical care and became a beloved figure. He built the Dalebrook Apartments in the 1920s, using the foundation and the roof of the old Vorhis mill. When he died in 1934, Dr. Mary Ridgway, who had grown up in the Willseyville Valley, took over his practice. She later married Dr. Martin Tinker and moved her practice to a house down the street, where it remains. Through her work with the Caroline Well Baby Clinics, she has overseen the immunization of several generations of children.

The trains were prominent in Brookton, sailing across the valley several times a day. Oldtimers remember loading hay, potatoes, and buckwheat into the boxcars, helping the station agent handle crates of eggs and chickens, sitting on the hill overlooking the track to watch the train go by. In addition to taking animals and produce to market and delivering packages from Sears and Wards, trains offered recreational opportunities. Locals could ride to East Ithaca, transfer to Freeville, spend time there drinking coffee and watching other trains come and go, and then return home.

Old Home Day, an annual celebration for Brookton, began in 1919 and continued into the 1940s. Originally held in the shade and flowers of Mason's Grove

(Greenway Farm), it later moved to the Federated Church; the event featured speeches and musical entertainment and reunions with friends returning from afar. In 1927 former teacher Will Graham noted the changes since his arrival in 1877: twenty-seven new homes, electric lights, macadam roads, and modern plumbing. The 1926 name change from Brookton to Brooktondale is not commented on, nor is the fact that street lights were installed in 1925. At Old Home Day in 1935 Professor Edwin Shurter proposed a memorial to Dr. Lockwood: those who wished to contribute could sign up "at the store." This store in the center of town, with the post office attached, had become, and remains, a village hub. Harry VanDeMark, famous as the local Santa, had another store at the eastern end of Brooktondale; between 1916 to 1947 he drove around the countryside to sell groceries from his wagon. Rural salesmen were common—in 1925, eleven made regular visits in the Caroline area. Jessie Brewer sold dry goods and had a lending library where Emily Mills's store had been. In 1934 Walt Arsenault bought the Beaver Brook Farm Dairy on Middaugh (formerly Bates) Road, which he operated until 1959.

Slaterville, which celebrated its Old Home Day at the school, still welcomed visitors who came in summer to escape the city heat. Mrs. Middaugh provided them with "ambered glass," to take home as a souvenir.[23] Irene Castle's *Exploits of Elaine* was filmed at that farm and featured John Middaugh's oxen, Buck and Bright.[24] Visitors were encouraged to purchase the famous Magnetic Water by the case, keg, or barrel. The butter and cheese factory established in 1902 served as a center for local farmers and a key economic support to the village until 1920. It later housed a bottling works. Clint Mulks had a sawmill at Krums Corners, where he provided sawdust for icehouses; he also took his portable sawmill to local farms. When electricity arrived in 1928, farmers and housewives were delighted to electrify pumps, milking machines, and irons. Radios, rare in 1925, were common by 1950.

Before World War II, Slaterville had two stores. Ferguson's Red and White sold fresh baked goods, groceries, gas, and oil. Blackburn's gas station sold groceries and miscellaneous items, including water from an artesian well, and later added a lunchroom. Local musicians liked to hang out at Blackburn's in the 1940s. A third grocery store appeared at the corner of Midline Road and Route 79 in 1944. The Masons moved from the phone exchange building to the school and then bought Ferguson's store in 1953, renting the front room to the post office. Grange members met in the former Slaterville House, where the firehall addition now stands.

In 1935 Ithaca pharmacist Edward Barrett bought the former James Mulks mill property in Boiceville. He called his place The Hobby and amused himself creating the parklike setting which still exists. Across the highway Dr. Genung remodeled his barns for poultry farming, the latest "industry." Dr. Gallagher, who died in 1921, and his son Lyman (who lived until 1945) promoted tourism, including Gallagher's Museum of Curios, Antiques, and Indian and Historic Relics. Lyman Gallagher wrote articles about Caroline history for the *Ithaca Journal*; his 1925 piece on the Catskill Turnpike expressed hope that federal money for new

31. The Fountain House. One of two significant hotels in Slaterville, it was built in 1872 and later enlarged to three stories. A brochure (May 1901) advertised "delightful scenery, fine roads for both carriages and bicycles; pure atmosphere, . . . absolute exemption from dampness, malaria and mosquitoes." The Fountain House burned in December 1911. Photograph courtesy of Caroline History Room.

central routes "for tourist traffic . . . through the Finger Lakes Region" would be forthcoming.[25]

"Filling stations" sprang up to cater to drivers and their cars. Brooktondale had three, including one built with materials from Ithaca's Lyceum Theater. Omar Mulks built a garage across from his house on Slaterville Road, and the stores in Slaterville provided services. In 1932 the Federated Church pulled down its horse sheds to provide room for cars. Church membership seemed to dwindle as cars became more common: some people went to bigger town churches, others took pleasure trips on Sunday. As automobile and truck traffic increased, train traffic decreased. When the Brooktondale trestle was damaged in the 1935 flood, it was abandoned by the Lehigh Valley Railroad and demolished for scrap. The Brooktondale and Besemer stations closed.

Caroline was hard hit during the Depression. The hill farms were not suited to mechanization. The gasoline engine that powered automobiles and tractors also wiped out the huge hay market for New York City horses. Farms were foreclosed or abandoned.[26] In 1929, on the advice of Cornell's farm economists, New York began offering farmers a minimum cash payment for their land. The state then planted trees to prevent soil erosion and to provide future timber and recreation sites. When Franklin D. Roosevelt became president, more land was bought through the Reforestation Act. Caroline presently has almost 7,000 acres of state

32. Morrell Mansion. This house was built in 1846 by H. K. Morrell on a 500-acre farm south of Caroline Center. Joseph McGraw of Dryden bought the property in 1865 and sold it in 1875 to Franklin C. Cornell, who rented out house and land. The building was carefully taken apart and rebuilt on the Martin Catherwood property on Highgate Road, sometime between October 1933 and the following spring, when the land became state property.

forest land acquired in the buyout.[27] Exploration of seasonal-use roads through the forest areas reveals an occasional lilac bush, apple tree, row of maples, or stone foundation. Some abandoned houses were substantial, but it was government policy that no buildings remain on the land. In 1929 Dr. Lockwood acquired a marble fireplace for his house before the Morrell Mansion was removed from Caroline Center.

From 1933 to 1941 a Civilian Conservation Corps camp on the Harford Road near Caroline provided work, housing, and a wage to many unemployed young men. They helped with reforestation on the new state lands and built the fire tower on Blackman Hill. They also became a part of the social and economic life of the community. The Resettlement and Land Utilization Administration operated site no. 9 out of the old school south of Caroline Center, providing a wage for men who came daily to cut pulpwood, plant trees, and take down buildings.[28]

Caroline, Caroline Center, and Central Chapel lost most population in the buyouts. Sinski's store in Caroline (Tobeytown) survived from 1919 until 1952, supported by gas rationing and the distance to Ithaca. The small church closed in 1910. Caroline Center had two country stores in 1925, but only one in 1944. The large church was little used, but local children attended the school until after the war. Central Chapel lost its church but kept a school. In the Willseyville Valley, high school students rode the train to Candor as late as 1932.[29] The station at Caroline Depot, on the Delaware-Lackawanna line (a different track from the one that had come through Brooktondale), existed until 1956 for freight and mail. After 1942 there were no more passengers, no more circus trains, no more student specials bringing city kids like E. B. White through the Caroline hills.[30] The two stores closed in the 1920s. In 1926 the newly formed Nazarene Church bought the old White Church and reconstructed it opposite Caroline Depot Road, then later moved to a new building down the road.

Children in Caroline attended one- or two-room schools before the war, even though opinion held that closing rural schools would save tax money.[31] The Central Chapel and Boiceville schools closed in the 1930s for lack of students. The Slaterville school provided the only high-school instruction. Anyone in Caroline could attend, but transportation was not provided. When older boys went off to World War I, high school instruction was discontinued. Students who went to Ithaca (or Candor) often boarded in town during the week. Some took a horse and buggy, or rode a milk truck, or, later, drove a car to school.[32] In 1918 Harry and Les Crispell used a Model T truck and in 1928 bought a small bus and transported students from Caroline. At first families paid for this kind of service, but in 1930 rural school districts began paying by annual contract.[33] The Crispells allowed nonstudents to ride to Ithaca or to locations along the way.

The Crispell Brothers, Caroline's enterprising family, later developed a regular bus service into Ithaca, at its peak making seven trips a day. The driver allowed passengers to step off for errands; and he brought back *Ithaca Journal*s as well as special items requested by stores or residents. When Crispell Brothers formed a charter service in 1929, the first trip took the Candor senior class to Washington, D.C. Later the buses made two trips to New York City every week and were hired by the colleges for music or athletic units or for field trips. Crispell also had a hauling business, carrying goods to and from New York City. And their moving vans operated until 1970.[34]

Speedsville declined when river commerce transferred to the railroads and when farmers left the Caroline hills. Fires took their toll where buildings were close together. In 1888 the Speedsville hotel and barn were destroyed. In 1902 two stores, a barn, and the meat market were lost. In 1928 a store facing the commons burned.[35] Old Home Days and family reunions continued to be held in the park. Local sawmills, now powered by electricity, stayed in operation.

Baseball was a favorite pastime in the 1920s and 1930s. As E. R. Eastman has pointed out, "If you never attended a baseball game between the teams of two neighboring villages 50 years ago, you have never seen a real ball game." The fans knew every player and were prone to spring onto the field at the hint of an argument.[36] When the war came and ballplayers went off to fight, a group of young ladies organized by Martha Lattin in Brooktondale gathered and edited news for servicemen. The circulation of the *Brooktondale Bugler* grew to five hundred. Mailings were finished at bees in various locations in Caroline as the newsletter became a community project. Issued from 1943 until 1946, it also published letters from servicemen and addresses so they could write one another. A booklet titled *Brooktondale, U.S.A.* was produced as a Christmas card in

1944.[37] Using extra funds and additional contributions, the *Bugler* group installed an Honor Roll commemorating local servicemen—near the Brooktondale ballfield.

Postwar Caroline

After the war, with better roads and cars and plentiful gasoline, it was easy to live in a pleasant (and less expensive) rural area and work in the city. As a result, the population of Caroline, at 1,617 in 1930 and 1,737 in 1940, rose to 1,900 in 1950. Cornell students, using Brooktondale and Slaterville as a sample, reported on what they called "the rural-penetrating movement." Where 58 percent of residents had been farmers or farm workers in 1925, only 17 percent were in 1950. Caroline had become a residential area for young people with growing families, whose wage earners worked in Ithaca, frequently at factory jobs, which typically paid better than farming.[38]

One Caroline organization that developed after the war was the volunteer fire company. Returning veterans familiar with vehicles and emergencies recognized that they could provide a badly needed service as well as take advantage of war surplus equipment. The Brooktondale Fire Company was organized at Tucker's Store in 1946, after a series of local fires and Ithaca Fire Department's outrageous offer to charge $100 for each call answered.[39] Trucks were kept in Frank Vorhis's garage until the station was built in 1951. Slaterville joined with Caroline to organize the Slaterville Fire Company in 1950. Their station was dedicated in May 1951, and a kitchen was later outfitted with Navy surplus equipment. Slaterville established an ambulance service in 1957 and added a community meeting room in 1963. The Speedsville Fire Company started planning in 1961, incorporated in 1965, and put up a building in 1966.

Another community force—little recognized until it was gone—was the local school, which focused people in a small community on a common cause. Brooktondale's two-room school had served both village and farm children. Slaterville's beautiful large building, with its playground and public water supply, was certainly the center of village activity. The various one-room schools were focal points for small communities. In 1956 all existing schools in Caroline were consolidated into the Ithaca City School District. In 1960 a new Caroline Elementary School was built—one of many in the Ithaca system—across from the Dutch Reform cemetery. It serves children from Caroline and from Ellis Hollow in the Town of Dryden.[40] Children in Speedsville now go to Newark Valley; those in the Willseyville Valley, to Candor.

The old school buildings were sold in 1959, some to become residences. A community association bought the Slaterville school for youth activities, then sold it to the town in 1966. The Brooktondale school was bought by the firemen as a meeting place for a local youth group called the Skip-Joe Club.[41] In March 1962 the club was reorganized as the Brooktondale Community Center to serve adults as well as youth. When the building burned in November of that year, the firemen donated the insurance proceeds and some of the former school land toward the building of a new community center, dedicated in 1964. Over the years, the Brooktondale Community Center has sponsored youth programs, a monthly newsletter, and an annual Apple Festival, as well as providing a location for family reunions and wedding receptions and a summer camp for children, for the benefit of all Caroline residents.

Boy Scouts were active after the war. In Slaterville, Meredith Brill organized the scouts in 1937 "after some boys climbed over Mr. Barrett's fence and killed the swans on his pond," as Hazel Brampton recalls. Brill played an important role in encouraging boys and families to take part in scouting activities. His brother Roland Brill gave land on Chestnut Road for annual camporees. In Brooktondale, Larry "Rep" Woodin became famous for his project SOAR, Save Our American Resources, an annual roadside cleanup that he organized by phone (he had been blind since 1958) and that involved many organizations and businesses. Both Rep Woodin and Meredith Brill received Silver Beaver awards for their contributions to scouting.[42]

In 1962 the Austin MacCormick Center was built as a youth recreation camp where the Morrell Mansion had stood. Dedicated by Governor Nelson Rockefeller as "a seat of learning for the boys who will be taught the principles of forestry, conservation, fire protection, fish and game work, landscaping and many other crafts," the project was expected to be an asset to the community, through payroll money, emergency assistance, and an increase in the value of "the forest plantations."[43] The camp was established on principles familiar to scouts, so it is not surprising to learn that Meredith Brill was chairman of a citizens advisory group associated with the camp.[44] Camp MacCormick is now a high-security detention center for delinquent boys.

After the war, Slaterville businesses included the post office in the Masonic Hall and two grocery stores. The corner store carried rifles, ammunition, china, penny candy, pottery, pet supplies, groceries, and a wheel of cheese. It had a checkerboard and a coffeepot for visitors. This store burned in 1981, and a convenience store was built closer to Midline Road in 1982. John Barnes bought Blackburn's Trading Post, which had been a local institution since 1934; his mother ran a luncheonette next door. St. Thomas's Episcopal Church has remained an active congregation since its beginning in 1894. After the Methodists joined the Federated congregation in Brooktondale, their church was used as a community center until it burned in 1957. The bell had been moved to St. Thomas's just before the fire.

Charlie Jones's telephone company was sold in 1955 to W. H. Caveney, who by 1961 had six hundred subscribers and two operators, at busy periods. Caveney began arrangements to sell to the Iroquois Phone Company in 1960. A public hearing revealed how poor rural service was, and the phone company was ordered to modernize and improve. Caroline was one of the earliest towns to have cable television because eager viewers living in the valleys set up their own systems. Anthony Ceracche eventually bought out the locals and was awarded the Caroline franchise. With more cars on the road, the Crispells noticed a decline in demand for bus service. In 1963, there were two round trip runs to Ithaca; by 1970 the service had been trimmed to one round trip per day, and even that was soon discontinued.

The Brooktondale post office, which had expanded operations when Caroline Depot closed in 1952 (and which now serves all of Caroline except Slaterville village and Speedsville), moved across the street when Jessie Brewer closed her store. In 1972, the Brooktondale Baptist Church built a new building on Slaterville Road, adding facilities for a school, which operated from 1972 to 1993. Their old church became an apartment building. Brooktondale activities then revolved around the remaining church, the fire hall, and the community center, in addition to the store and the post office.

When the Brooktondale Fire Company celebrated its first twenty years in 1966, residents were smug about progress since the war. The village had a fire company, natural gas, cable television, consolidated schools, a community center, telephones with direct dialing (no toll to Ithaca!), and now was looking forward to getting a safer road for school buses. From 1962 to 1967, Route 330 through Brooktondale was upgraded, for the first time since 1914. The improvements were greater than anyone expected. The Route 79 intersection was totally changed, and the entire road from there to 76 Road was "modernized." Whole avenues of maples were lost; the abandoned upper mill was subjected to a spectacular "practice burn" in the summer of 1964; the bridge in front of the store was reconfigured. The old Shurter House, which had survived several floods in its day, was bought for one dollar and moved to its present location at 447 Brooktondale Road. Those who objected to the "Rape of Valley Road" complained that the road went nowhere, because it ended at 76 Road. Caroline Center residents and neighboring dairy farmers defended the improved connection to Speedsville and Tioga County, which was used daily by trucks carrying milk, gas, and feed. When the highway crews finished with Brooktondale, they started on Slaterville. Many village trees were lost there, some houses were moved, other buildings were removed altogether. The new wide road helped traffic hurry toward Ithaca. The Crispell business moved to Slaterville Road, where highway workers had removed a large gravel bank and left enough room for buildings catering to truck maintenance. The location is within the Town of Dryden, but Crispell Automotive is still considered a Caroline business.

When Walt Arsenault died, his sons, George and David, began a farm equipment business at the former dairy on Middaugh Road. Arsenault Tractor Sales continued as a John Deere dealership until George died in 1985. In the 1990s, Tioga Transport moved to these buildings from Newark Valley. Many Caroline commuters now use this public transportation to get to work in Ithaca. Nearby, University Sand and Gravel continues to be one of Caroline's major businesses, digging and separating the glacial deposits that formed the terminus of prehistoric Lake Brookton.

As the larger villages became residential after the war, small centers became invisible. The track was torn up at Caroline Depot, and nearby fields have given way to housing. The Nazarene Church joined the Ithaca congregation but keeps its property on White Church Road for summer camp meetings. Caroline Center used the local church intermittently for services and regularly as a polling place; the building now houses an active congregation. The remaining store has became a nightclub under several successive owners. Caroline is a farming and residential area. Speedsville has held on to a local grocery store, an active Episcopal church, a community association that owns the old church and maintains the park, and a fire company. Residents are local farmers or commute to work in Ithaca or Tioga County. Fish fries, church dinners, horseshoe tournaments, and the annual dirtbike Enduro still draw visitors. The bandstand in the park was rebuilt in 1976.

A senior citizens' group was organized in 1970 to provide social events for all Caroline seniors. Members worked hard to establish a senior housing project, which opened as Fountain Manor in Slaterville in 1988. In 1976 town residents renovated the Slaterville school to create a meeting room and two offices for town business on the first floor. The second floor then became a repository for papers and artifacts dealing with local history. A history of Caroline was published in 1976 and expanded for the town's 1994 bicentennial. In 1989, when the bookmobile from the Finger Lakes Library System was discontinued, a reading room was installed at the Town Hall.

Today Caroline has 3,044 residents and a scattering of small independent businesses as well as a heritage of seven historical farms.[45] Caroline residents are militantly opposed to zoning, with the curious result that little development has occurred there compared to other towns. On the other hand, the housing projects at Farmer Lokken's, Sarsy's Acres, Landon Road, Speed Hill Road, and Besemer Road are all examples of level farmland taken for housing after World War II.

In 1991, Caroline witnessed a spontaneous outburst of yellow ribbons in support of servicepeople in the Persian Gulf War and their families at home. Drawing on past memories and fed by a desire to contribute, volunteers decorated trees all over the town with enormous yellow bows—in quite the same spirit that the *Brooktondale Bugler* had been mailed in the 1940s.

3 Town of Danby

Linda McCandless

In Danby, residents get more snow and less spring than in the rest of Tompkins County, but they relish their hardwood-studded hills and verdant valleys. Neighbors have a nodding acquaintance, and the family names on the rural mailboxes still match the names of the roads.

The history of Danby is the story of Danby, South Danby, and West Danby, three communities that straddle one of the most unusual geological phenomena in the county: the Danby Divide. It runs through the Michigan Hollow wetlands and Jennings Pond and separates two watersheds, one that drains north via Buttermilk Creek, Cayuga Lake, and the St. Lawrence River, and another that drains south to the Atlantic via the Susquehanna and Delaware rivers.

The first Iroquois residents used the watershed for farming and hunting, returning to the more temperate Cayuga Lake floor for the winter. Year-round white settlers arrived in 1795. All of the early pioneers lived a hardscrabble existence, battling the backwoods with self reliance, faith, tribe or family. Early settlements—South Danby, North Danby, the Beers and Adam settlements, Michigan Hollow, and West Danby—were well supplied by Cayuga Inlet, Buttermilk Creek, Six Mile Creek, Lick Brook, Danby, Miller, and Sulphur creeks, Jennings Pond, and an abundance of underground springs. The settlers found moderately fertile soil, mixed gravel and shale loam in the valleys, and shallow, poorly drained, rocky topsoil on the hills.

Danby has always been sparsely populated. In 1858 the population stood at 2,331. In 1990 it was 2,858, only 3 percent of county residents.[1] Today, seventy miles of roads in Danby are paved and nearly one-quarter of the town's 34,143 acres is owned by the state.

First Settlers

The earliest Danby settlers were "Mound-Builders," a peaceful, intelligent people whose culture is largely a matter of conjecture.[2] The Iroquois succeeded them.[3] The Cayugas, known by the name Gueugwehono, "the people of the mucky land," set up farms and orchards south of Cayuga Lake and made excursions into the Danby hills. In the summer they erected temporary shelters near

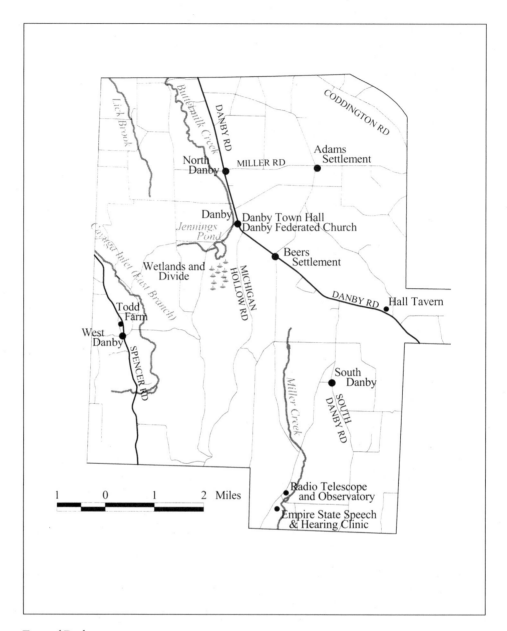

Town of Danby

the headwaters of Buttermilk Creek and planted corn, beans, squash, pumpkins, and tobacco. A historical marker at Jennings Pond reads: "Cayuga Indian Village—probable birthplace of Chief Logan."

When a contingent of Sullivan's army destroyed Indian villages at the head of Cayuga Lake in 1779, troops also burned a village of about one hundred log houses a few miles up Inlet Valley, near what later became West Danby.[4]

In the spring of 1789 eleven white men left Kingston, New York, to explore the wilderness west of the Susquehanna River. They returned with their families in September and built three log cabins on four hundred acres on the north side of Cascadilla Creek in what is today Ithaca.[5] The group consisted of Isaac Dumond, his wife, and three children; John Dumond and his wife; Jacob Yaple, his wife Maria (Isaac Dumond's sister), and their three children; Jacob's younger brother John; Peter Hinepaw, his wife, and their five children—twenty people in all.

Because an unscrupulous agent failed to pay taxes in Albany, these settlers lost title to their land in 1795 and were forced to relocate. Isaac and John Dumond and Jacob Yaple moved about four miles south and settled a short distance northeast of the bridge that now crosses Buttermilk Creek.[6]

Although most of Tompkins County was surveyed in military townships by Simeon DeWitt between 1784 and 1790, and claimed by Revolutionary War veterans in lieu of pay, the southern portion of the county lay beyond the Military Tract. Danby, Caroline, and Newfield were part of the 336,380 acres of the Watkins and Flint tract. Robert and Samuel W. Johnson, land speculators from Connecticut, who had extensive holdings in New York, purchased much land in what would be known as Danby.

In the spring of 1797, about six miles south of the Dumond and Yaple homestead, Lewis and Jabez Beers purchased one hundred acres of land each from the Johnsons, who were neighbors of theirs in Connecticut. Their homestead would soon become known as the Beers Settlement (later, South Danby). By the end of July they had cleared a small garden, planted potatoes and turnips, and erected "squares" for two cabins. In September they returned with their families, including Lewis's wife, Phebe Curtis Beers, his brothers Abner and Jabez, the latter's wife and children, and two apprentice boys, Joseph Judson and William Collins. Brother Nathan and Lewis's parents joined them later.

Within four years Lewis Beers and his family had bought a yoke of oxen, cleared sixty acres of land, built a "good house and barn," established the first post office (1801), were running a small inn in their 20′ × 22′ home—and tending to the sick, for Lewis was a doctor.[7]

West Danby was settled in 1808 by Moses Barker, who had moved to Spencer with his father Joseph in 1794. He organized the West Danby Baptist Church in 1810. In 1812 he married 19-year-old Amy Spaulding, whose family had moved from Vermont to Spencer in 1798 and to West Danby in 1807. Amy, a true pioneer child, helped her two brothers fend off rattlesnakes and traded a pig she had earned by milking a neighbor's cow for her first pair of shoes. The couple lived across from the Baptist church that Moses had founded, on 125 acres of land he had bought for $4.25 an acre. The property later became the Todd farm, a dairy farm of some repute in the 1950s.[8]

The Ithaca-Owego Turnpike and Incorporation

The turnpike that put the villages of Danby and South Danby on the map was envisioned by Dr. Lewis Beers when he took advantage of an initiative by New York State to settle remote areas by selling charters to build and operate toll

33. Lewis Beer's house at 2081 Danby Road. The first family home of this doctor, innkeeper, postmaster, and turnpike visionary was a cabin. This later residence, pictured here c. 1919, is now the home of Wendell and Jane Bryce.

roads. On April 7, 1807, Beers established the first corporation to build the first turnpike in the area. It was to link Owego—an important port on the Susquehanna River and a vital link in the New York–Philadelphia trade route—with Candor, Danby, and Ithaca. Twenty-seven citizens joined Beers in the charter, selling stock at $20 per share. It took two years to raise the $8,000 (one-fifth) necessary to begin.[9]

Construction of the 66-foot-wide turnpike began in 1808. Skilled laborers earned $1 for a 12-hour day; less skilled workers received 30 cents a day. Contractors were mostly farmers who worked the road between farm chores. The 37-mile-long highway was completed, inspected, and approved to open in December 1810. It came in under budget, at $37,000, and the corporation was $1,000 in debt.

The toll road was free to persons on their way to church, funerals, blacksmith shops, gristmills with grain for family use, or to secure the services of a physician or a midwife. Jurors, witnesses, state and federal troops, and people who lived within a mile of the tollgates were also given free passage. Rates were assessed at three gates: one at each end and one in the middle. Commercial shippers moved grain, livestock, flour, tar, potash, lumber, plaster, and salt from Ithaca to Owego and from there to Philadelphia and Baltimore via the Susquehanna River.[10] The War of 1812 was a boon to north-south commerce along the fledgling road. The

34. The Hall Tavern, c. 1940. Photograph courtesy of Linda and Gene Getz.

war cut gypsum supplies from Nova Scotia and as many as eight hundred teams hauled plaster daily along the turnpike.[11]

The end of the Ithaca-Owego Turnpike Corporation came on schedule in 1840. The corporation was dissolved, and stockholders recovered their original investment plus interest at 10 percent per year.[12]

The construction of the turnpike transformed Danby, so-called by pioneer families who came from Danby, Vermont, and brought the name with them. Their town had been named after the earl of Danby, onetime prime minister of England, who received a large land grant in the northeast.[13] Danby was organized on February 22, 1811, when it was taken from the Town of Spencer in Tioga County. The town remained in Tioga County until March 22, 1822, when it was annexed to Tompkins County. On April 29, 1839, a small part of the town of Caroline was annexed to Danby.[14]

The first town meeting was held on March 12, 1811. After officers were elected, one of the first orders of business was to dictate that boars over two months old were not to run at large, under penalty of 25 cents payable to the complainer.[15]

Havens for travelers and their animals sprang up along every well-traveled turnpike and there were at least five stagecoach stops in Danby. Among the best documented is a tavern opened in South Danby in 1811, in a structure that still stands at 2613 Danby Road. Documents dating from 1828 to 1837 confirm that the tavern was licensed "to sell strong or spirituous liquors and wines to be drank at this dwelling" and to be operated by Leonard Hall, a man "of good moral character." Succeeding generations of the family owned the Hall Tavern until the 1920s, when Virginia and Frank Sprague bought it, renamed it Hillview, and took in tourists.

Among other architectural curiosities, the house has a small upstairs ballroom with a spring floor and a wooden ceiling arch that separates the main floor from the orchestra pit. The current owners, Linda and Gene Getz, are the proud inheritors of Leonard Hall's trunk which is trimmed in leather held by brass tacks that spell out the initials L.H. The trunk contains deeds and receipts in Leonard Hall's hand.

Some musicians who played to the ballroom crowd at Leonard Hall's tavern were undoubtedly members of the county's first brass band organized in 1829 by ambitious young musicians from Danby. The band was the pride of the whole county for nearly twenty years. It played at the dedication of the Clinton House in Ithaca in 1832. For many years the bandstand that stood on the north side of the Danby Town Hall was the site of their concerts.[16]

Jennings Pond and Buttermilk Creek, 1805 to Present

The source of the falls in Buttermilk Falls State Park is Buttermilk Creek, home to beaver, deer, herons, and other wildlife. Over the years it has supplied water-power for several enterprises, including a sawmill built in 1797 by Isaac and John Dumond and a gristmill built in 1799 by Jacob and John Yaple, both near Comfort Road. Another mill, the Elm Tree Flour and Sawmill, was organized in North Danby by Ellis, Johnson, Beers, and DeForrest in 1853 and became one of the most important manufacturing interests of the time. In 1856 ownership of the Elm Tree passed on to Thomas J. Phillips, who added steam power. The building was destroyed by fire in 1868 and the land remained vacant until 1875, when Frazier and Krum built a mill whose proprietor became W. R. Gunderman. In 1879 the mill had three runs of stone, ground about 50,000 bushels of custom work, and the sawmill turned out 100,000 feet of lumber a year.[17]

The property at the headwaters of Buttermilk Creek was originally owned by Lewis Beardsley, who sold it to Joseph Judson in 1805, when Judson was 24. (Judson had come to Danby apprenticed to Lewis Beers, in 1797.) Judson dammed the creek to form Judson's Pond and operated grist- and sawmills there. Benjamin Jennings arrived at the same location in 1802 and secured the water rights.[18]

In the late nineteenth century the Ithaca Water Co. acquired the rights to develop a watershed for the city's water supply, carved out a 40-acre pond in 1895, named it Jennings Pond, but never used it as a reservoir.

In the early 1930s the Jennings family conveyed 10.75 acres to New York State. The parks commission built an earthen and flashboard dam which they used to control the flow of water over Buttermilk Falls into the 751-acre Buttermilk State Park. In exchange, residents of Danby were allowed to use the pond for swimming and bass fishing; motorboats were prohibited.

The dam caused Danby's first and only tidal wave in 1987, when it gave way while being rebuilt by the state. According to Ric Dietrich, who was on the Danby Town Board at the time, state engineers drained the inner pond in the fall but forgot to calculate the back pressure that it provided for a larger, semicircular earthen dam that held back the bigger pond. Under pressure from the spring runoff the dam collapsed, sending a wall of water "25 to 30 feet high" coursing through Danby, causing property damage and near loss of life. Alan Mooney, for instance, was asleep in the basement apartment of the old fire hall at 23 Bald Hill Road. He awoke and escaped but water was 4 to 5 feet above the outside windows and 6 inches deep inside. Property owners along the creek successfully brought a class action suit for damages against the construction company.[19]

Agriculture in the Nineteenth Century

By 1858 Danby was a thriving agricultural town whose residents supported sixteen schools and eight churches. Two out of every three acres had been improved by the population of 2,331 people. They owned 954 horses, 1,946 working ox or cattle, 1,342 cows, 7,051 sheep, and 1,467 swine; produced 7,838 bushels of winter wheat, 148,763 bushels of spring wheat, 3,453 tons of hay, 17,791 bushels of potatoes, 49,142 bushels of apples, 130,978 pounds of butter, 4,019 lbs of cheese, and 1,547 yards of domestic cloth. Local businesses included general stores, gristmills and sawmills, boot and shoe shops, blacksmith shops, wagon and carriage shops, churches, schools, post offices, an express and telegraph office and railroad depot on the Lehigh Valley Railroad.[20]

The tenor of the town in 1879 can be assessed by noting burial lists and prices at the local general store. Burial permits were issued for people who had died of pneumonia, cancer of the throat, heart disease, angina pectoris, paralysis, apoplexy, pistol shot and shock, and spina bifida. A broom cost $0.30, five pounds of nails $0.25, a new horseshoe $0.45, a bushel of wheat $2, one pound of coffee $0.28, and five gallons of kerosene $0.75.[21]

One farmer of the time was Nelson Howard Genung, whose family moved from the Cayuga Lake flatlands where malaria was rampant to forty acres of good land fourteen miles to the south, atop Mount Ararat. In "A Tribute to South Danby," which he wrote in 1934, Genung recounts that there was "not an abandoned farm in this entire neighborhood" in 1875. "All the inhabitants were happy and in comfortable circumstances. There were no renters. Each man owned his farm and tilled the soil, sent his children to the district school. . . . Many of the children later attended the High School in Ithaca and several went to Cornell."[22]

Genung refers to a "colored" family named Simms that rented the Hildoup Farm near Arthur Charles Howland's farm in South Danby from 1880 to 1895. By Simms's account, he had escaped slavery in Virginia, starting on April 3, 1858, with seven others, avoiding roads and tramping through nearly impassable gullies at night. Because of a three-day Easter holiday, the escape was not discovered until April 7, when the fugitives were almost to Pennsylvania.

When they arrived at Carlisle, the seven separated and Simms headed toward

Harrisburg. He told Howland he nearly starved as he was forced to crawl on hands and knees to relieve his feet. When he arrived in Montrose, he worked for two weeks for a black man named Warren, received $4 in wages, then went on to Binghamton where he met a distant black relative named Thomas whose preacher brother took Simms to Ithaca.

Simms remained in Ithaca for sixteen years, holding a steady job in Esty's tannery. After sharecropping a farm on Snyder Hill in the 1870s, he moved to the Hildoup farm in South Danby, acquiring a wagon, a team of horses, and such farming tools as a plow and harrow. Howland remembers Simms as a good farmer, "in some ways quite in advance of his white neighbors, especially in the use of fertilizers for his crops." It could be argued that Simms was one of the first organic farmers in the community. Whenever he heard of the death of any domestic animal within a ten-mile radius of home, he fetched the carcass, boiled it in a big iron kettle, reduced the material to a thick broth, mixed it with wood ashes, and spread it on his plowed land. The result was that Simms's crops were good even though the land was poor.

Simms and his wife attended the Methodist Episcopal church in South Danby. "He was well-liked by all the neighbors and treated on a basis of perfect equality," said Howland. "Mr. and Mrs. Simms were the only Negroes I ever saw until I went away to school."[23]

Railroads, Schools, Churches, and the Finnish Migration

If Danby and South Danby rose to prominence on the back of the Ithaca-Owego Turnpike (now Route 96B), West Danby's claim to fame was the railroad linking Ithaca to Athens, Pennsylvania, which ran its first train on August 21, 1871. By 1877, after coming under control of the Lehigh Valley Railroad Company, the Geneva, Ithaca & Athens lines were considered the way to travel the 463.5-mile stretch billed by the company as "the Switzerland of America."[24] The Black Diamond Express, the Lehigh's flagship, transported newlyweds and travelers in pullmans through West Danby in high style to Niagara Falls. At one time five trains a day chugged through West Danby; two stopped.

The Lehigh Valley eliminated passenger service through Ithaca in 1961, but the 21-mile Van Etten-to-Ithaca branch, which links with the 14-mile line to Milliken Station in Lansing, is still used daily by ConRail. As many as 17,000 cars a year travel through West Danby; 13,500 of them are loaded with coal bound for Milliken. None of them stops.[25]

Rural sociologists could argue that a community's prosperity can be measured by the number of churches and schools the residents support. In Danby in 1860 there were sixteen schools for 880 children. One- and two-room schoolhouses were still being used in 1941. Augusta Chapman, a lifelong resident of West Danby, graduated from the two-room, eight-grade schoolhouse on Valley View Road in West Danby in 1929. George Peter and Ken Traver graduated from the one-room, eight-grade, eight-student schoolhouse on South Danby Road located next to the old general store and post office in 1930 and 1941, respectively. The

35. Vacation Bible School in West Danby, 1926. For many years Augusta Chapman (née Fairchild) regularly attended the school held at the West Danby Baptist Church on Valley View Road. Sitting second from the right in the first row, she was nine when this picture was taken. Other pupils included Mildred Loomis (now Knapp), Joe Loomis, Frances Todd (*top row, left*), and Edith Lewis (*top row, center*, later wife of pastor Sidney Fisher). Photograph courtesy of Augusta and Walter Chapman.

schoolhouse in West Danby is gone; the schoolhouse and post office on the South Danby Road still stand.

By the 1860s there were eight churches in Danby, one unheated church for every three hundred people. Services usually ran for three hours. Dr. Lewis Beers preached at the Swedenborgian church (the Church of New Jerusalem) at the Beers Settlement, which he organized in 1816. The South Danby Methodist Episcopal Church was established in 1830 and also served as a community center. Now it is a private residence that has been restored and enlarged by the Turner and Reasor families.

In Danby proper the First Methodist Church was established in 1811. The Presbyterian Church was founded in 1807 and later became known as the Congregational Church. In 1954 the First Methodist and Congregational churches merged to become the Danby Federated Church. They alternated church sites until 1974, when the members decided to preserve and refurbish the 161-year-old Congregational church building and use it exclusively. A stately, graceful structure in the middle of town, it is the oldest original church building in the county. The Methodist Church was torn down.

The Christ Protestant Episcopal Church was established in 1826 and located in

36. Danby Congregational Church, 1908. Following merger with the First Methodist Church in 1954, it became the Danby Federated Church. Photograph courtesy of Susan Hautala, Town of Danby historian.

South Danby near Peter Road. The same year, the Baptist Church of Danby was also organized.

West Danby was the home of the West Danby Baptist Church, established in 1810 by Moses Barker across from his farm on Valley View Road. A new church was built along Route 96/34 in 1976 after which the abandoned church burned. The West Danby United Methodist Church was organized in 1869 and is still active.[26]

Many service organizations centered around church life then as they do now. In Danby at the turn of the century these organizations included the Danby Young People's Society of Christian Endeavor and the King's Daughters. In West Danby many young people's social activities were centered around Danby Pioneer Grange no. 230, located at the corner of Valley View Road and Maple Avenue, which was organized in 1874. It was used until it burned to the ground in the 1980s.

37. Reverend Frank Tobey, c. 1933. Photograph courtesy of Susan Hautala, Town of Danby historian.

Among Danby's most influential and colorful ministers was the Reverend Frank Tobey, "the grand old man of Congregationalism," who rode into town in 1894 in a buggy drawn by an "Indian pony," expecting to stay one year. He retired in 1934, with the reputation as "the marryin' parson of Tompkins County." He had married over sixteen hundred people.[27]

By 1994 religious influence had waned in Danby, and just three active churches remained: the Baptist and Methodist in West Danby, and the Federated in Danby.

The edifice that became the Danby Town Hall was built in 1826 as the Baptist church and used as a church until 1866. By 1896 it had become the town hall. On July 4, 1866, the Soldiers' Monument Association was organized to build a 29-foot-high Italian marble shaft in front of the town hall and display the names and dates of death of the forty-five local men who died in the Civil War. The monument still stands.

The town hall has been the focus of frequent debate in Danby, as the community questions whether the historic structure meets the town's practical needs. The Danby Town Board proposed to demolish it in 1974. After weeks of heated discussion, 267 Danby residents voted down the suggestion on March 5, 1974, by a two-to-one margin. The town hall was then refurbished for $25,000 by the Novarr-Mackesey Construction Company, which had also renovated the Federated Church (at the time John Novarr was a resident of Danby).

Between 1890 and 1935 a great many Finlanders left lumber and mining camps in Michigan and Minnesota to resettle in Spencer and Van Etten. Their political and social organizations spilled into the neighboring communities of South and

38. Danby Town Hall, c. 1900. The building has been used for grange meetings, band concerts (bandstand on the right), town meetings, and visits from Santa Claus. The Soldiers' Monument in front was dedicated in 1870.

West Danby. Some established residents considered the Finns a strange, clannish tribe who "ate raw fish" and "boiled their blood" in steam baths set right out in the yard. Others claimed there were no better neighbors.

Among them were Red, Socialist-leaning Finns and White Nationalists. Many outsiders were slow to see the distinction and resented them all—especially during the Red Scare of 1923–1924, again during the war years of the 1940s, and the McCarthy years of the 1950s. From time to time crosses were burned in the yards of the leading members of the Finnish Farmer Society, the so-called Red Finns.

The Finns bought many rundown dairy farms and converted them into thriving poultry farms. At one time, virtually all the farms in the Crumtown Valley were owned by Finns, including most of the establishments in South Danby.[28]

The Danby State Forest and County Camp

The 7,259-acre Danby State Forest is located in South Danby and is one of Tompkins County's great natural resources, an undeveloped terrain of marshes, lowlands, and 1,600-foot ridges rife with wildlife. The forest contains a portion of the Finger Lakes Trail, wetlands along Michigan Hollow Road formerly managed by

39. DeWitt Traver (1854–1932). This South Danby farmer kept sheep, once telling his family, "If you keep cows, you lead a dog's life." Here he is cutting oats in a 30-acre field on a McCormick binder, one of the first of its kind, c. 1920, with his son Fred.

the Department of Fish and Wildlife and by Jennings Pond. Most of this land was acquired in 1933 as part of the Resettlement Program initiated by the Roosevelt Administration to help alleviate the Depression.

"The land in South Danby was the world's worst soil," remembers George Peter, whose father owned a dairy farm on Peter Road at the time. "We could barely eke out a living with 22 milk cows. We mixed manure with clay and rocks and tried to grow crops." Local farmers in imminent danger of foreclosure sold out for as little as $4 an acre and were resettled on better land near Ovid and Genoa.

Some families refused to move. DeWitt Traver, who had accumulated eight hundred acres of land in South Danby by the time he died in 1932, was considered thrifty in his accumulation of assets and stubborn in his refusal to take anything but cash for his livestock and his crops. A recognized oxen handler and crack rifle shot, Traver kept sheep and practiced his marksmanship on the groundhogs who were a constant threat to his crops.[29] His descendants still live on South Danby Road.

The land accumulated during the Resettlement Program was transferred to New York State in the 1950s. Today it is actively managed by the Department of Environmental Conservation (DEC). Of fifty state forests administered by the DEC's Cortland County office, it is the largest in six counties. In 1995 the land was valued at $1,000 an acre.

40. Summer Camp on Fisher Settlement Road. This rear view of the main lodge dates from the 1930s. Today the Empire State Speech and Hearing Clinic offers education here to more than 150 youngsters every summer. Photograph courtesy of Town of Danby history collection.

The government turned part of the land acquired through the Resettlement Act, 519 acres on Fisher Settlement Road, into a Civilian Conservation Corps camp for adult men in 1933. They planted many of the abandoned farms in trees. When the corps moved out in 1939, the Protestant churches of Tompkins, Tioga, and Cortland counties held interdenominational youth summer camps there until 1945.

In 1939 the New York State Bureau of Handicapped Children and the New York State Department of Education recognized Ithaca College professor Ralph Jones for ten years of speech and hearing therapy in the Ithaca City schools and requested that he found a clinic. First housed downtown with seven children enrolled for the summer, the clinic moved to the camp on Fisher Settlement Road in 1946 when Ithaca College sublet it from the government. The camp was leased to other organizations for summer programs, among them the Quakers, who held conferences on social issues, including nonviolence and world peace.

Ed Badger joined the staff in 1947. Named director in 1956, he was elected chair of the board in 1978 and continued at the camp until his death in 1989. Under his directorship the clinic secured a ninety-nine-year lease from the state in 1963.

During the 1970s helping the hearing-impaired became a major service activity of Lions International, and the group became active supporters of the camp. In 1980 Lions Camp Badger became home of the facilities of the Empire State Speech and Hearing Clinic, Inc., a program funded by the New York State Education Department. For six weeks every summer it serves about 150 youngsters with 70 staff people, of whom about 50 are students in speech pathology and special education. The second oldest institution of its kind in the country, the clinic has been at the forefront of creating public awareness for special needs education for children with multiple handicaps.[30]

Danby Fire District and Modern Elementary School

Churches and schools were the primary service organizations of the nineteenth century, but among the most influential in rural America during the last fifty years are fire and rescue teams staffed solely by volunteers. Danby Fire Company No. 1 was established in January 1947. Among the thirteen charter members were Henry Makarainen, Fred Hill, Ray Millspaugh, R. H. Wilbur, and four others, eight of whom listed their occupations as "ag." In 1947 dues were $1 a year and meetings were held once a month (as they still are). Out of a total membership of 105, 15 to 25 members showed up at meetings (also still true, according to Danby Fire Commissioner Ralph Bowles).[31]

The fire company was under the aegis of the Danby Fire District governed by five publicly elected commissioners who collect and spend tax money for buildings and equipment. At one time the district supported three fire companies—in Danby, West Danby, and Coddington Road.

The original Danby fire station still stands on Bald Hill Road. A new, three-bay, cinderblock fire station designed by architect William Downing was built in 1968 on the former two-acre school lot at the corner of Danby and Gunderman roads for $125,000. As of 1994 it housed two pumper/tankers, an Initial Attack pickup truck, and the Danby Rescue Truck.

In West Danby the old fire station stands empty on Maple Avenue. A new fire station was build on Sylvan Avenue in 1994. The fire house on Coddington Road is no longer in existence. Homes in that locale are now served by the Brooktondale Fire Company.

In May 1959 more than eighty parents formed the Danby School Advisory Group and petitioned the Ithaca School District for a new school to consolidate students in the district. Holt & Downing Architects designed the school, which was located on Gunderman Road and for eighteen years served as the only public elementary school in Danby for kindergarten through sixth grades. (Some residents of West Danby were placed in Newfield schools, while some South Danby residents attended Spencer schools.)

Despite local opposition the Ithaca School Board reorganized the district and closed the school on June 27, 1980. The district then sold the building and twenty-two acres to the DIVI Corporation for $80,000. The property became the headquarters for Ithaca Theatre Lighting and for DIVI, owner of the Ramada Inn formerly in downtown Ithaca and resorts in the Caribbean. After business turned sour for DIVI, the school district bought back the building at a tax sale for $800,000—ten times what it was sold for.

Modern Land Issues and Notable People

In 1961 Cornell University erected the precursor to Arecibo—a 17-foot-diameter radio telescope on the roof of a concrete block laboratory built on the former 210-acre Jones/Miller Farm, located on Fisher Settlement Road. According to George Peter, born and raised on nearby Peter Road and director of laboratory operations at Cornell for the National Astronomy and Ionosphere Center at that time, solar flares were observed from the lab and the results reported to the National Bureau of Standards. The site was so remote, he said, that researchers were frequently forced to snowshoe to the lab from South Danby Road, two miles away.

After five years Cornell built on the site an 84-foot-diameter radio telescope whose dish was a spherical reflector. The "Danby Dish" was mounted on the hillside and aimed at the same sections of the sky being concurrently monitored by radio telescope operators in Puerto Rico.

To protect the reflector from the elements, the university covered it with a heavy nylon bubble. On March 25, 1974, researchers discovered a 12-inch slash in the bubble. Initially vandals were blamed, but later reports in the *Ithaca Journal* cited "defective material" under a "heavy snow load." Regardless of the cause, $30,000 in damages proved fatal to the project. The Danby laboratory was closed, and operations moved to Brown Road in Lansing.[32]

In 1985 Warren and Jan Schlesinger bought the land and buildings from Cornell, deeding 171 acres to the DEC for additional state forest land. They turned the lab into a home and dismantled the 17-foot telescope.

In 1986, under the chairmanship of Tompkins County representative Frank Proto, the county Solid Waste Committee started a new landfill siting process and closed Tompkins County's Sanitary Landfill on Hillview Road in West Danby. Known as the Danby Dump, the 25-year-old landfill straddled the Tompkins-Tioga county line. Because it was located on or near the Danby Divide

41. Danby Dish, c. 1970. Cornell University erected this radio telescope in 1966 as part of its laboratory in Danby. Today most of the land originally owned by Cornell is part of the Danby State Forest. Photograph courtesy of Cornell University Library.

wetlands, landfill leachate had contaminated wells and wetlands both north and south of the site.[33] The huge hummock was capped and seeded in the early 1990s, and a new county transfer station was built in downtown Ithaca in 1994.

In the last 150 years Danby has had its share of notables, including William Grant Egbert (1869–1929), founder of the Ithaca Conservatory of Music, which later became Ithaca College. Egbert, a well-known master violinist, is buried at the Curtis Road Cemetery. Another Danby notable was Wilson Greatbatch, who was named to the National Inventors Hall of Fame on February 10, 1986, for his patent of the implantable heart pacemaker in 1962.

Milton and Janice Todd were the last in a family that farmed for 152 consecu-

42. Dawes Hill Community. Residents and friends gather for a communal meal on July 25, 1977. *Clockwise, from the top,* Nancy Lowenthal, Kathy Mason (and Corey, two days before his birth), Bob Kaputkin, Paul Legreze, Debbie Bliss, Steve Zimmerman, Joan Spielholtz, Karin Lowenthal, and Dave Mason. Dawes Hill was in existence from 1969 until 1981. Photograph by Kathy Morris.

tive years in West Danby. Their 1830s home was built on the site of the original Moses Barker log cabin, and still stands on Valley View Road. Milton Todd's interest was breeding Holsteins. Recipient of the first Century Farm Award in Tompkins County, the farm had an official milk production of 13,960 pounds, first in the county for two consecutive years.[34]

Roswitha and Fritz Daemen-Van Buren, who live on Howland Road in South Danby, were among the first to import Trakehner broodmares to this country in 1974. They founded the American Trakehner Association.

Helene and Erwin Locker immigrated from Germany to Ithaca in the 1960s and founded H&E Machines, Inc., on Comfort Road, in 1976. In 1994 H&E employed 130 people and was rated Tompkins County's thirtieth-largest employer. The company manufactures steam and gas turbine blades; gross annual sales are over $9 million.

In the 1970s and 1980s several communes sprang up in West Danby where residents practiced a back-to-the-land lifestyle centered around spirituality, self-sufficiency, and loyalty to the "Family." Meals, money, and chores were usually shared. Architecture was anything but four-sided.

The original West Danby commune was called Yea God and revolved around a whirling dervish named Freedom, who was the group's spiritual leader. He read auras and gave to residents such names as Silver Cloud, Twinkle, Flower, Let, and Banana Tree.[35] Yea God evolved into the Beech Hill Pond Community. Dawes Hill, known for its honey, is located less than half a mile away. Lavender Hill, Ithaca's original gay and lesbian community, was just over the line in Newfield.

In the last half of the twentieth century, Danby residents frequently commute elsewhere to work, but continue to be well educated and independent minded. Building contractors, a few remaining dairy farmers (the Van De Bogarts and Sczepanskis), Wilbur Lumber, Danby Hardwoods, Angelheart Designs, Auto Salvage of Ithaca, Rick Dobson Enterprises, Benjamin's, the Danby Market, and H&E Machines constitute the economic base. Sales tax revenues for the town run between $150,000 and $175,000.

A small corps of civic-minded residents serves on the Danby Community Council and the Planning Board, runs the fire companies and town garage, and puts out the *Danby Town News*. The Danby Historical Society has operated under the leadership of longtime Danby resident Susan Hautala since the late 1970s.

With fewer than three thousand residents, Danby's small-town countenance requires close scrutiny on the part of outsiders who seek to determine its character, but, to insiders, it is a friendly visage, deeply lined by friends, family, and a sense of place.

4   Town of Dryden

Rachel J. Dickinson

A 1911 booklet written to promote the Village of Dryden describes it thus: "There are neither dingy hovels nor palatial mansions, paupers nor millionaires, in Dryden village. The great majority of the people own their homes and the per capita wealth is seven times that of the average of the Nation. The man of means is not above manual labor and the laborer is a small capitalist. The simple, wholesome ideals of William Morris become an actuality in this model village."[1]

When the first white settlers came to Dryden to claim their military lots within Military Tract lot no. 23, they found heavily forested rolling hills and numerous streams. In 1797 Amos Sweet, the town's first settler, traveled the Bridle Path —built by the state in 1795 and so named because it was wide enough only for a single horse—and constructed his small log cabin in what is now the Village of Dryden. The cabin was 10-feet square, with one door and one 18-inch window with greased paper over the opening; it had an open fireplace and a hole in the roof to let out the smoke. Sweet's claim to his lot was invalidated a couple of years later, and so George Robertson is credited as the town's first resident freeholder.[2] Daniel White came to what would become Freeville in 1798 and had established a gristmill on Fall Creek by 1802; subsequent settlers could have their grain milled locally rather than grinding it by hand or hauling it over to Ludlow's mills (Ludlowville).

The first quarter-century of the town's history is filled with pioneer commonplaces. Sawmills sprang up along the waterways as lots were cleared of their white pine and the lumber was prepared for the growing towns to the east and south. Sheep were raised, because they could graze around the stumps of the felled trees, and woolen mills were established to process their fleece. Farming was of the subsistence variety, as settlers had to work hard just to survive. Joel Hull, a surveyor by profession, opened the first store in Dryden in 1802; when Dryden organized as a town in 1803, he was elected the first town clerk. In 1804 the first schoolhouse was established in the log cabin that Amos Sweet had abandoned a couple of years earlier. The post office in the Village of Dryden was established by 1811, and the Presbyterian church was started in 1808. The church was built on what is now the four corners in the Village of Dryden, ensuring that

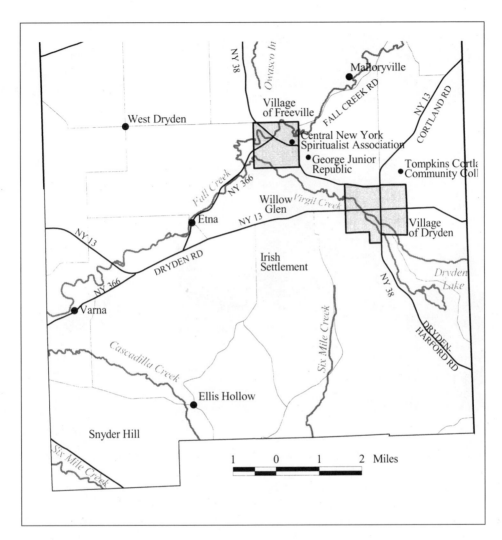

Town of Dryden

the village would grow at that end of the town rather than a couple of miles up the Bridle Path at Willow Glen.

Peleg Ellis came to claim lot no. 84 of Dryden in 1799, in the locality now known as Ellis Hollow. He cleared the land and built on the headwaters of Cascadilla Creek. His brother John came to Dryden in 1801 and lived nearby, in the Ellis Hollow region. Known as King of Dryden, John Ellis was judge of the Court of Common Pleas after Tompkins County was organized in 1817. He was also supervisor of the town for twenty-seven years and a member of the State Legislature in 1831 and 1832.

43. Amos Sweet's log cabin. This replica was built on the Dryden Agricultural Fairgrounds in 1897 for the Centennial Celebration. Photograph courtesy of Dryden Historical Society.

Between 1794 and 1803 Township no. 23 and Township no. 22 were combined under the name of Ulysses. In 1797 the population of the whole Town of Ulysses was 52, but by 1800 the census shows a headcount of 927. At the town meeting of Ulysses in March 1802 it was voted "that the township of Dryden be set off from Ulysses" (confirmed by the state legislature in 1803). Unlike most of the towns carved from the Military Tract, Dryden has changed very little in original size and is still almost one hundred lots square, each lot containing six hundred acres.[3]

By 1824 Spafford's *Gazetteer of the State of New York* lists the Town of Dryden with a population of 3,951; "number of neat cattle 3,670; 674 horses; 6,679 sheep; 37,300 yards of cloth made in families in 1821; school districts, 20; public monies received in 1821, $576.05." Spafford also lists "6 grist mills, 26 saw mills, 2 fulling mills, 4 carding machines, 5 distilleries, and 4 asheries."[4]

During the nineteenth century the town included the villages of Dryden, Free-ville, Etna, Varna, and Ellis as well as places with names not so familiar today: Willow Glen, West Dryden, Malloryville, Irish Settlement, and Snyder Hill. Varna, Etna, and Freeville survived because they lay along waterways and the state road. In the latter part of the century railroads came through these villages and so secured their survival. The Village of Dryden became the site of town government and was the first incorporated village within the town (1857).

Etna, originally called Miller's Settlement, then Columbia, and finally Etna in 1820, was first settled by Rev. William Miller and his brother Arthur sometime around the turn of the century. The first religious society in the town was organized in 1804 at the home of William Miller. Etna's early history is one of mills and distilleries. In fact, anecdotal history has it that Etna was so named because the smoking distilleries and asheries on the numerous small islands in Fall Creek reminded observers of the smoldering Mt. Etna. Goodrich writes in his 1898 history that

> fifty years ago Etna had a hard name, being noted for its horse running and liquor distilling proclivities, there being no less than ten or twelve stills within two miles square of this section of town. While the general business of the place has not increased in recent years the character of its inhabitants and industries has very much improved, and a stranger who now visits Etna finds it very pleasantly located upon the opposite banks of Fall Creek, which are here connected by a very substantial iron bridge, one of the largest and best in the township.[5]

The Village of Dryden, known as Dryden Corners early in the nineteenth century, might have looked different had the provisions of an 1812 deed been carried out. Abram Griswold, Nathan Goddard, Joshua Hall, and John Taylor willed to "the good people of Dryden" thirty-six square rods of land on each side of the Dryden four corners to provide for a village common. The payment was to have been "one peppercorn and one oat yearly." But the agreement did not last, for the business district grew across this common land. In 1836 John Southworth built a brick store on the southwest corner, and in 1840 Joseph McGraw built his brick store on the corner opposite. Goodrich writes that at about the same time, two of the best dwellings in the village were erected on Main Street. "Both are said to have been raised on the same day, one with the use of liquor for the workmen, which was the established custom on these occasions, but at the other raising a supper was substituted, being the first effort to promote the cause of temperance which we are able to record in Dryden village."[6]

Freeville, the second-largest village in the town, was first settled in 1798 by Elder Daniel White. He established a gristmill on Fall Creek around the site of present-day Mill Dam Park. White's son John moved the site of the mill upstream slightly, and built a considerably larger solid frame building which stood until 1941.

It is not certain how Freeville got its name. According to A. B. Genung's history of the village, at first it was simply White's Mill and then White's Corners. But Elder White "himself vowed that in this new country the place names ought not to perpetuate some man's name merely because he got there first." He was supposedly the one who suggested the name Freeville, which was then recorded in the circuit rider's recordbook.

Not much happened during Freeville's first fifty years—West Dryden and Willow Glen (or Stickles Corners) were bustling metropolises in comparison. The county map of 1853 shows only about ten families clustered in the vicinity of the lower four corners, where Mill and Johnson streets meet Main Street. The Meth-

44. West Dryden Community Center in the 1960s. Built as a Methodist Episcopal church in 1832, the structure is currently being refurbished by the community with help from Historic Ithaca and New York State. Photograph courtesy of Dryden Historical Society.

odist church was built near the lower four corners in 1848, and the first school stood on a knoll beside Virgil Creek on Johnson Street.[7]

From about 1830 to 1860 the Village of Dryden experienced a period of prosperity. The stone Woolen Mill was built by A. L. Bushnell, providing employment for a considerable number of inhabitants. Jeremiah W. Dwight built his stone block on Main Street, and P. M. Blodgett built a three-story wooden building, the Blodgett Block, directly west of Dwight's building. The first Methodist church was built on the four corners in 1832 (the current building dates from 1874 when the church was rebuilt after a fire). The Presbyterian church had gone up a few years earlier, in 1824 (it was rebuilt in 1940 after a 1938 fire). The first newspaper published in the village came from the handpress of H. D. Rumsey in 1856 and was known as *Rumsey's Companion.* It published a series of articles known as "The Old Man in the Clouds," a lively account of the early days of Dryden's history. From 1856 Dryden had a weekly newspaper almost continually until the *Dryden Rural News* ceased publication in the early 1980s.[8]

The Village of Dryden was incorporated in 1857 with a population of about four hundred and 999.25 acres included within the corporate limits.[9] At that time the village included mercantile, hardware, and grocery stores, churches, schools, mills, hotels, lawyers, a doctor, a debating club, and an individual who served as both undertaker and furnituremaker.

The first post office in Freeville was established in 1864 through the efforts of Rev. Isaac Harris. He was not only Methodist minister but also appointed first postmaster, using a front room of his house for a post office.

In 1869 the Village of Dryden made an arrangement for the Southern Central railroad line to pass within its boundaries on its journey from Owego to Auburn. Farmers now had the advantage of shipping items to a larger market. According to Goodrich, however, the new railroad did not produce an immediate change in the affairs of the village. The merchants soon found that profits from reduced freight rates and quicker transportation were offset by their customers' new ability to travel to and trade in larger towns.[10]

Economic depression hit the little village in the 1860s as the woolen mill, tannery, and several other businesses failed. A major fire burned a portion of Main Street in 1866, including the Blodgett Block and the neighboring hotel; these lots lay empty for a couple of years, and there was very little new construction in the village.

In 1870 Freeville's fortunes changed. The Southern Central laid its tracks within a half-mile of Freeville's lower corner. A shanty, with the word "depot" nailed over the door, became the first building in "new Freeville." By the following year the railroad that would eventually became the Elmira, Cortland & Northern (EC&N) crossed the Southern Central tracks, creating a junction in Freeville. A local company, the New York & Oswego Midland Railroad, was formed and began running trains in 1880; the Lehigh Valley bought all the local lines in 1890. Genung writes that an "interesting aspect of the railroads in those days was their local—almost neighborhood—character. The roads were always ready to give a special train to any group who wanted to go somewhere for a day's outing. There was little formality or red tape and the charges for such excursions were comparatively light."[11]

The orientation of the Village of Freeville changed almost overnight, from north-south to east-west, as new settlement sprang from the railroad junction. Houses were built, businesses were started, hotels flourished. Freeville was experiencing an economic boom.

Meanwhile the Village of Dryden was working hard to improve municipal works and to create institutions that would benefit the public. The first public

45. Freeville's railroad station, c. 1897. A train waits at the newly constructed station. The Junction House, a hotel, stands to the left. Photograph courtesy of Dryden Historical Society.

school, held in Amos Sweet's abandoned cabin, was joined by at least two public school buildings in the village by the middle of the century. On the corner of Main and Lewis streets was a private academy where Edward Ruloff, later convicted of the murder of his wife and daughter, served as headmaster in 1842. In 1860 the Dryden Seminary was built on the site of the present school grounds. It served as a private academy for about ten years until the property was purchased by the school district and run as a public union free school and academy. In 1876 the village hall was built to accommodate not only the workings of the government but also fire-extinguishing apparatus. In 1892 the village voted, at an expense of $25,000, to establish a municipal gravity-based water system.

The most ambitious enterprise ever seen in Freeville was the glass factory. It began as a stove factory in 1885, but the deal with the promotor fell through and the subscribers cast about for a tenant. A Belgian glass manufacturer, Cleon F. Tondeur, who already had factories at Canastota and Oneida, agreed to buy the property in 1886 and moved in equipment for manufacturing cathedral window glass. The EC&N extended its tracks to Sylvan Beach to haul the fine white sand used in the factory. Tondeur manufactured colored glass here until his patents lapsed in about 1890, resulting in his financial failure. When the Methodist church was relocated to its present site in 1890 (to be closer to the new center of town), the windows were replaced with some made in the Tondeur factory. One hundred years later another glass manufacturing firm, Serviente Glass Studio, established its studio about two hundred yards from the site of Tondeur's factory.

46. Main Street in Dryden at the turn of the century. This winter view looking down Library Street shows the newly built Southworth Library on the right and the Dryden Opera House, the first building on the left. Photograph courtesy of Dryden Historical Society.

Freeville was incorporated in 1887, including within its corporate limits the square mile of territory comprising lot no. 26 of Dryden township. It had 300 inhabitants at the time. In 1900 Freeville had a population of 440; the 1990 census recorded 449.

The year 1894 saw the completion of the Southworth Library on Dryden's Main Street. This beautiful gothic building, constructed of Ohio sandstone, was designed by William Henry Miller of Ithaca and stands as a memorial to several of Dryden's founding families. Jennie McGraw Fiske was born in Dryden in 1840, the daughter of local millionaire John McGraw and granddaughter of John Southworth. When she died at the age of 41, she left $30,000 to the village for the building, support, and maintenance of a public library. The library holds two primitive oil paintings of Jennie's parents and a wooden eagle carved from local applewood by Jansen Miller, Dryden native and world-renowned violin maker. The most valuable document owned by the library is an original manuscript of Lincoln's second inaugural address. It was given to John Dwight, a congressman from Dryden, by Robert Lincoln, the president's son, in appreciation of his efforts in propelling the Lincoln Memorial Park to full congressional approval.

In 1875 A. C. Stone, a developer who lived in Freeville, built the Lyceum Hall on Freeville's Union Street. This hall not only served as a theater and forum for community meetings but also became popular as a dance hall and roller skating rink. Stone renovated the hall in 1905–1906 as a country playhouse, with new seats, a balcony, and new scenery. After Stone's death the Lyceum Hall was

47. Dryden Lake. For many years extensive ice harvesting was done at this location. This photograph, showing the railroad tracks going down onto the frozen lake, was taken on February 1, 1921. Photograph courtesy of Dryden Historical Society.

bought by the village and served as a community center. The Lyceum has served as the site of several ventures including the Honey Butter factory and a plant that tie-dyed T-shirts; it was sold by the village in the early 1980s.

Under the leadership of John Dwight, $3,500 was raised to build the Dryden Opera House on Library Street in 1893. The opera house seated up to six hundred and served as the entertainment center of the village. The village's first motion picture was shown there in 1906. But the opera house could not compete with larger communities, and the corporation sold the building in 1936. It was converted into apartments the following year. The last public event held in the opera house was the graduation exercises of Dryden High School class of 1936.

On the outskirts of the village is Dryden Lake. Prior to refrigeration (1890s–1932), extensive ice harvesting provided employment there for up to one hundred men from mid-December into March. As many as one hundred railroad cars packed with ice could be shipped out in one day. When the Borden Milk Plant was built in 1905, it laid a direct railroad line to the lake for ice. Today Dryden Lake is a popular recreation spot for anglers, bird watchers, and picnickers and is part of the public greenway from Ithaca to Dryden.[12]

From 1890 to 1900 the residents of Freeville enjoyed Riverside Park, built and managed by Harris Roe on the bank of Fall Creek behind Main Street. Riverside Park had a broad, low-roofed auditorium, where Chautauqua programs were held on Sundays, and an oval pond stocked with goldfish and black bass. But the most popular attraction was the steamboat *Clinton*, which could take up to a dozen people on its regular run between the Mill Dam and Brooklyn Bridge. The fare was five cents a trip.[13]

The Dryden Springs Sanitarium was once located on what is now Spring House Road. Built as the Dryden Springs House in 1845, this hotel was bought by Dr. Samantha S. Nivison in 1862. Dr. Nivison, the first woman physician in the county (and involved a few years later in a controversy surrounding the building of Cascadilla Hall, which became part of Cornell), developed and promoted Dryden Springs as a place for the water-cure treatment. The medicinal spring waters, discovered by the Lacy brothers while prospecting for salt in 1820, had long been touted by the local community for their curative powers. The Dryden Springs Sanitarium had three doctors on staff and functioned as a summer resort. No longer used as a sanitarium after 1900, the building burned to the ground in 1945, and today the only trace of grounds once beautifully manicured is a slight terracing to the overgrown landscape.[14]

Two unique institutions, both still extant, were established in Freeville in 1895. The Central New York Spiritualist Association began as a tent camp in 1895 in Riverside Park. In 1897 the association purchased the land where the camp is located today, on Route 38 heading toward Dryden. As early as 1907 families came to spend weekends at the camp, where they could rent tents and cots. The camp soon expanded to include many summer cottages, a dining hall, auditorium, chapel, hotel, healing temple, and prayer garden. Through the years many world-famous healers and mediums have spent time at the Freeville campgrounds.

In July of 1895 William R. "Daddy" George founded George Junior Republic on a 48-acre farm on the southeast edge of the Village of Freeville. Daddy George was

A Court Scene, George Junior Republic, Freeville, N. Y.

48. George Junior Republic, early 1900s. Citizens are gathered for a trial in their courtroom. Photograph by Verne Morton, courtesy of Dryden Historical Society.

born near West Dryden and went to New York City as a young man. There he developed plans to improve the opportunities and lives of young people. He began bringing "fresh air fund" children to West Dryden and Freeville in the early 1890s and "observed that the unearned gifts of food and clothing had a debilitating effect on families when the youths returned home after a summer in Freeville."[15] From that observation arose the George Junior Republic motto, "Nothing without Labor." The young people there divide their time to this day between educational pursuits and gainful employment in a variety of service tasks.

George's educational ideas and methods, his commonsense ideas of individualism, self-government, belief in God, love of country, humanitarianism, and his concern for youth interested penologists, social workers, reformers, and philanthropists all over the country. By 1910 the Republic had over four hundred acres and many buildings including cottages, hotels, a bakery, hospital, laundry, shops, gymnasium, jail and courthouse, and farm buildings. There were 250 "citizens"—boys and girls between 12 and 21 years of age—and 50 helpers.

Many famous and remarkable people came through Freeville and spent time there because of the George Junior Republic; among them were Thomas Mott Osborne, Gerritt S. Miller, Calvin Derrick, Kate Fowler, Theodore Roosevelt, Eleanor Roosevelt, and Helen Keller. The Republic celebrated its centennial in 1995, and although it has changed since its inception (it now has only male citizens, most placed there by courts or the state), it is still a remarkable example of the provision of education and the experience of participatory democracy for an at-risk population.

49. Washington School in 1914. Teacher Nita Hall stands with her students in front of the District no. 23 school, on Caswell Road outside of Freeville. Photograph courtesy of Dryden Historical Society.

Because of the town's rural nature, the education of children took place in twenty-eight rural schools and several private academies. In 1827 school district no. 5 (outside Etna and Varna) built an unusual brick building, the Eight-Square School House, which still stands today and is the property of the DeWitt Historical Society.[16] By the latter part of the nineteenth century the villages of Dryden (1872) and Freeville (1898) both had union schools, or free public schools, that offered high school instruction. In 1936 the Town of Dryden centralized its school districts. Primary instruction was provided in the villages of Dryden, Freeville, McLean, and Etna, and secondary instruction was centralized at the Dryden Central School on Union Street. Freeville built a handsome new brick school in 1936 on Main Street and eventually tore down the wooden school across the street. The last rural school district, Turkey Hill, was brought into the new centralized district in 1959. Today Dryden is also home to Tompkins Cortland Community College (TC3), which opened in Groton in 1968 and moved to its Dryden campus in 1974. TC3 is part of the State University of New York (SUNY) system, and its students can earn a two-year associate's degree.

Every town has a history of disasters, and Dryden has had its series of fires, floods, and tornadoes. Among the most significant were the 1866 fire that burned part of the downtown Village of Dryden, the 1931 fire that destroyed several downtown Freeville buildings including the old Roe store, the fire that burned down the Dryden Presbyterian Church in 1938, the fire that destroyed the Dryden town hall and firehouse in 1944, the 1954 fire in the Dryden Central School that caused $400,000 in damage and led to a year of school in quonset huts, and the fire that destroyed the Dryden Hotel in 1995. There have been at least three significant floods: the flood of 1935 put the Village of Freeville under water and devastated the part of Dryden nearest Virgil Creek; the 1981 flood severely affected properties along Virgil Creek, causing the Village of Dryden to modify the creek for flood control purposes; and the flood of 1996 cut off the Village of Freeville from Etna for several days as Fall Creek rampaged through "Wernickville." There have been at least two recent tornadoes in the Village of Dryden, one in 1969 and the other in 1994. The 1994 tornado ripped the roof off the Empire Livestock Pavilion, and Dryden made the national news with a story about a cat which was apparently sucked into the funnel and then dropped from the sky, unharmed, in front of a startled onlooker.[17]

The Town of Dryden has had its share of communitywide events over the years. The Ellis Hollow community has sponsored the Ellis Hollow Fair annually since 1953. The Freeville United Methodist Church celebrated its twentieth annual Freeville Harvest Festival in 1995. The Dryden Grange has been sponsoring Dryden Dairy Days since the 1970s. For almost fifteen years (1970–84) Etna sponsored the Fall Creek White-Water Derby, a five-mile race from Etna to Varna. The villages of Dryden and Freeville have both had centennial celebrations.[18]

Throughout Dryden's history one finds such social organizations and clubs as the Ellis Hollow Women's Club (est. 1959), the Etna Women's Community Club (est. c. 1920), the Dryden Fortnightly Club (est. 1896), and the Dryden Needle Club (est. during World War I). Two clubs are especially noteworthy. Dryden's Spit and Whittle Club (1931–40) attracted considerable attention because of the name, and its membership included an assortment of Dryden "characters" who met in a club room in the old Ranning's Hotel on Main Street. The other club, Freeville's Knights of Pythias, sponsored the Freeville baseball team from 1930 until World War II. This ball team played in the Intra State League, then the Municipal League, and finally the Post Standard League, and was one of the finest baseball teams in central New York.[19]

A few of the individuals with significant links to the town's history are listed below. In addition to Jennie McGraw Fiske, Dr. Samantha S. Nivison, and Daddy George, there were A. K. Fletcher, editor of the *Dryden Rural News* from 1933 to 1970; John Miller, raised in Dryden and first governor of North Dakota in 1889; John Southworth, with an estate worth $1 million when he died in 1877; Jeremiah Dwight, land speculator and timber man, who in partnership with John McGraw had the country's largest lumberyard, in Michigan in the late nineteenth century; Warren Ellis Schutt, student at the Hibbards Corners school in Ellis Hollow and first Rhodes Scholar from the United States; Dr. Homer Genung (d.1933), village doctor in Freeville for fifty years; George Goodrich, who wrote Dryden's centennial history (1898); A. B. Genung (d.1963), chronicler of Freeville's history; and H. Emilie Cady (d.1941), homeopathic physician and metaphysician, author, and healer in the Unity Church.[20]

50. Main building of the Dryden Agricultural Fair. This unusual duodecagon structure once stood on the site of the present town barn on East Main Street in Dryden. Photograph courtesy of Dryden Historical Society.

The history of the Town of Dryden also involves the history of agriculture in Central New York, for Dryden's settlements developed in the middle of rich and fertile farmland. Spafford writes in 1824 that this "township has a great diversity of soil, surface and timber . . . the general surface is level, yet tossed here and there, into some pretty lofty ridges. A great proportion of the land is of superior quality and the farmers enjoy every thing that farming opulence can desire."[21] As noted earlier, sheep outnumbered cattle in the early nineteenth century, probably because sheep were easier to protect from wild animals and had an easier time grazing the recently cleared land. As more land was settled and improved, the dairy industry began to establish a foothold. As Goodrich writes in 1897, "the disposition of the Dryden farmers to devote their efforts to dairying instead of grain-raising has tended to improve rather than diminish the natural resources of the soil. In place of the original pine timber, excellent farm buildings have been supplied, and the Dryden farmer is no longer ashamed to acknowledge the location of his home."[22]

In 1856 the Dryden Agricultural Society was organized, as proposed in *Rum-*

51. Borden Milk Plant. Workers pasteurized, bottled, and shipped milk to New York City via the railroad. Pasteurizing and bottling stopped in 1936, but bulk shipments of milk continued until the plant closed in 1960. Photograph courtesy of Dryden Historical Society.

sey's Companion of that year. The society sponsored the Dryden Fair for sixty-two years (1856–1917), and, according to A. K. Fletcher, was "touted the greatest township fair in all of New York State before dissension wrought its doom in 1917." The fairgrounds, now the site of the livestock pavilion for Empire on East Main Street, boasted a racetrack, a grandstand, horse and stock barns, and the main fair building, a duodecagon built in 1857. Goodrich writes that "this building is a model in its way, for the purpose for which it was designed, having been imitated by numerous agricultural societies in the West, and no one ever claims to have seen a building so completely adapted to the requirements of a country fair."[23] At its high point, in 1906, the Dryden Fair drew a crowd of 30,000. Fletcher called the fair house one of the "7 wonders of Old Dryden." After 1917 it was used by the Dryden Town Highway Department to house machinery and equipment. The building was razed in 1953.

In 1951 there were about 2,800 dairy cows in the town, practically all of them on commercial dairies, of which there were about one hundred. In 1905 the Borden Milk Plant was established in the Village of Dryden. Twenty workers pasteurized and bottled the milk, which was then shipped to New York City. In 1936 Borden stopped pasteurizing and bottling, and milk was shipped to New York in bulk. A 1951 booklet promoting the Town of Dryden stated that "dairymen here are prosperous. They are located on good farms and conduct the most important income-producing business in the township."[24]

Dryden is close to Cornell University and is home to many Cornell employees, so the town often receives the scrutiny and the benefit of this relationship.

52. Munsey Little, a farmer and owner of a meat market in the 1930s, taking a break from field work. Known for its rolling farmland, the Town of Dryden to this day supports several dairy farms. Photograph courtesy of Dryden Historical Society.

Master's and Ph.D. theses have been written about the agricultural and sociological state of the town; classes in rural sociology have interviewed the inhabitants and advanced theories about why the people of Dryden thought what they thought.

One important tangible benefit of the Cornell-Dryden relationship was the Pioneer Co-op Dairy Cattle Breeders Association, started in 1938. Professor Stanley J. Brownell of Cornell's School of Agriculture approached some county extension agents and a group of Dryden farmers about starting a dairy cattle breeding program. The farmers organized and went to Fay Stafford, president of the First National Bank of Dryden, who reportedly said, "Sounds like a good idea to me—how much do you need?" The program was financed, a veterinarian hired, and the business set up in George Monroe's barn on West Main Street in Dryden. The Pioneer Co-op, the first cooperative in the United States organized and completely financed by members exclusively for the purpose of artificial breeding, was successful beyond expectations; it became the Central New York Artificial Breeding Co-op in 1940 and moved its headquarters to Baldwinsville, N.Y.[25]

The booklet "Dryden: The Township, the Village," written in 1951, also points out a development that would become more evident in the years to come. The author writes, "Of the total number of residences, it is evident . . . that a little over half of them (58%) are in the open country, and of these in the country, half are rural residences of people who gain their living elsewhere than from the land. This trend appears to be continuing so that more city folks are coming to the township to make their homes." As the Town of Dryden becomes criss-crossed with better roads leading to and from Ithaca, Cortland, and Syracuse, it finds itself within what is developing as a major transportation corridor, one that has affected settlement patterns and the types of businesses springing up along the major artery, Route 13. Developments have been carved out of former dairy farms, small high-tech firms are housed in nineteenth-century buildings, and fast food restaurants and service stations line both sides of the road as one leaves the Village of Dryden and heads toward Syracuse. With the disappearance of dairy farms and the small family businesses that catered to the local economy, elements once considered essential to its character, Dryden has entered the next phase of its development.

5 Town of Enfield

Susan Thompson

The Town of Enfield, approximately six miles square, spreads across a valley dotted with rolling hills, ponds, streams, woodlands, residential homes, farms, stores, a private airport, and a school. The town, located approximately seven miles west of the City of Ithaca with a mean elevation of 500 to 700 feet above Cayuga Lake, can be viewed from various locations on Harvey Hill and Enfield Center roads. Five Mile (Enfield) Creek winds through the town and leads south into a beautiful gorge in the upper portion of Robert H. Treman State Park, known as Enfield Glen and filled with steep winding pathways and thundering waterfalls.

The area we call Enfield was first settled in 1804 by John Giltner. Soon thereafter Judah Baker, his wife Lydia Chase, and their children settled Enfield Center. Other families with the names of Applegate, Baker, Budd, Grey, Griffins, Harvey, Lovell, Newman, Noble, Pell, Privets, Purdy, Rolfe, Rumsey, Vankirk, and Wilkin, soon followed.[1]

Samuel Rolfe, John Applegate, Charles Ink, Judah Baker, and Moses Lovell of the Town of Ulysses first registered the area to become a town in November 1820, and Enfield was officially registered with the State of New York on March 16, 1821. It was reputedly named after Enfield, Connecticut, because a great number of the first settlers originated from Connecticut. The town was formed from thirty-six lots (nos. 34–39; 42–47; 50–55; 58–63; 66–71; 72–77) of the southern portion of Military Township lot no. 22, Ulysses.

Agriculture

Agriculture was the way of life for many residents, and by 1865 80 percent of the town's land was used for farming.[2] Farmers not only grew crops and raised livestock but were also involved in the timber business. According to an 1866 topographical map, five sawmills were operating on Five Mile Creek.[3] Lumber is still milled at the Rothermich and Eddy farms.

Like the rest of the country, Enfield had hard times after the Civil War. To help, the federal government encouraged the establishment of farmers' organizations.

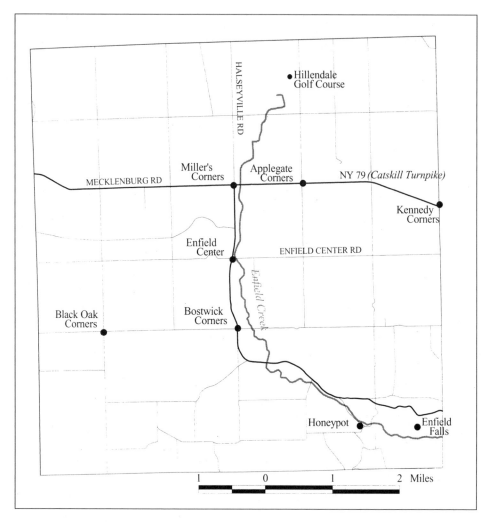

Town of Enfield

The Enfield Valley Grange no. 295 organized in February 1875, at the home of John Theall. Members of this grange were offered discounts on household goods and farm and family insurance, and they provided a place where families could gather for social events. The group participated in county fairs, showing everything from vegetables to livestock. In 1925 the Enfield Grange built a grange hall in Enfield Center, and the hall has served as a place for grange meetings, town election dinners, and harvest festivals. The Enfield Grange is still in operation today, and by 1995 it was the only Tompkins County grange to own and maintain a building.[4]

In 1875 there were 318 operating farms, averaging 73 acres per farm.[5] Sixty-five years later the number of operating farms had dropped to 191, but average size

53. High bridge near Lucifer Falls in the Enfield Glen, c. 1910.

increased to 107 acres. Larger farms could be managed with fewer people because of improved farm technology and techniques.[6]

In the late 1950s very few teams of workhorses and oxen remained in service; tractors had taken their place. A local farm owner, Hulsa Smith, traveled from farm to farm with his thrashing machine and ensilage cutter to fill silos with corn. Neighboring farmers would come to work for the day with Hulsa. A midday meal was always served at the farmhouse where the silo was being filled.

In the 1970s the town was designated part of Agriculture District No. Two by the county legislature. This designation was to protect agricultural land from nonagriculture development. In the next decade the U.S. Department of Agriculture bought out approximately 25 percent of the town's dairy farms.[7]

Three dairies in the town were designated Dairy of Distinction by the New York State Beautification Program in the 1990s—Larchmont, G-Quist, and Stargo farms. According to the 1990 U.S. Census Enfield contained ninety operating farms.[8]

Two nationally known farm-related companies currently operate within the town—ISA-Babcock Industries and Eastern Artificial Insemination Cooperative.

Businesses and Professions

Over the years many businesses have thrived in Enfield. The list contains general stores, boot- and shoemakers, coopers, blacksmiths, farmers, seamstresses, broom makers, sawmills, gristmills, and car repair.

The Ferris family in 1812 operated a sawmill on Five Mile Creek, south of the Baker family settlement. In the main Enfield Falls area on Five Mile Creek, near a small waterfall, Isaac Rumsey built a gristmill in 1817 which ground local grains. Enfield Center, located near Five Mile Creek, grew quickly. During the 1860s and 1870s there were thirteen blacksmith shops and seven country stores in Enfield Center.[9] Will Rumsey's peddler wagon (established in the 1920s–1930s) is well remembered among town residents. Rumsey came to town once a week, stopping at various homes, bringing such necessities as sugar and flour. The main bartering currency was eggs.[10]

Wortman Hall, located at Enfield Center, is one of the town's oldest remaining buildings once used as a general store. In this hall John Wortman began his business in about 1866 as the local undertaker and carpenter. Since Wortman's time the Wright, McFall, and Newhart families have run general stores in Wortman Hall. The McFalls had one of the first gas pumps in the town (1926). Many community dances, church fundraising "donations," minstrel shows, and grange meetings have been held in this hall. Currently the building is a private home.

Jervis Langdon, father-in-law to Samuel Langhorne Clemens (Mark Twain) operated a general store in Enfield in 1827. He stayed for a few years and eventually moved to Elmira in 1845.[11]

Millers Corners was another business center for the town. Before 1926 Mrs.

54. Main Street in Enfield Center, 1916. On the left is Will Rumsey's store, which according to its sign sold SOCONY gasoline.

Coon operated a small store there. The building resembled a chicken brooder house with a canopy on top, and at night Mrs. Coon would close the canopy down. Schaber's General Store and Gas Station was located on the northeast corner. In the field behind the Schaber store were held many community picnics and baseball games. This store burned shortly after the new Enfield Elementary School was built in 1957. Currently Partner's Market, built in 1963 as Gregg's Junction Market, and Valley Korner, built in the early 1990s, are located on the site.

New York State Historical Markers indicate where four taverns were located in the town. Wallenbeck Inn, on the corner of Fish and Buck Hill roads, is still there, though it has been a private home for many years. It was built in about 1826. The marker for Applegate Tavern is on the corner of Applegate and Mecklenburg roads; this tavern was operated by the John Applegate family and burned during World War II. VanDorn Tavern, on the corner of VanDorn and Mecklenburg roads, was owned by Peter VanDorn. A Catskill Turnpike milestone once stood at the edge of this intersection but is no longer there. The tavern was torn down in 1916.[12] A farm, located halfway between the Applegate and VanDorn taverns, was used as an overnight resting stop by livestock drovers. Drovers would come out in the early morning to recapture their turkeys among trees in the pasture.[13]

The VanMarter Hotel, operated by Elizabeth and Aaron VanMarter, was located in Enfield Center. In about 1875 Moses L. Harvey bought the hotel and renamed it

55. Applegate Tavern, located at Applegate Corners, with the historic marker in front.

Harvey Hotel. In 1893 or 1894 the hotel again changed hands and thereafter was operated by Frank Teeter under the name Teeter Hall. The hotel was noted for its many dances held on a "floating" dance floor (heavy coil springs were placed under the corner floor boards). It is now a private home.

The town no longer has taverns, but it does have similar establishments for social activities. Kuma Night Club, built before 1948 as the Woodside Inn, is located on Mecklenburg Road; Newhart's Lodge opened in 1960 on Griffen Road; and Willowwood Campsite and Lodge is located on Rockwell Road.

For its first century and a half Enfield supported many doctors in general practice. Doctors O. C. Comstock and Parvis Williams practiced in 1818 in the Enfield area, when it was still Town of Ulysses. By 1874 eight doctors had practiced in Enfield, and from 1874 through the late 1930s, from Charles T. Kelsey up to and including doctors Minor McDaniels and David Robb, another eight were recorded with general practices in Enfield. These doctors, most of whom were born and raised in the area, had offices in their homes and made "sick calls" at their patients' homes.

During the 1920s medicine shows visited the town. A big tent with circus seating was set up at Miller's Corners. Entertainment of some sort started the show, and then snake-oil liniments advertised to cure everything were sold, two or three bottles for $1.00. These shows came and went overnight. The town also had a local patent-medicine doctor—Dr. Louis F. L. Humphrey.[14]

56. Enfield Park, c. 1890. According to this photograph's label, these are "Half-Breeds" standing outside a cabin. Long before the glen area became a state park, many visitors used the reservation's facilities.

Enfield Falls and Robert H. Treman State Park

Enfield Falls is located in the southeastern part of Enfield, in upper Robert H. Treman State Park. This park, originally Enfield Glen Reservation, is named to honor Robert H. Treman who, with his wife Laura, presented the land to New York State in 1920. A historic marker at the upper main entrance to the park designates the location of the Catharine's Town–Cayuga Lake Indian Trail. A stone house built by the Woodward family in 1822, near the upper park on Stone House Road, is one of Enfield's oldest existing homes. The Grist Mill located here was constructed in 1838–1839 by Jared Treman and was in use until 1916. Robert H. Treman (Jared's grandson) bought the mill in that year; by 1927 the mill building had been restored and opened for public viewing. Today tours of the building are offered when the park is open. At one time the Enfield Falls Hotel, started in the 1830s by the Wickham family, was also located in the area. The

57. Pinhole view of CCC camp at upper Enfield, taken August 8, 1941.

gorge was also used for part of the movie *The Great White Trail*, produced by the Leopold D. and Theodore W. Wharton Movie Studios of Ithaca in 1917.

In 1933 President Franklin D. Roosevelt established the Civilian Conservation Corps (CCC). Camp SP-6 used the park as their home. Over one hundred young men lived at the camp until 1941. These men were responsible for carpentry and masonry at the park. When flooding occurred throughout the county on July 7, 1935, CCC men were there to help repair damage to the park.[15] The town included camp residents in the community. As locals later recalled, "when the Grange and church held dances they would bring up a truck full of the boys from the camp to join in on the fun."[16]

To the northeast of the park is the Gray Road area, also referred to as Enfield Falls. Located there are Budd Cemetery and the Enfield Falls Community Building (the latter, the scene of many community organizational suppers and dances, is no longer in use). Also in the vicinity at one time but now gone was the one-room Budd School House.

Crossroad Communities and Hamlets

Town roads received their names from local families, such as Rothermich, Fish, and Stevenson. Roads were also named for the vicinity, such as Enfield Center Road.

58. Budd School, District no. 14, Enfield Falls. The district school on Gray Road receives a visit from a library bookmobile in 1928–1929. Photograph by a staff photographer of the National Geographic Society.

Enfield's first official highway was an extension of the 1804 Jericho Turnpike (Catskill Turnpike to Bath), constructed in 1825. By 1876 this road had been abandoned, and the turnpike reverted to the town for maintenance. Now the turnpike (Route 79) is called Mecklenburg Road.

Four years after its establishment, on April 4, 1825, the town passed an ordinance that all roads and road districts in the town should be surveyed and numbered by road commissioners. This survey began at the east end of town and numbered north and south roads first.[17] During the early years town citizens took care of the roads themselves. In the winter, according to one Enfield resident's diary in 1896, the men and boys shoveled snow off the roads, and at some points the snow was six feet deep.[18] Not until 1960–1961 were name signs placed on each road. Roads are currently managed by town, county, and state.

Residents also used family names and descriptions of the land to refer to some of the more populous areas.

Applegate Corners, at the intersection of Applegate and Mecklenburg roads, was settled by the Applegate family (John, Mary, and their seven children) in 1807.

Enfield Center is at the intersection of Enfield Main and Enfield Center roads. The Baker family (Judah, Lydia Chase, and seven children) in 1804 settled halfway between Enfield Center and Miller's Corners (Military Lot no. 52). Judah

59. Miller's Corners, heading north, 1933.

Baker was a Revolutionary War soldier, though the land he settled was not allotted to him. The original Military Tract owner was John Mundon from the 2d New York Regiment.

Black Oak Corners, at the intersection of Harvey Hill and Black Oak roads, is said to have received its name because of the trees that grew there. At one time a large black oak stood at the intersection; in 1927 the town cut it down.[19]

Bostwick Corners, at the intersection of Bostwick, Harvey Hill, and Enfield Main roads, probably received its name from the Andrew Bostwick family, which settled that area in 1820. Kennedy's Corners is where Sheffield and Mecklenburg roads intersect; four Kennedy families are listed on the Enfield map of 1853. As for Miller's Corners, at the intersection of Enfield Main, Mecklenburg, and Halseyville roads, the Miller family was living in the area according to the same map. Honeypot [Meadow Brook] was a sparsely populated community along the Enfield Falls Road just west of the upper entrance to Treman state park; other such communities are Christian Hill (at Waterburg and Iradell roads) and West Enfield, at Georgia and Mecklenburg roads.

Schools

Enfield once had fourteen public schools within its borders, but now it has just one elementary Ithaca city school. Students from the town attend schools in the

60. Stone schoolhouse on Applegate Road, in the 1880s. This District no. 5 school, built in 1809, was demolished c. 1940. Shown, *left to right*, are Charles Voorhis, Joe Wallenback, George Arnold, Alice Norton, Edna Arnold Stark, Maude Newman (teacher), Nellie Rumsey Meyer, Grace Norton.

City of Ithaca, Trumansburg, Newfield, and Odessa, depending on the location of their home in the town.

The town considered education important from the start; by 1824, eight school districts reportedly existed in the town. These schools were kept open six months a year.[20] By 1865, fourteen public one- and two-room schools were open. These schools each had one teacher who taught kindergarten through eighth grade.[21] After graduation some students continued their education downtown at Ithaca High School.

The original schools had no electricity or running water. Students who attended them still recall them with enthusiasm—sled rides down Enfield Center Road West and Harvey Hill Road; long "rope walks" home from school in the middle of a 1920 blizzard; Mrs. Hubbell's scalloped potatoes for hot lunch; Regents exams at Enfield Center School; fund-raising dances at Enfield Grange Hall for a graduation trip to New York City; end-of-the-year picnics at Enfield Falls.

The last of these scattered schools closed when Enfield Elementary School opened in 1959 at Miller's Corners. Currently four of the one- and two-room schools still stand, and all are being used as private homes.

Enfield Elementary School has gone through many changes since it opened its doors for students from kindergarten through sixth grade. In 1987 Nancy Siembor-Brown became the school's first woman principal. Sixth-graders were directed to attend middle schools, and in 1986 Enfield sixth-graders were the first group to attend DeWitt Middle School. (Students had previously been attending Boynton Middle School.) The new state "Compact for Learning" program at the Enfield school encourages more general community involvement, and is designed to engage town residents.

Churches and Cemeteries

Enfield supported five churches in the first 25 years of its existence.[22] One of the first to organize in the town was the Baptist Church, in 1817. Elder John Lewis functioned as the first pastor of the church, which had twenty-six members. Services were held first in the home of Jonathan Rolfe and then in the Woodard School, at the intersection of Woodard and Hines roads. An official house of worship was built in Enfield Center in 1842, on the east side of Enfield Main Road. This church building was moved to the west side of the road and rebuilt in 1881; it still stands today.

The Christian Church of Enfield was constituted in 1821. The church building was located on the east end of Fish Road, and Elder Ezra Chase was the first pastor. The church was disbanded in later years and the church building torn down; the building materials were used in various cottages along Cayuga Lake.[23] Christian Cemetery is located where the church once stood. The oldest recorded headstone is that of the son of David and Rebecca Beach, who died September 7, 1827.

The Presbyterian Church was organized at Bostwick Corners on February 14, 1832, by Rev. William Page. A church was built at Enfield Center in 1835–1836. The church organization was disbanded in later years. A Presbyterian cemetery is located in Enfield Center. The oldest recorded headstone there is of Bethiah Newman, wife of James Newman, who died on March 30, 1828.

The Methodist Episcopal Church, with its first pastor Joseph Pearsall, held meetings in barns at Bostwick Corners in January 1835. A church was built in June 1835. By March 1876 the church was voting to remove the church to Enfield Center. In June 1878 the new church building, on West Enfield Center Road, was dedicated. The church and its building are still in existence today.

The Methodist Episcopal Church at Kennedy's Corners was organized in 1844, with Elias Lanning its first leader. The members first held church classes at the North School House. The church was built in 1844, and an addition a few years later. On October 16, 1917, a fire started in the sheds next to the church, and the buildings were destroyed. One year later a new church was built, and on December 29, 1918 the new building was dedicated at a special service. The church was disbanded in 1983, and the building is currently a private home.

In the fall of 1982 John and Helen Smith donated land on South Applegate Road to the Agape Church. This organization was started in summer 1980 by Rev. Kenneth Hoover and had been looking for a permanent location. The congrega-

61. First Baptist Church in Enfield Center, 1963.

tion moved into the new building in July 1983. It currently has regular attendance of over one hundred persons and runs many community-oriented help projects.[24]

Jonathan Rolfe started a cemetery near his home on Applegate Road for the town. On June 10, 1876, a group of townspeople met and elected nine cemetery trustees; a society was organized and incorporated as the Rolfe Cemetery Association. The oldest recorded headstone is that of Ephraim Rolfe who died on May 27, 1818.

Other Enfield cemeteries are the Kellogg/Teeter Cemetery on Gray Road; Rumsey Cemetery on Trumbulls Corner Road, where the oldest recorded headstone reads Eliza. E. Fortner/June 30, 1816; Summerton Family Cemetery on Hines Road, oldest recorded headstone says John Summerton/1803–1891; Woodard Cemetery on Woodard Road near Enfield Falls (overgrown today with just a few stones related to the Woodards of Enfield Falls), the oldest recorded headstone is for Polly Ogden who died October 13, 1826; Taber Cemetery on Enfield Center Road near Sheffield Road. Located in the vicinity of Enfield Falls on Gray Road is the Budd Cemetery where the oldest recorded headstone is of Gilbert L. Rightmire, son of Daniel and Tamar who died February 26, 1834.

The town now manages all of these cemeteries and has a cemetery committee that gives advice on cemetery matters.

Organizations and Recreational Activities

Enfield has established organizations to deal not only with fires and other emergencies but also with social activities for the many age groups in the community.

Enfield supported at least two units of the Women's Christian Temperance Union (WCTU)—Enfield Center and Kennedy's Corners.[25] The groups held their meetings in members' homes and in local churches. They recorded many community projects, such as sewing and providing sunshine boxes for sick people. During World I they purchased unbleached muslin and rolled bandages to send to the front. Comfort bags were sent to soldiers during both world wars. Information was circulated in the community informing people of the perils of alcoholism and tobacco addiction.[26]

In the early 1930s Enfield had a town baseball team. Its home field was Miller's Corners. Some of the teams they played were the Taughannock Vets, Gunners (Gun Shop, Ithaca), and Allen Wales (National Cash Register, Ithaca). The team played until at least 1965.[27]

In 1933 Rev. Dutton S. Peterson and his wife Martha started a mothers' club. This club gave women a place to go for a break from everyday routine. It held monthly meetings and went on day trips and a few week-long trips to Happy Valley Homes in Lisle, New York. The club operated until the 1980s.[28]

During the 1940s, when the town population began to grow again, people became concerned with fire coverage for their properties. In February 1948 a group of residents formed the first volunteer fire company in town. By July 1949 the fire company not only had completed a firehall but had purchased their first truck. A second firehall was constructed in 1989, northwest of the original building, which was then sold to the town and is now the Enfield Community Building.[29]

For many years the fire company held an annual firemen's carnival at Miller's Corners in Schaber Field. This carnival has more recently been replaced by such fundraisers as chicken barbecues and an annual car show (in August).

The Ladies Fire Auxiliary was organized in 1953. Its members are relatives of fire fighters, and the group assists in fundraisers and provides support during fire and rescue calls.

Hillendale Golf Course is both business and recreation. The golf course of nine holes, on the west side of Applegate Road, was built in the mid-1930s by Ernest Buteux.[30] The course, closed during World War II, was sold to Edgar and Alberta Sebring in 1960; the Sebrings made various improvements and additions. In 1978 the course was sold to Anthony and Angela Durante, and in 1980 to the current operator, Mary Novickas. It is an eighteen-hole golf course today.

The Enfield Senior Citizens Organization was started in the late 1970s and is comprised of nearly eighty men and women of the town. The group disseminates information about county services available to seniors and organizes many activities, such as boat tours of the Finger Lakes.

The Enfield Community Council has been providing community programs since 1974, with funding from the town, fundraising, and the United Way. Programs cover the very young (e.g., Enfield Cooperative nursery school), older children (Summer Camp, and After School Day Care and Enrichment programs), and adults (woodworking, ceramics, and exercise). In October 1975 a harvest festival was held to celebrate these programs and to raise funds for them. This festival has become an annual event in the community. The council is constantly improving its programs and adding more, all for the benefit of the community.

Government and Post Offices

Enfield's government operates like that of most other small New York towns. Space for the officers and employees of the town is located at the Enfield Town Hall, built in 1966 at Enfield Center.

Walter Payne was elected the first town supervisor, in 1821. Very few early records exist, but one 1821 book records "Marks and Strays." The town clerk recorded the ear notches of animals belonging to town citizens. For example, Nathan Benedict marked his livestock with a crop of the left ear and slit in the crop. The fence viewer who inspected boundary fences in the town and helped settle disputes over wandering animals used this Marks and Strays book.

Early town business meetings were held at various private homes and in a hotel in Enfield Center.[31] The Pig's Ear building, reportedly owned by an Enfield private men's club, was purchased by the town in 1923 to be used as a town hall. The building was then moved from West Enfield Center Road to Enfield Main Road in Enfield Center, and an addition was built on. Election booths were permanently installed inside. The town hall was used not only for town business and elections but for card-playing parties and other social events. Currently this town hall is used for storage of items belonging to various social groups. Stevenson Contractors built a new town hall and town garage in June 1966, west of the old town hall. An addition on the south side for more storage was completed in 1977. Most town business and the sessions of the town court are conducted in the town hall.

The Depression of the 1930s affected everyone. The town was able to help "all able bodied males" by hiring men to work at 25 cents an hour to cut brush and perform other needed work. Hourly wages for town highway employees went from 35 to 30 cents and back again in six months in 1931. The town also kept up with recreational activities, allowing town machinery to be used to keep the baseball grounds in shape.[32]

In 1977 Mabel Purdy, town clerk, and Edna Palmer, tax collector, retired after twenty-five years of service to the town. Thereafter their jobs were combined. That same year the justice of the peace lost *ex officio* designation as a voting member on the Enfield Town Board.

Before November 1985 the town was represented by one representative on the Tompkins County Board—Newfield District 8. Representation changed when the 1980 census showed growth in District 8 and a decrease in Ulysses District 15. To create equal population districts, the town is now represented by two Tompkins County Board members.

Enfield's first woman town supervisor, Etta Gray, took office on January 1, 1986.

At one time there were four post offices in the town.[33] On December 29, 1822, the Enfield post office was established at the Applegate Tavern and John Applegate was appointed first postmaster. This post office, discontinued and reestablished at various times, was closed permanently in November 1902. On March 14, 1832, the West Enfield post office, located on what is now Georgia Road, was established. It was discontinued on February 10, 1841. Enfield Centre post office, at the northeast corner of Enfield Main and Enfield Center roads, was established on July 11, 1846, and Solon P. Sackett was appointed first postmaster. The post office officially changed spelling from Centre to Center in 1893; it was discontinued in 1918. The Enfield Falls post office, established on May 31, 1882, was located near the mill at upper Treman state park. Charles Budd was appointed the first postmaster there. On August 30, 1902, the Enfield Falls post office was discontinued, and Rural Free Delivery service was established from Ithaca that same year.

Military History

Many town families sent members to serve during the country's wars. Between 1863 and 1864, 118 men were mustered into the army from Enfield to serve in the 109th Regiment of Infantry. They fought from the Battle of the Wilderness, Virginia (May 1864) to the Battle of Petersburg (April 1865).

Twenty-two men served in World War I, 108 in World War II, and 40 in the Korean War.[34] The Sergeant Reynold J. King Army Reserve in Ithaca is named after Reynold King of Enfield. Sergeant King was killed near Fort Eminence in France on August 15, 1944.

Population

The Town of Enfield started in 1821 with an approximate population of 1,304.[35] The population in 1840 reached 2,340, only to drop by 1850 to 2,117.[36] Thereafter the loss of residents was continuous. By 1880 the town had lost 527 residents, probably because life in the country was not easy and industrial growth in the City of Ithaca and nearby enticed residents to move.[37] In the 1870s hope was lost when the Pennsylvania Sodus Bay Rail Road, which was to go through the town, was not completed, and the Catskill Turnpike was abandoned in 1876.[38]

Between 1880 and 1930 the town lost another 1,008 residents, 53 percent of the population. During the 1940s, however, the population started to come back, as was true all over the county.[39] It went from 939 in 1930 to 1,082 in 1940, then to 1,316 in 1950. The town was growing so much that in 1965 Sandy Creek Trailer Park opened to provide more housing opportunities.[40] What had taken eighty years to lose, the town more than gained back in sixty. Residents numbered 3,054 in 1990.

6 Town of Groton

Margaret Hobbie

In the northeast corner of Tompkins County lies Groton, a small town with a remarkable history. Its past was built on industry; its present and future revolve around concerns for the material and social well-being of its citizens.

Unlike the other eight towns of Tompkins County, Groton is situated in the Owasco Lake watershed rather than that of Cayuga Lake. The town is only tenuously connected to the rest of the county through Fall Creek, which drains to the south and eventually into Cayuga Lake. For reasons of geography, transportation, and business affiliation, Groton has until recently looked to Cortland—rather than to Ithaca—as its market town.

Groton is moderately hilly, the highest point in the town being 1,506 feet above sea level. One unusual natural feature is Bear Swamp, a wet, wooded area of several hundred acres located in the southwestern portion of the town. The soil in general is gravelly loam, underlaid by slate, well suited to crops and animal husbandry. Agriculture and agricultural services have been at the heart of Groton's commercial and industrial growth.

Early Settlement

Groton was originally part of the Town of Locke, Military Tract Township no. 18, named after the English philosopher John Locke. Much of what we know about Groton's early history was recorded by M. M. Baldwin, principal of the Groton Academy, who wrote *The Beginnings of Groton* in 1868. By that time the pioneers had all died, but several of their children were still living; Baldwin interviewed them along with other early residents.

What is now Groton was, according to Baldwin, probably settled in 1797 by the Perrin, Williams, and Carpenter families, all natives of the northern Berkshires in western Massachusetts. Lot no. 75 of the Town of Locke had been granted to Major Benjamin Hicks of Canajoharie, who hired John Perrin to clear, survey, and sell off portions of the lot. Perrin and his wife Hephzibah, along with Ebenezer Williams and Ezra Carpenter, journeyed by wagon over beaten paths and blazed trails until they reached lot no. 75. For the first month their home was a rude

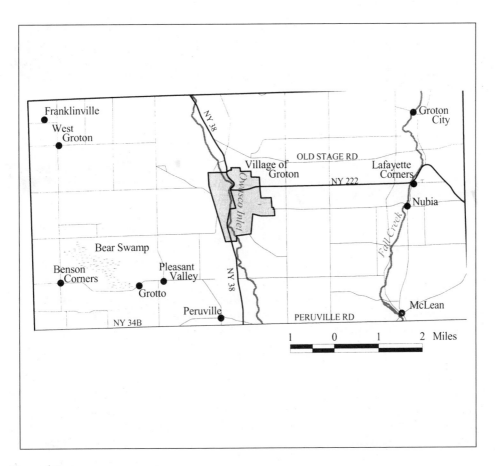

Town of Groton

shelter built against the upturned roots of a fallen tree. Then they moved into a log cabin they had built. Ebenezer Williams, a trained surveyor, walked to Cortland to borrow a compass and chain, surveyed the lot, and subdivided it into portions suitable for farms. The Perrins passed the 1797–1798 winter alone but were joined in the spring by John's father, Lemuel, and others. In the following years more families, primarily from New England and Pennsylvania, came to the area. Some important early names were Crittenden, Branch, Bennett, Hathaway, Loomis, Ingalls, Stuart, Atwood, Avery, and Morton.

The story of Groton's name has been repeated at least once since Baldwin's history appeared in 1868. The Town of Division was set off from the old Town of Locke on April 7, 1817, ten days before it was made one of the original six towns of Tompkins County. (Locke had been divided precisely in two, whence the name Division for its southern half.) Baldwin states that on March 13, 1818, the name Division was changed to Groton upon the petition of residents, many of whom had come from Groton, Massachusetts, or Groton, Connecticut.[1]

That residents petitioned for the change of name is not in question. But of the dozens of New Englanders who had settled in Groton by 1815, not one appears to have been from either Groton, or from towns anywhere close (or, for that matter, from Groton, Vermont). The only New England Grotonian was George Fish, who was born in Groton, Connecticut, and settled in Locke in 1816. At the time the name Groton was chosen for the New York settlement, Fish was a nineteen-year-old newcomer, but he may have suggested the name of his birthplace for his new home. A majority of his Yankee neighbors would have been familiar with the name from New England, and they appear to have supported the choice, although Baldwin reports that many favored the name York. The hamlet that later became the Village of Groton was known in the early days as Perrin's Settlement or, more commonly, as Groton Hollow.

In 1817, when the Town of Division was established, this hamlet contained about seven log cabins and seven frame buildings, including a store, a tavern, and a schoolhouse. By 1825 a carriage shop, a fulling mill, a large residence known as the Mansion House, and several other houses and public buildings had been added.

In 1817 Groton Hollow contained no church building. The area's oldest church, commonly called the Old East Church, had been organized in 1805 as the East Congregational Church in Locke and held services in a log meetinghouse two miles east of the hamlet. It was replaced by a large frame meetinghouse in about 1818, built with contributions of "labor, grain, and neat cattle."[2] This church declined as a Congregational church developed in Groton Hollow, and in 1864 the Old East Church building was moved into the hamlet and converted into the town hall.

The First Baptist Society was incorporated in 1818 and its house of worship on Cortland Street boasted the hamlet's first church bell. The Methodist church was incorporated in 1836 and built a meetinghouse in 1842. A Congregational church was founded in 1849 and its building, dedicated 1851, contained the first church organ.

The first log schoolhouse, a structure 30 by 25 feet, was built in Groton Hollow in about 1805. It burned in 1813 or 1814 and was replaced by a succession of other buildings. A library was started in 1834, but its functions were taken over by the Groton Academy a few years later.

The Groton Academy opened in 1837 with S. W. Clark, a recent graduate of Amherst College, its first president. The school attracted students from the village and "those of far distant sections" of the town.[3] Baldwin eventually became owner and president of the school; he claimed that the academy was a crucial factor in the growth and importance of the village.

Prior to the erection of the Academy, public opinion was greatly divided as to where the main village in the town would eventually be. But, as soon as this institution began to pour out its blessings upon the community, that question was decided. Those seeking new locations at once gave this the preference. Many have been the families which have settled here, mainly on this account.[4]

On January 31, 1839, a neutral weekly newspaper, the *Groton Balance and Democrat,* began publication in Groton Hollow. After its first year, it published thirty-five issues as a partisan paper called the *Groton Democrat.*

In 1860 the hamlet of Groton Hollow voted (by a vote of 68 to 55) to incorporate as a village. The new municipality encompassed 433.9 acres, and the population was 596. An atlas of Tompkins County published in 1866 showed the Village of Groton as by far the largest settlement in the town, with a basic configuration much as it is today, concentrated on South Main and Cortland streets. The village's businesses and industries included the office of the Justice of the Peace, several stores, town hall, two manufacturers of carriages and sleighs, a drug store, a grocer, three physicians, a manufacturer of threshing machines and boxes, three Protestant churches, School House no. 8, the Groton Academy, two merchant tailors, a dental office and daguerreotypist's studio, a sash and blind maker, several mills and smithies, the Groton Hotel, a cheese factory, a millinery, the First National Bank of Groton, and two cemeteries. A new warehouse built by the Perrigo brothers was called Fremont Hall, after John Fremont, because the owners allowed meetings to discuss the novel doctrines of the newly formed Republican party. Groton was also home to Masonic Brethren, of Groton Lodge 496, Free & Accepted Masons.

The Hamlets

The 1866 map of the Town of Groton is dotted with place names—almost every major road intersection seems to have attracted enough settlers to qualify as a hamlet. Many of these settlements were established about the same time as Groton Hollow and some had rivaled it, but by the middle of the nineteenth century the future village had exceeded the other hamlets in importance.

McLean

The largest of these settlements today is McLean, on Fall Creek at the southern edge of the town. Part of the hamlet lies in the Town of Dryden, and its most important institution—Cassavant Elementary School—is part of the Dryden school system. McLean was settled in about 1806 and at first was called Moscow. When a post office was established in 1824, the name Moscow could not be used (there was already a post office of that name in Livingston County). The hamlet on Fall Creek was named McLean instead, in honor of the newly appointed postmaster general of the United States.

McLean pioneers settled on both sides of the Groton/Dryden town line. Before 1850 they established several churches, among them Baptist, Methodist, Universalist, Zion Protestant Episcopal, Roman Catholic, and Episcopal. At one point the hamlet boasted seven sawmills.

In the 1890s McLean was a settlement of about four hundred souls, whose industries included a foundry and machine shop, a barrel factory, a tannery, a

62. Elm Tree Inn, c. 1910. This McLean landmark is still standing, though the elm tree is gone. Photograph by Verne Morton.

large creamery and cheese factory, a gristmill, a cidermill, several small shops, two general stores, and a drug store. In 1897 the hamlet's industrial era came to an abrupt end when fire wiped out the tannery, foundry, mills, and several residences.

One of the first buildings in McLean was a log tavern constructed by Amasa Cobb a little east of Fall Creek. Later, the tavern was replaced by a two-story hotel called the Elm Tree Inn in honor of the great tree that stood on the Cortland-McLean Road. That elm fell victim to blight in the 1970s, when about two hundred years old, but a large cross section has been preserved and still stands in front of the building, now shaded by a large black locust.

The children of McLean's pioneers were taught for a few weeks a year in private homes until the first of several school buildings was constructed. By 1850 the school had 137 students, and in the 1890s a Union Free school was established that took students through tenth grade. They could finish their high schooling at Dryden, Groton, Cortland, or Homer.

In 1930 the Board of Education supervised the construction of a modern brick school building, with six classrooms, a library, a gymnasium, and restrooms. The new school's first principal was J. H. Cassavant, whose name the school now bears.

Peruville

Peruville lies on the Owasco Inlet a short distance north of Route 34B. The origin of its name is obscure, but there is a Peru in Massachusetts near the birthplace of many Groton pioneers.

Although the hamlet is now a quiet residential community, for much of its history it was a thriving industrial center. Earlier histories and memoirs mention a pail factory, cidermill, sawmill, cheese factory, blacksmith shop, general store, axe shop, casket builder/undertaker, hotel with dance hall, tavern, milliner, cabinet shop, post office, print shop, and distillery. Some of the factory buildings have survived and are now used as warehouses, garages, and residences.

A New York State Historical Marker honors Charles W. Sanders, creator of an early spelling book used to prepare students for higher education. Sanders worked out of a small print shop on Old Peruville Road, which was later moved to the Sobers farm and used as an outbuilding.

West Groton

Much of the westernmost part of the Town of Groton is referred to as West Groton, but the heart of the settlement is at the intersection of Cobb Street and West Groton Road. West Groton was settled in 1797 by Isaac Allen, a master bridge builder from Vermont. Allen built the settlement's first store at the southwest corner of the intersection. Captain John and Olive Guthrie were also early settlers. The area grew quickly in the 1810s, about the time of the formation of Tompkins County and the Town of Groton.

In 1816 five West Groton residents established a Congregational church, the West Church of Locke. The building they constructed on West Groton Road in 1832 still stands and serves as a house of worship and community meetingplace. The church today, having merged with the East Lansing Baptist congregation, is an independent evangelical church serving families in Groton, Lansing, and Dryden. The First Christian Church of West Groton was founded in 1831 and met in the schoolhouse until a house of worship was built in 1833 on the east side of Cobb Street. In 1879 the church was described as "here yet, but it has no society, no congregation, no pastor."[5]

In the 1850s, in addition to the two churches, West Groton claimed two stores, a tavern, a wagon shop, two shoe shops, three blacksmiths, a tannery, two cooperages, a carpet weaving shop, a public school, and a select school.

Groton City

Groton City, on Fall Creek in the northeast part of the town, was first known as Slab City because of the many sawmills in the area. It claims to have been in the early 1800s a more important business center than was Groton Hollow.

From 1824 to 1841 this hamlet's post office was known as Fall Creek. The post office was reestablished in 1849 as Groton City and retained that name until discontinued in 1902, after the establishment of Rural Free Delivery.

Sanders' New Series.

THE

SCHOOL READER.

THIRD BOOK.

CONTAINING

PROGRESSIVE LESSONS IN READING, EXERCISES IN
ARTICULATION AND INFLECTION, DEFINITIONS, &c.

BY CHARLES W. SANDERS, A.M.,

AUTHOR OF SPELLING BOOK, SERIES OF SCHOOL READERS, ELEMENTARY AND
ELOCUTIONARY CHART, YOUNG CHOIR, YOUNG VOCALIST, ETC.

NEW YORK:
IVISON, PHINNEY & COMPANY,
48 & 50 WALKER STREET.
CHICAGO:
S. C. GRIGGS & COMPANY,
39 & 41 LAKE STREET.
1863.

63. Title page of *Sanders' School Reader,* Third Book, 1863. Charles W. Sanders
compiled his primers in Peruville. Photograph courtesy of Roger Haydon.

Today Groton City is a tidy collection of residences and farms, but in the past it boasted a general store, a free meetinghouse (which served as the community center), several sawmills and gristmills, and a Masonic hall. Baldwin noted that Groton City had never had a tavern.

Several smaller hamlets have appeared on Groton maps over the years. Lafayette is a small settlement on Fall Creek at the intersection of the Groton-Cortland and East Side Creek roads. George Fish built a gristmill here in 1824 and named it the Lafayette Mill in honor of the general, who at that time was on his great tour of the United States.[6]

Less than a mile south of Lafayette is Nubia, which was known first as Gooseville and later as Footsville. The name Nubia was imposed by the U.S. Post Office in 1893 over the objections of local residents. The post office was discontinued in 1902. One of the first bridges constructed by the Groton Iron Bridge Company spanned Fall Creek at Nubia from 1877 to 1981, when it was moved to Bank Swallow Park in the Village of Groton.

Franklinville was located in the northwesternmost corner of Groton in old lot no. 51 of the Town of Locke. In the 1820s several mills and textile factories were built here on Hemlock Creek, which flows through a narrow ravine called the Devil's Den, producing abundant waterpower. Baldwin records that "later a freshet came and washed the business away."

Benson's Corners or Bensonville lies at the intersection of Buck and Benson's Corners roads. It was named for its first postmaster, Nelson F. Benson, in 1833. A mile or so farther east on Buck/Pleasant Valley Road lies Grotto, whose name was almost certainly derived from Groton. The next intersection is called Pleasant Valley, a small collection of houses around a church. It was made notable by a memoir written by Joseph P. Hester, who grew up there in the early twentieth century.[7]

Other place names that appear on town maps are Pierson Corners, Mosher's Corners, Morton Corners, Riggs Corners, Ludlow Corners, Smith Corners, Jones Corners, Carey Corners, Fitts Corners, Stevens Corners, Mud Schoolhouse Corners, Peruton, Merchants Corners, and Hart Corners. The existence of one-room schools throughout the town helped reinforce the identity of these often tiny settlements.

Groton Businesses

Until about 1866 there was little to distinguish Groton from many other small upstate towns. It was an agricultural community dotted with hamlets and a village that primarily provided services for farmers. Between the Civil War and World War I, however, Groton developed a series of significant businesses. Very few towns of Groton's size can claim such a rich industrial history.

The manufacture of carriages in Groton began as early as 1820, according to Baldwin's sources. In 1876 several small shops, including Hicks, Adams & Davey (formerly Powers and Pennoyer) and Williams and Carpenter, merged to form a stock company, the Groton Carriage Works. The factory produced carriages, cut-

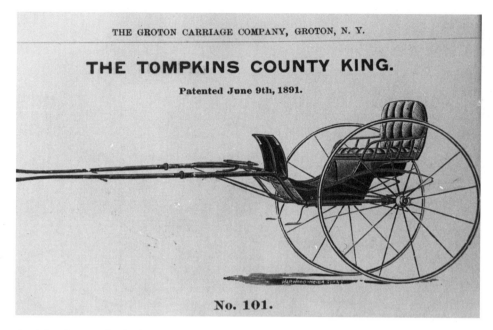

THE GROTON CARRIAGE COMPANY, GROTON, N. Y.

THE TOMPKINS COUNTY KING.

Patented June 9th, 1891.

No. 101.

64. Advertisement for the Groton Carriage Company, 1893. The ad appeared in the *Tompkins County Business Directory* of that year.

ters, carts, and delivery wagons. By the time the firm liquidated in 1908, it was producing five thousand vehicles a year.

By the end of the nineteenth century Groton was known around the world for the design and manufacture of metal truss bridges. This industry started modestly in the 1870s, with the merger of an agricultural machine manufacturing company and an iron foundry. The former enterprise, the Groton Separator Works, had been founded in 1847 by Daniel Spencer. By 1867, when it was known as Perrigo and Avery, the firm's markets extended to the Midwest and California.

The brothers Charles and Lyman Perrigo founded the Groton Iron Works in 1849. By the 1870s the foundry's markets too reached to California. In 1877 the firm began to manufacture iron truss bridges under the name Charles Perrigo and Company, and shortly thereafter the Groton Iron Bridge Company was formed. Groton bridges were distinguished by their use of railroad rails for bridge piers (an early example of industrial recycling), the strength of vertical piles, and stiff bracing systems.

The records of William Williams, who worked as an agent for the company, tell us something about business life and travel in the last quarter of the nineteenth century. His 1887 account book reveals that he traveled by train, horseback, and stagecoach ("bus"). Groton lay on the Southern Central Railroad line, but at the start of a journey Williams usually traveled on horseback to Auburn or Owego to connect with the New York Central or the Lehigh Valley. Train fare from Auburn to Geneva or to Syracuse was 52 cents. Williams generally paid 50 cents to $1.00

for meals and was reimbursed 2 cents for every mile he traveled on horseback. He paid $1.00 for a hotel stay for himself and $1.50 for livery for his horse. He used the telegraph system frequently to communicate with customers and the home office, and made at least one telephone call during his sales career (on May 2, 1887).[8]

In 1887 the firm reorganized as the Groton Bridge & Manufacturing Company and expanded its product line to include steam engines, grain separators, and heaters. It established an insurance program for employees and branch offices in other parts of the United States. Its factory covered several blocks on the west side of Main Street around Railroad Street in the Village of Groton, and employed dozens of workers.

Carriages and bridges were not the only industries in Groton at the end of the century. The town was also home to Booth Brothers woodworking, the Monarch Road Roller Co., and the Excelsior Skirt and Manufacturing Co. Grotonian Nelson H. Streeter, working on his own as an inventor, obtained patents on a folding mirror, a better mousetrap, a cold-handle flatiron, and about seventy other products.

The Conger family is one of the most important in the history of Groton. Although family members later became associated with the bridge and typewriter industries, their first important enterprise was a store. Corydon W. Conger and his eldest son, Frank, opened a general store in about 1870, dealing strictly on a cash basis with suppliers and customers. By 1879 two other sons, Jay and Benn, had joined the expanding business.

In addition to its cash-only policy, the Conger store was notable for its service. The Congers built three horse wagons to serve a thirty-mile radius from the village. Every wagon had its own route and kept its own books. Each made weekly trips lasting four or five days, stopping at farms to deliver supplies of dry goods, shoes, tools, and to pick up orders for the following week. A contemporary journalist described the enterprise as "in every respect . . . a large department store, with a manager for each branch and a corps of travelling salesmen."[9]

Charles Perrigo, a founder of the bridge company, also helped establish the First National Bank of Groton in 1865. The Banking Acts of 1863 and 1864 had sought to stabilize U.S. currency by requiring banks, which in those days issued their own paper money, to pledge U.S. Bonds with the treasury to secure the notes they issued. The acts also established the Office of Comptroller of the Currency to monitor the soundness of charter banks. The comptroller took a dim view of the Groton petitioners' attempts to found a bank in such a small community, with a capitalization of $50,000, but relented when local businessmen raised $100,000.

The bank almost immediately demonstrated its willingness to further the economic interests of the community. In 1867 it purchased $25,000 in Town of Groton bonds and 25,000 shares in the Southern Central Railroad. The health of this financial institution, in which all local industries invested, fed the prosperity of the town and in turn laid the groundwork for industrial expansion.

In 1896 Welthea Marsh became president of the bank upon the death of her husband, Dexter H. Marsh. She is believed to be the first woman bank president in New York, possibly in the nation. Not all businesses were as forward looking

65. Conger Store delivery wagon, c. 1890. This wagon and others like it delivered goods from the village store to area farms.

as those of Groton, however, and throughout her tenure Mrs. Marsh prudently signed all documents "W. M. Marsh."

Telegraph service was established in Groton in 1865, and four years later the Southern Central Railroad was brought to the town by local subscriptions of $50,000. This line, later part of the Lehigh Valley Railroad, linked Lake Ontario at Fair Haven with the Pennsylvania coal fields at Sayre and ran through Auburn, Moravia, Groton, Freeville, and Dryden. At Freeville travelers could transfer to the Ithaca & Cortland line, which later also became part of the Lehigh Valley.

The foresightedness of Groton's citizens and elected officials contributed to the community's prosperity and continued growth. In 1888 the village government purchased forty acres around springs lying northeast of the village to ensure adequate water supply. Water from the springs was collected in a settling basin and then ran to a reservoir high enough to furnish high pressure for fighting fires.

In 1896 the village decided to build its own electric lighting plant. It was paid for with village-issued bonds at 3.5 percent interest. Electricity was generated at a coal-burning plant on Cayuga Street north of Cortland Street and provided power for private consumers and street lighting until midnight (following a "moon-

66. Welthea Marsh, president of the First National Bank of Groton, c. 1900. W. M. Marsh, as she was known, may have been the first woman bank president in America.

light" schedule). The Groton Bridge & Manufacturing Company had its own generator, and the village purchased some power from the factory for day service.

The dawn of the twentieth century found the Village of Groton a prosperous, progressive community. It boasted a well-disciplined fire department, village-owned waterworks and lighting system, rail connections to larger communities, a thriving retail district, and manufacturers providing jobs for hundreds of people.

The largest employer in 1900 was the Groton Bridge & Manufacturing Company, with 160 employees. That year, however, brought radical change. The firm was purchased by J. P. Morgan's American Bridge Company, which was attempting to wipe out competition. The Groton factory closed in 1901 and its machinery was dismantled.

The following year, Jay and Benn Conger bought back the plant and purchased new equipment, doing business as the Groton Bridge Company. It prospered for another twenty years, finally brought down by new state regulations, competition from the larger Pittsburgh firms, and the growing involvement of the Conger family in another enterprise—typewriters.

Many crucial developments in the history of typewriter design and application occurred in Central New York—in Syracuse, Ilion, Ithaca, and Groton. The Crandall Typewriter Company was the first to manufacture in Groton. Its crown jewel, the Universal, won a gold medal at the Paris Exposition in 1893 and made a wealthy man of its inventor, Lucien Crandall. The machine was notable for permanent alignment, interchangeable type, and visible writing. (Up to the early 1890s most typewriters printed "blind" on the underside of the platen; it was

67. Unidentified men with examples of Corona typewriters, c. 1920s. Of its many products, Groton is most closely identified with the typewriter.

impossible to see what had been written without lifting the carriage.) Unfortunately the Crandall company was too small to keep pace with expanding competitors and declared bankruptcy in 1896.

That same year, the Smith brothers, natives of Lisle, broke away from the Union Typewriter Company of America over the issue of visible writing. The Smiths wanted to introduce this feature into Union typewriters. When their partners balked, they formed their own firm: L. C. Smith. By 1904 they had also introduced such revolutionary features as two-color ribbons, stencil cut-outs, and interchangeable platens.

Benn Conger was president of the Groton Bridge Company and a state senator when he became interested in typewriters in 1909. On a train to Albany he came upon another passenger using a Standard Folding Type-Bar Visible Writing Typewriter—the world's first practical portable—which was being produced by the Rose Typewriter Company in a New York City loft. Conger and two friends formed the Standard Typewriter Company and bought Rose's patents and rights. They moved the manufacturing operation to Groton, found a home for it in a building recently vacated by the Groton Carriage Works, and eventually changed its name to the Corona Typewriter Company. The Smith and Corona companies continued to refine their products and became leaders in their respective areas of typewriter manufacturing—for the office and the home. In 1926 they merged to form L. C. Smith and Corona Typewriters, Inc., and expanded their manufactur-

68. Beeyard in Groton, 1897. W. L. Coggshall instructs his sons Brown and Archie. The Coggshall honey tradition extended to a third generation with grandson Millard. Photograph by Verne Morton.

ing plant in Groton. In 1927 the firm absorbed Corona Portable Calculator, another Groton manufacturer, and by 1928 there were Smith-Corona plants in Syracuse, Groton, Cortland, and Illinois. The company continued to expand throughout the following decades.

The Photographs of Verne Morton

In 1896 a young Groton teacher, the descendent of early settlers, began taking photographs of flowers and ferns. Verne Morton not only was a talented nature photographer but had a keen interest in the rapid agricultural, technological, and social changes that were taking place around him. He sought to document them. During the next forty-nine years, Morton took over ten thousand photographs of natural and social life in Groton and surrounding communities. He lived simply in the family homestead on Old Stage Road with his younger brother, Neil.

Verne Morton's images help us understand life in Groton at the beginning of the twentieth century. His early photographs, those taken before World War I, show farmers using horses and oxen and their own backbreaking labor to plow, harrow, sow, harvest, load, and transport crops. Only in the 1920s do tractors and other engines appear. Morton, conscious of the passing of traditional agriculture,

69. Groton children at play, 1932. This photograph by Verne Morton shows "Dumpville" station with Ronald Butts, *seated,* and two other children. Morton's slice-of-life photographs were in fact carefully posed.

strove to document agricultural processes and eventually compiled series on beekeeping, harvesting, building dry stone walls, cultivating pumpkins, raising poultry, and maple sugaring.

Morton's roots as a teacher reveal themselves in his many photographs of children at school and at play: children and teachers walking to their one-room schools, raising the flag, taking rollcall in plain wooden rooms warmed by pot-bellied stoves, studying quietly at their desks, reciting, calculating, spelling at painted wooden blackboards, and playing games at recess. Many images show children at work outside school—helping with the corn harvest, drying dishes—and at leisure—tending to pets, riding bicycles and sleds, re-creating adult tea parties and workplaces.

The Village of Groton in Morton's pictures is a tidy, prosperous place. Substantial Victorian homes fronted by tall elms line Cortland Street. The business district boasts two- and three-story brick and frame commercial buildings, the Groton Hotel, and a bandstand at the Main/Cortland intersection. Groton-built bridges span the inlet. Photos of the lumberyard to the northwest of the business district, and the typewriter factory to the south, indicate an abundance of jobs.

Despite the presence of an internationally famous factory, everyday life in Groton was much like that in other upstate New York towns for most of the

70. Main Street in Groton village looking south, 1908. Photograph by Verne Morton.

twentieth century. A 1935 Cornell University term paper, written by Groton native Priscilla Stringham, depicts life in Groton in vivid detail.[10]

Stringham describes a town slowly rebuilding from the hard years of the early 1930s. Corona typewriters, the only factory in town after the demise of the bridge and road-roller plants in the early 1920s, had gone from employing 800 men and women in the late 1920s to 600 in the early 1930s, but had recently rebounded to a payroll of 1,030 and was running on four shifts. Corona employed workers from Groton and surrounding communities, including part-time farmers and many farm women.

The improvement of the roads to Cortland and Ithaca in the early 1930s had affected Groton's retailers. Although the food suppliers were prosperous, clothing and shoe retailers and others were languishing, unable to compete with bigger stores elsewhere. Almost every home had a radio and telephone service; mail was delivered daily on Rural Free Delivery and twice daily in the Village of Groton. The weekly *Groton Journal & Courier* carried news of civic affairs, community events, and personal notes.

There were still twenty-one rural schools, each with one or two rooms, in the Town of Groton. The Village of Groton had five churches, and places of worship were located throughout the town.

Stringham describes a homogeneous, close, gregarious community. Neighbors had responded generously to aid victims of the Great Flood in the summer of 1935. There were dozens of social clubs, lodges, study groups, church-affiliated organizations, granges, scouts and other children's clubs, and volunteer fire companies. The library, founded by Dr. Miles Goodyear in 1917, was heavily used and supported in part by school taxes. The Groton Opera House on the second floor of the municipal building had become a movie palace, the Corona Theater.

Informal gathering places could be found throughout the village and town. Popular spots in the village were the Jones and Hayden drug stores, Pete Hoffman's billiard parlor, and the Corona Club. Pierson's store filled this community function in West Groton, Thomas's store in Groton City, Mericle's and Powell's stores in McLean, and the blacksmith shop in Peruville.

Groton reached its peak as a small industrial community in the 1950s and 1960s. Both government and industry contributed to the area's prosperity. In 1953 the Groton Memorial Park on Sykes Street in the village opened, and district voters approved bond issues for a new central school on Peru Road. Natural gas service was introduced in 1956. Smith-Corona continued to expand, merging with a calculator manufacturer in 1958 to become Smith-Corona-Marchant or SCM.

A 1972 planning study described Groton as having many of the characteristics of other central New York towns.[11] It was served by two main thoroughfares, Routes 38 and 222. Manufacturing and commerce were concentrated in the village. Most of the housing units were single family homes, and much agricultural land along country roads had been given over to new houses as small farms ceased operation or merged with other small farms. McLean, Peruville, West Groton, and Groton City were all recognizable communities with strong identities.

The only developed area with a "suburban" character lay just north of the village. Many fine old village homes had been preserved and bespoke the affluence of the early twentieth century. Groton Central School housed students from kindergarten through twelfth grade on two campuses in the Village of Groton. Tompkins Cortland Community College still made its home there. Several churches and meetingplaces in the village and throughout the town helped bring the community together.

Throughout the 1970s a group of committed Groton citizens, led by Dr. Stephen Blatchly and Dr. and Mrs. Willard Short, worked to improve the health and housing of local residents. Their original purpose was to build better housing for seniors; they accomplished this goal, at the same time founding a child development center, an ambulatory care unit, and a nursing home. The facilities were built with government grants and community donations.

In 1983 Groton abruptly entered the postindustrial era when SCM Corporation withdrew from the village. Its buildings were torn down in 1985. Groton residents were unruffled by SCM's departure, much to the astonishment of the rest of Tompkins County. But in fact, by the time the village factory closed, its dominance in the community's economy and identity had waned. Its contribution to the village property tax base was small ($30,000), due to an agreement reached several years earlier. The majority of out-of-town workers came from other parts of central New York and had little attachment to Groton outside the workplace. Finally, SCM's share of the village workforce had fallen to less than 32 percent (250–350 workers out of 1,100); many of these workers were transferred to the Cortland plant and continued to live, shop, volunteer, and pay taxes in Groton. Thus even before SCM departed, the Village of Groton had evolved from a factory town to a bedroom community serving Ithaca and Cortland.

Groton's perception of itself had also changed. Its citizens took justifiable pride in the progressive policies that had made possible the establishment of the Groton Community Health Care Center. The center continued to expand its programs and the area it served. By the mid-1990s it ministered to the needs of 8,500 patients a year and had added an intermediate care facility, a dental clinic, and a nursing home. The center affiliated with Cortland Memorial Hospital in 1989 and established a satellite dental clinic on the Ithaca Commons in 1994.

Volunteers working with the Groton Beautification Council improved the appearance of the village and coordinated the rescue of the Nubia bridge (manufactured by the Groton Iron Bridge Company in 1877) and its relocation to Conger Boulevard in 1981. The Groton Historical Society, founded in 1972, worked to preserve the record of the town's rich past, establishing a museum in the Old Baptist Church on Main Street in 1985. Groton's pride in its past was also reflected in Grace LePage's mural in the 1972 First National Bank Building, which depicts Main Street at the turn of the century. The bank is committed to remaining small and independent. The Goodyear Memorial Library doubled in size in 1981 and continues to be a major community asset, with a 30,000-volume collection, parenting and career resource centers, a children's section and story-hour program, and an informed and energetic staff.

71. Groton High School. Built in 1921, the high school was later the first home of Tompkins Cortland Community College. Photograph courtesy of Tompkins Cortland Community College.

The history of a prominent village building is a microcosm of the village in the twentieth century. The Groton High School building was built to house Groton Central School in 1921 at a time of economic growth and local boosterism. Its function did not change until the post–World War II boom years. It became the elementary school after the high school on Peru Road was built in 1954, and it was sold to SCM Corporation in 1962 when the new elementary school on Elm Street opened. SCM used the building for offices until 1967 and then donated it as the home of the new community college for Tompkins and Cortland counties.

Tompkins Cortland Community College used the building for seven years until it moved to its new Dryden campus. In 1975, after offering the building to both the village and the town, SCM sold it to a Cortland businessman for $2,600. It was purchased in 1979 by developer John Caveney and during the 1980s housed several apartments, a business, and a small Baptist congregation. The building was named to the National Register of Historic Places in 1992.

In 1992 the building took on new life as a subsidized apartment building for senior citizens. The conversion to residential use involved the restoration of many original features, including tin ceilings, moldings, and two murals depicting early settlers.

Changing employment, transportation, and shopping patterns have altered life in the Town of Groton in the mid-1990s. Its residents tend to work and shop in other communities, and ties with Ithaca grow stronger each year. But Groton remains fiercely proud of its history and its ability to adapt to change.

7 Town of Lansing

Louise Bement

Situated in the northern part of Tompkins County, the area now known as Town of Lansing, with Cayuga Lake its western border, has attracted people for thousands of years. The lake softens the winter temperatures and allows respite from the summer heat as Lansing residents flock to their parks and cottages to enjoy the water and its views. And Lansing has views! Rolling rich farmland, hanging valleys with their falls and gorges, glimpses of the lake; where is there a more beautiful place to live?

The lake provided food and transportation for the first settlers in the region, the Am-eo-lithnic or "early dawn stone" Native Americans whose bone implements have been found along the shore of the lake.[1] These Native Americans were followed by the Algonquins and the Cayugas. The Cayugas had a "museum" near the Salmon Creek Falls where on the trees they recorded their exploits in war with paintings and carvings.[2] To the north in Cayuga County the Cayugas had a castle, fields of grain, and orchards. Lansing seems to have been a hunting and fishing area with small villages along the banks of Salmon Creek where ravines and cliffs protected the Cayugas from their enemies. By 1790, when white settlers arrived upon the scene, only a few Native Americans were living in Lansing.

The settlers of the early 1800s were farmers, merchants, millers, and black-smiths who came from Pennsylvania, New Jersey, and New York to claim military lots or to buy cheap frontier land. They came to an area of one hundred military lots, a town named Milton in the county of Cayuga. It was not until 1817 that Tompkins County was formed and Lansing removed from the Town of Genoa (formerly Milton). At that time Lansing received sixty lots, and Genoa was left with the remaining forty.

The early settlers came in the winter or early spring, using the frozen water-ways for transportation. The only roads were Native American trails and the overgrown paths made by Sullivan's conquering armies in 1778. Mills to grind grain, make boards, and finish homespun fabrics were built along the flow-ing streams of Lansing, and the forests were cleared to make fertile fields. The trees were burned to make potash, to be sent down the lake, over to the Hudson River, and thence to Albany and New York to be sold or bartered for needed supplies. Eventually the clearing of the lands affected the streams so that they

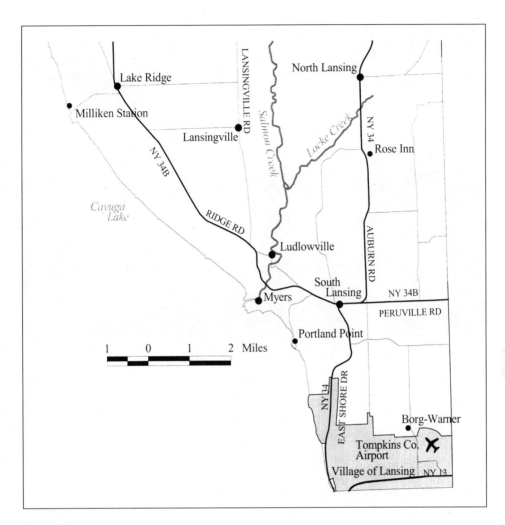

Town of Lansing

either flooded or ran dry, thus hampering the mills that depended on a steady flow of water.

The early communities of Lansing carried settlers' names: Northville, Beardsley's Corners, Teetertown, Myers, Ludlowville. Of these only Ludlowville and Myers remain, the rest being given other names when their post offices came in. Lansing's roads also carry the names of early settlers: DeCamp, Esty Drive, Armstrong, Bill George, Lockerby Hill, and Teeter. Asbury Road is named for the Methodist Church, Auburn Road for the route to Auburn, and Algerine Road for a street in London, England, which was the home of thieves and others of questionable character.[3]

Ludlowville is named for Silas, Henry, and Thomas Ludlow. They came from Long Island in March 1791 and bought Military Lot no. 76, six hundred acres,

72. Last operating mill in Ludlowville. It was destroyed by fire on October 30, 1934. Photograph courtesy of Town of Lansing archive.

for $60. Near the Salmon Creek falls they built a log cabin and a gristmill. They added a tavern to their buildings to house the customers of their mill. Soon other settlers followed, from New England, Pennsylvania, and New Jersey. Among them were Oliver Phelps, who started the first store in Lansing and supervised the building of the first two steamboats on Cayuga Lake; Daniel Thayer, who built a wheel spoke factory and iron foundry; Daniel Clark, who built a dye and cloth-dressing establishment; and Amasa Wood, who built a tannery. Ludlowville grew rapidly into a thriving village mainly because of the water-power that supplied its mills and factories. In time it had many shops and stores and was the largest shopping area in Lansing. Calvin Burr founded a store there in 1812. He was also one of the incorporators of the old Bank of Ithaca in 1829. In 1848 James Burr bought out Calvin and formed a partnership with Henry B. Lord. The firm of Lord and Burr lasted eighteen years.[4]

Myers is named for Andrew Myers, who settled at the mouth of Salmon Creek in 1791 and built boats to carry settlers' goods. After his father's death Andrew Myers Jr. also ran boats and added a gristmill to the family enterprises.[5] Myers was a small hamlet of fruit farmers, millers, and boatmen until 1891, when people who worked at the International Salt Plant came to live there. Then it became more of a community, with a store, a barber shop, and boarding houses.[6]

North Lansing was originally called Beardsley's Corners. John Beardsley of

73. Myers Road looking toward Route 34B, c. 1910. On the road are C. H. Haring and his milk wagon. Photograph courtesy of Town of Lansing archive.

Stratford, Connecticut, built one of the first frame houses there in 1796. This house had the first glass windows in the community and also a chimney stack. Beardsley was justice of the peace and county judge in 1793. Other early settlers in North Lansing were John Bowker, first justice of the peace, supervisor, and constable of the Town of Milton; Daniel Bacon, who ran the tavern where the Ithaca-Auburn stagecoach stopped; and William A. J. Ozmun, who built a sawmill. Ozmun was instrumental in securing a railroad station, and he became station agent and express agent; he also erected stores and a wagon repair shop. A beautiful historic home survives in North Lansing, the Rose Inn, built in 1854 by Abram Osmun in the Italianate style and containing a notable spiral staircase.[7]

Lansingville was originally Teetertown, named for Henry, Peter, and Coonrod Teeter, who built taverns in Lansingville. Henry's tavern burned in spring 1804. His wife died in the fire, and Henry died about six months later.[8] In 1792 Samuel Baker set up his blacksmith shop in the hamlet. Deilman Bower, born in Germany, settled in Lansingville in 1794. Eight or more large farms came to be occupied by Deilman and his sons, and this area of Lansingville came to be known as the Bower Settlement. A German Lutheran church, built of logs, was also used as a schoolhouse. Besides blacksmithing and farming, other industries were soon started: a shoe shop, a tannery, a hat shop, a tailor, a wagon shop, a store, a cabinet shop, and a veterinary. At the lower end of Ford Hill Road the Ford's mill occupied a spot on Salmon Creek.[9]

South Lansing was first named Libertyville. In 1830 a large hotel was built there by General D. D. Minier to service stagecoaches on the Ithaca-Auburn run. He named his hotel the Central Exchange, as stagecoach horses were exchanged

74. Rogues Harbor Inn in South Lansing, c. 1900. Photograph courtesy of Town of Lansing archive.

there. The hotel became known as Rogues Harbor; even the planting of trees and the name Elm Tree Inn has not stopped the residents from calling it Rogues Harbor to this day. The hotel played an important part in Lansing's history. After 1838, when William H. Seward became governor of New York State, a room was reserved for him at the hotel whenever he traveled back and forth to his home in Auburn by stagecoach from Albany or Washington. He was a U.S. senator in 1849 and secretary of state in Lincoln's administrations. The hotel was known as a stop on the Underground Railroad, and during the Civil War the militia drilled on the grass behind the hotel.[10] South Lansing had a cornet band from 1884 to 1887. Its uniforms were dark trousers, cream-colored shirts, and blue capes. The band owned a bandwagon drawn by four horses.[11] Today South Lansing is an important center of the large Town of Lansing. The consolidated school buildings are there, as is the town hall.

Industry in Lansing

Two familiar area names are Syrian Hill and Portland Point, in the central part of the town along the lakeshore near Salmon Creek.

Syrian Hill was developed after 1891 when an incorporated company was

75. International Salt Company in Myers, c. 1960. The plant was destroyed by fire in the early 1960s. Photograph courtesy of the International Salt Company, a part of Akzona, Inc., and Town of Lansing archive.

formed to obtain the salt from deep beneath the surface of the land at Myers Point. A plant was erected, and salt wells were drilled near the mouth of Salmon Creek. The brine from these wells was evaporated in open pans to give a coarse salt. By 1893 a nine-foot vacuum pan and a rotary dryer had been added, and the production of high-grade salt began. At this time the plant had a capacity of 140 tons daily and employed one hundred persons. In 1904 the plant consolidated with the International Salt Company, and enlargements necessitated the hiring of more workers. A large percentage of the people who came to work at International Salt were Syrians. Whole families came and encouraged relatives from Syria to join them. The company houses on the hill overlooking the plant became the Syrians' village.

In the summer of 1962 the Lansing plant was closed, and its business was transferred to the firm's plant at Watkins Glen, New York. Some employees chose early retirement, some chose to work in Watkins Glen, others found jobs in Lansing. The houses on Syrian Hill were sold to the people who occupied them.[12] Syrian Hill, with its small Syrian church, is today peopled with Syrians and later newcomers to Lansing. Land north of Ludlowville that the salt company owned was given to Lansing for its rod and gun club. The land south of the mouth of Salmon Creek was given for the town park, and the land north of the mouth of Salmon Creek was obtained by New York State for future recreational purposes.

Portland Point was named for the portland cement processed from the vein of Tully limestone under the area. Joseph Shurger first owned this point; his daughter married Harts Collins, who mined and processed the limestone and sold it to the Ithaca Glass factories. After the death of Harts his son Sherman formed the Portland Point Cement Company. The next owners, in 1900, started as the Cayuga Lake Cement Company, founded by Marcus E. Calkins, Charles E. Treman, LcRoy H. Smith, Robert H. Treman, Mynderse Van Cleef, and George S. Livermore. This corporation was dissolved in 1915 and the property sold to J. G. White Management Corporation of New York City. Under this management the company's steam operations were replaced with electricity.[13] Before long the company came under the management of the Penn-Dixie Cement Company of Nazareth, Pennsylvania.

The hamlet of Portland was begun May 3, 1901, with the construction of a row of ten houses. By 1903 the community consisted of thirty residences and hotels, and contracts had been let for the building of twenty new homes.[14] Employees of the plant lived in this village, while the supervisors and office workers lived in Ithaca and came to work by train. The people living in the village had electricity and water supplied by the cement company. They heated their homes with coal. These villagers came from Italy, Syria, Poland, Germany, Ireland, Czechoslovakia, Hungary, Russia, and England.[15]

The Portland Cement Plant closed in June 1947 when labor disputes and the difficulty of mining the limestone rock at the quarry made the plant inefficient.[16] The plant was abandoned and the equipment sent off to the company's other plants in December 1950. The plant had been in operation forty-eight years. The cement silos were used for grain storage in the 1950s; in the 1960s the Cayuga Cement Company stored cement there, using the last of the big barges on the lake to transport the cement. The quarry is worked today by Cayuga Crushed Stone, producing rip-rap, gravel, and paving materials.

These two industries, with their company-owned villages, changed the make-up of Lansing's population from pre-Revolutionary family farmers to a combination of farmers and factory workers from Europe and the Middle East. Many of the original families worked at the salt and cement companies, but one-room district schools tended to isolate newcomers from the Lansing mainstream until the schools were centralized in 1948.

Another industry just north of Portland Point was begun in 1915 when John Clute formed the Rock Salt Corporation and put down a mine shaft to the 1,500-foot level. The salt at this level was of poor quality. Not until 1921 was the Cayuga Rock Salt Company formed by Frank L. Bolton and John W. Shannon and a better vein of salt found at the 2,000-foot level. This level was mined until 1968, when work began at 2,300 feet. In 1970 Cargill bought the mine rights and modernized the facility.[17] A long strike in 1986 almost closed the operation and caused hard feelings in the town. During the strike some workers were brought in and trained to replace the striking miners. The workforce today is made up of many second- and third-generation "Rock Salt" people.

Beside the Rock Salt Mine there is another corporate presence in the northern part of the town today, the New York State Electric and Gas Company (NYSEG)

Power Generation Station at Lake Ridge. In September 1950 a 500,000-kilowatt steam electric-generating station was begun, named Milliken Station as a tribute to Arnold W. Milliken, vice president and general manager at the time. The station opened in 1955. In 1990 Milliken Station burned soft coal mined in Pennsylvania and delivered to the plant by rail. Approximately 800,000 tons of low-sulfur coal was burned each year, and the station had a maximum generating capacity of 317,000 kilowatts. Ninety-two people were employed.[18]

On Warren Road in the Village of Lansing is Borg-Warner Automotive Inc. Borg-Warner began in Tompkins County as the Morse Chain Company, making bicycle chains and other products. The Industrialized Machine Products Plant in Lansing was opened in 1975, and in 1980 ground was broken for the Automotive Products Plant.[19] This industry has landscaped, parklike grounds, which include a large swimming pool for the employees and their families.

In 1990 Lansing was not totally an industrial community. Many people living there worked at Cornell or Ithaca College or at Ithaca businesses. There were still large, wealthy farms and a rural feeling in the central and northern parts of the town.

Origins of the Village of Lansing

The southern part of the town was also made up of large farms until Route 13 was rerouted out of Ithaca and up the hill beside the lake to Lansing in 1963. The southern area quickly experienced explosive growth. Apartment projects, motels, car dealerships, and shopping malls went up rapidly, transforming the area. A need for zoning led to formation of a village of Lansing in 1974.

The town council at first agreed to form a water district for the area south of Waterwagon Road, and for the same area an intermunicipal sewer district that would use the sewer plant of the Village of Cayuga Heights.

Congested traffic and difficult intersections along North Triphammer Road led residents to press the town council to regulate land use. When the process lagged, residents sought a referendum to form a separate village. Both the right to hold a referendum and the ultimate result were challenged unsuccessfully in court.[20] A referendum on December 3, 1973, approved the Village of Lansing, 204 to 179. A final court challenge was set aside a year later, and the village came into being on December 19, 1974.

By 1990 the village had a population of 3,269, 35 percent of the town's total residents, and by 1996 it contained 43 percent of the town's assessed property values.

Travel

The town has been served by a variety of routes since its earliest days, starting with trails used by the original inhabitants, progressing to developed roads and highways, to railroads, and finally an airport.

The original main route through the town was known by Native Americans as the "Warrior Trail." This trail entered the town along roughly what is now Route 34B above the lake, turned toward Ludlowville, wended its way near the present South Lansing T intersection, and then descended roughly the Esty hill to the valley floor.[21]

The main highways through the town today are Route 13 at the south, Route 34 from Ithaca to Auburn, Route 34B (which includes the Peruville Road to the east and continues north from the South Lansing T, nearer to the lake than 34), and Warren and North Triphammer roads running north and south.

According to the Town of Lansing Directory, eighty-four miles of town roads are fully maintained year round by the Lansing Highway Department. An additional forty-seven miles of country roads are plowed and cindered by town crews during the winter. The highway department is housed in the town barns just off Route 34.

Several railroads operated over the years. Traces of some abandoned railroad grades can still be seen in fields. The first (and only surviving) line in the town was the Cayuga Lake Railroad, which ran from Ithaca along the lakeshore to Auburn beginning in February 1872. The Lehigh Valley Railroad system acquired the line in 1879 and abandoned it in 1950. Trackage was reopened in 1954 as far as the Milliken power station for coal delivery. Conrail took over operations in 1976.

A New York & Oswego Midland Railroad opened soon after the Cayuga Lake line in December 1872 and ran north from the present Route 34 about a half mile north of Peruville Road to Auburn, and also south and east to Freeville and thence to points northeast. It stopped service in October 1889.

The Auburn portion of this line was reopened in December 1908 as the New York, Auburn & Lansing Railroad, with a new section south to Ithaca, situated east and above today's Route 34 down to the city's Stewart Park. The line, on occasion stalled by formidable snow drifts, was reorganized as the Central New York Southern Railroad, then abandoned for good in May 1924. A short spur built by Colonel J. V. McIntyre to his Rogues Harbor hotel was used between the summers of 1909 and 1920.[22]

In July 1956 the Tompkins County Board of Supervisors voted 11 to 4 to float a $2 million bond issue to buy the Cornell University Airport in the Town of Lansing and run it as a county facility. By 1965 the county airport employed three people and was undergoing $370,000 worth of improvements, including a new taxiway, runway extensions, and lighting.[23] Some 220,000 people used the airport in 1989 and its runways could accommodate large jet planes, although in the summer months a longer runway was needed for the same weight load. In April 1990 four air services—USAir, TW Express, Continental Airlines, and Mohawk Airlines (a commuter line founded by the son of a president of the former Mohawk Airlines)—were flying out of the airport, and a move was made to build a new terminal. Design work had been approved as part of a five-year airport master plan that included an extended runway, a new terminal building, and extended parking lots.[24] The project was completed, and the new terminal opened on April 1, 1994, at a cost of $11 million: $5 million came from a federal tax on air passenger tickets, $3 million over twelve years from a $3-per-ticket charge on passengers using the airport, $1 million from New York State, and $2 million over ten years in charges to airlines using the facility.[25]

Lansing Schools and State Centers for Youth

In 1813 Richard Townley, school commissioner, divided the town into twenty-two districts, sold the public school lots, and gave deeds for them.[26] These district schools were organized under the Common School laws of New York State, and each was under the supervision of its own school board. Every one-room schoolhouse was similar in size and design, and these small country schools survived until the mid 1940s.

In 1930 the Ludlowville Union School, which consisted of a grade school and high school, replaced its school building in Ludlowville with a large brick building near but outside the hamlet. By 1948 eight of the thirteen district schools of Lansing were contracting to send all their pupils to this modern building. To educate the children for a reasonable tax rate Lansing voted to centralize in 1948. One-room schools were put back into use when needed to accommodate an overflow of grade-school students, but they were not used as district schools. Rather, in 1950 first through third grades went to North Lansing, kindergarten and first grade went to South Lansing, first through fourth grades went to Ludlowville, and fifth through twelfth grades went to the high school. There were 474 students in the centralized district.[27] As the population continued to grow, an elementary school was built in 1958, and 1974 saw the construction of a new high school. Fifth through eighth grades then attended school in the 1930 building, and it was called the middle school. In 1990 there were 1,050 students in the district.

The campus of the Tompkins-Seneca-Tioga Board of Cooperative Educational Services (BOCES) is located in the village, providing the three counties' school systems with vocational and other special student programs.

The South Lansing School for Girls was opened in August 1968 by the New York State Department of Social Services in facilities that had been a training center, called Kingdom Hall, for the Jehovah's Witnesses organization. It was intended as an upstate alternative to the Hudson Training School, and it could hold up to sixty delinquent girls from nineteen counties. In 1974 the facility was turned over to the New York State Division for Youth. After the closing of the large training schools statewide, South Lansing became the only training school for girls in New York State, with a capacity of fifty of the most difficult girls in the system.

The facility more than doubled in size in 1992 and now houses 113 delinquent girls. The effectiveness of the program has allowed qualified students to attend local schools and work in the community. Groups of students from the center are frequently involved in community day, 4-H activities, competitions, and Teens Helping Teens peer-counseling programs. Several local families serve as satellite foster homes for girls from the facility. The facility also hosts annual meetings of

76. District no. 13 school just north of Route 34B on Conlon Road, c. 1914. Martha Quick was the teacher. Josephine Conlon (Ernstein), later a longtime Ithaca High School teacher, stands at the right end of the second row and is marked by an X on her skirt. Photograph courtesy of Town of Lansing archive.

the local Lions and Rotary clubs, which with several other groups, including the Lansing Faculty Association, support the facility at holiday times. In 1993 the Division for Youth opened a similar facility for delinquent boys, the Lewis Gossett Jr. Center, next to the center for girls. By 1997 the Gossett center was serving 150 boys.[28]

Churches

The Town of Lansing had seven churches in 1990: the All Saints Roman Catholic, the Asbury Assembly of God, the Faith Baptist Fellowship, the Grace Baptist, the Lakeview Christian Life, the Lansing United Methodist, and the West Groton–East Lansing (a Baptist congregation).

Lansing had very few Roman Catholics before Slavic and Hungarian families moved in to work in the salt plant at Myers, and All Saints Church did not exist until 1910, when Mass was held for one or two years in an empty tenant house belonging to Frank Gallagher. When the house was occupied, the benches and altar were removed to Gallagher's large dining room, where services were conducted for a year or more. The first Catholic chapel in Myers was built in the spring of 1913. The present church was built in 1932.[29]

Grace Baptist Church was incorporated in its second year, 1961, and purchased a 2.5-acre lot from Merton Argetsinger. It was a branch chapel of the Tabernacle Baptist Church of Ithaca which met in the South Lansing Grange Hall until its church was built.[30]

The Faith Baptist Fellowship of North Lansing began on a Wednesday evening in early fall of 1966, when a group of Christians met at a home for Bible reading, prayer, and hymn singing. Everyone enjoyed it so much that they decided to meet every week. In October 1966 Sunday school and worship services were started. Rev. Walter Weiss was called as the first pastor. The fellowship was incorporated as a church in February 1967 and the former North Lansing Methodist Church building was purchased.[31]

The West Groton–East Lansing Church was constituted at the home of Philmore Barney on March 27, 1808, and was called the Second Church of Milton. The congregation first worshiped in Barney's barn and later in Benjamin Buck's barn. In 1832, after much discussion, a building was erected in lot no. 74 "in the Town of Lansing and adjoining the east and west road from Luther Barney's to the Groton line." This building, last used as a church in 1979, is now a private home. The congregation today meets in Groton.[32]

The Lansing United Methodist Church was formed out of the larger Lansing parish, which consisted of churches in Ludlowville, North Lansing, Asbury, Lansingville, East Genoa, and Myers. In 1796, when the small local Methodist churches began, two Methodist groups were formed: one at the home of Jonah Tooker a mile west of Ludlowville, another at the home of Robert Alexander south of Lake Ridge. By 1797, two log meetinghouses had been erected, one at Asbury and one at Teetertown (later Lansingville). The Lansingville church burned in 1938.[33] The Asbury red church was built in 1811. When in January 1844 the red church burned, the present church was constructed. The last Methodist service was held at Asbury church in October 1962. It later was used temporarily by the Asbury Assembly of God Church, and today it is a private home.

The Ludlowville Methodist Society was formed in 1822 and built its first church, Zion's Chapel, in 1825. During 1867–1868 Zion's Chapel was moved into Ludlowville from the hill on which it had stood. The last service in this church was held in October 1962. In the mid-nineteenth century the people of North Lansing met for worship in their homes, then organized to build a church in 1851. The last service held there was in 1961. Myers Church was built in 1907 and the last record of service there is on June 26, 1946, but Myers Church was not used regularly after 1933.[34] By January 1963 plans were under way to build a new church to replace the parish churches that were too small and in need of repair. In 1987 this active church built a large addition to the original church with meeting-rooms and an office for the minister, which was dedicated in January 1988. Large rummage sales in the spring and fall, a fall antique show, and a popular Christmas Fair help raise money for the church.

Services of the Asbury Church of the Assemblies of God were first held August 17, 1969, in the old Asbury Methodist church building. The church was begun by

77. The Asbury Methodist Church, c. 1900. Built in 1844, it is located on the corner of Asbury and North Triphammer roads. Photograph courtesy of Town of Lansing archive.

a group of six families who had formerly attended Assembly of God Church in Ithaca. The Asbury Methodist church building was being sold, and so the congregation needed to buy land on which to build. They contacted Helen Atwater, who surprised them by donating land on North Triphammer Road. In December 1969 the congregation moved out of the drafty Methodist building and into Duane Ray's welding shop on Atwater Road, which was beautified with new carpets and fresh paint. In May 1971 construction started for a parsonage on the new land, and the congregation began meeting in the parsonage garage. From November 1973 to the following March volunteers worked with used lumber to build the church. On April 27, 1974, a dedication service for the new building was held.[35]

The Lakeview Church of Christ was started in 1974 by a group of about thirty people, many of whom had previously been associated with the downtown Ithaca Church of Christ. The group chose the name "Lakeview" before moving to 56 Burdick Hill Road in Lansing—where it truly does have a lake view. The association of Lakeview with the Churches of Christ lasted for only a few years, and the group then renamed itself the Lakeview Christian Life Fellowship.

Lakeview has never been a large group, but it has always focused on children. In its first year several Lakeview mothers established an independent Christian nursery school, the Robin's Nest. This nursery school was the first formal education for hundreds of Lansing area children and was still going strong in 1990.[36]

Another religious institution is the Watchtower Bible and Tract Society (Jehovah's Witnesses), which in January 1935 purchased a six-hundred-acre tract of land north of the community of South Lansing and began farming operations under the name Kingdom Farm. This large farm produced food for the Watchtower Society's international headquarters in Brooklyn, New York. After years of painstaking effort an excellent herd of Holstein-Friesian cattle was established. Dormitories, a greenhouse, carpenter shop, swimming pool, outdoor theater, library, mill elevator, and milk plant were added. In 1953 the farm spread over approximately eight hundred acres.

In February 1943 a ministerial training school was added to this complex. After graduating 3,638 students from Kingdom Farm, the school was moved to Brooklyn in 1960. Until 1967 the facilities on the farm were used for short refresher courses. In 1968 the school buildings and some of the farm buildings were sold to New York State for the Lansing School for Girls.[37]

Lansing Volunteer Fire Department

Today's fire department originated from four early fire companies: the Ludlowville, the South Lansing, the Lansingville, and the North Lansing.

Before 1915 Lansing had no fire companies. When a fire got beyond control of the bucket brigade, the town depended on fire apparatus brought from Ithaca by train.

In 1990 the Lansing Fire Department provided fire protection and ambulance service to the Town and Village of Lansing. The department was composed of four fire companies and a fifth company (an ambulance and rescue squad). Fire Company 1 and 2 (the Ambulance and Rescue Squad) were located in the central station in South Lansing on Route 34B. Fire Company 3 (Lansingville) was located on Route 34B in the northwestern part of the town, Fire Company 4 (North Lansing) on Route 34 in the northeastern part of the town, and Fire Company 5 in the southern part of the town on Oakcrest Road, Village of Lansing. Ambulance service was discontinued in August 1992. Members of the fire department are all volunteers who donate their time to maintain the equipment and obtain the necessary specialized training.[37]

Government

Lansing's government today consists of a town board of four council members who serve four-year terms and a supervisor who serves a two-year term. The town board appoints boards and commissions that exercise considerable responsibility for the formulation of policy. Residents are encouraged to provide input to the town board through letter writing, attendance at board meetings, or direct personal contact. The town supervisor is responsible for coordinating staff assistance to the town board. Additional elected officials are the town clerk and the highway superintendent. Appointed officials include a town attorney, auditor, engineer, park superintendent, recreation director, code enforcement officer, and historian. Lansing's Municipal Court has two justices, each elected for a four-year term.[38]

The Village of Lansing's government consists of a mayor and four trustees. Other village offices are: clerk and treasurer, code enforcement officer, deputy clerk, ombudsperson, superintendent of public works, attorney, and engineer.

The Town of Lansing has had a Lansing Post Office designation since May 1, 1973, when the last of the small village post offices was closed. The town's population was 9,290 at the 1990 census, and its property assessed at $661.5 million by 1996.[39]

8 Town of Newfield

John Marcham

The first white settlers of Newfield quickly discovered how hard it was to scratch a livelihood out of the area's densely wooded, hardscrabble hills. In the early 1800s Newfield was one of the last corners of present-day Tompkins County to be populated.[1]

Farming, and with it the town's population, waxed and waned for many years.[2] No single occupation or industry took hold, but merchants came to provide services to residents. For years now, the Newfield Central School District has been the town's largest employer.

The best land in Tompkins County was in the northern towns. In a treaty that ended U.S. action against Indians in central New York, the state acquired land that included the area that is Newfield today. Speculators bought large holdings, or patents, and sent out agents to sell lots to individuals and families.

The land that is now the Town of Newfield was originally part of 336,000 acres bought from New York State for 75 cents an acre by John Watkins, Royal Flint, and five other men who expected to make a great deal of money by reselling it. This land included the present towns of Newfield, Danby, and Caroline in Tompkins County and part of Cayuta in Schuyler County. Two other men later bought all the present acreage of Newfield from Watkins and Flint and then sold one-third of their holding to two brothers from Connecticut. One of the brothers owed school taxes in his home state and in settlement gave the state the land in western Newfield that became known as Connecticut Hill. Two generations of the Estabrook family came to Newfield as agents to sell the land, the last of which was not sold until 1879.

The land of the present-day Town of Newfield was originally a part of the Town of Spencer in Tioga County. In 1811 the area was taken from Spencer and named Cayuta. In 1822 the town was renamed Newfield, and it was officially annexed to Tompkins County in 1823. Final changes took place in 1853 and 1854 when the western one-fourth of the town's area was removed and annexed in two parcels, one to Chemung County and the other to Schuyler County.[3]

By 1790, a few trails through the woodlands were the main evidence that remained of the earlier presence of Cayuga, Catawba, and Saponey Indians, the

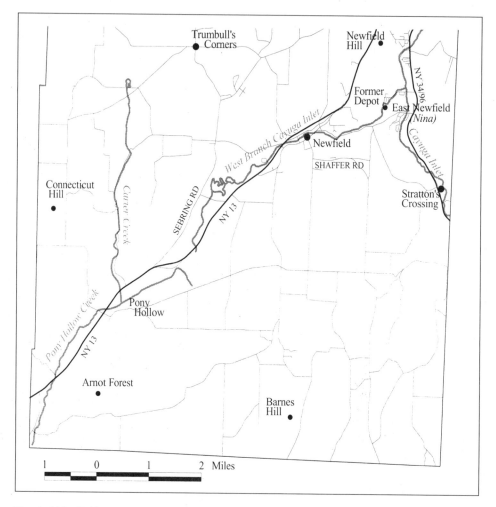

Town of Newfield

last recalled in the name Poney Hollow (more recently Pony Hollow) given the valley southwest of Newfield village, through which Route 13 runs to Elmira.[4]

Pioneer Years

Indians had abandoned the area when the first white settlers started arriving. James Thomas took up land in Pony Hollow in 1800, followed in 1801 by Joseph Chambers and 1804 by John White. Eliakim Dean of Ithaca bought land the next year on the west branch of Cayuga Inlet, where water in a deep valley could power mills. The settlement in the northeast corner of the town came to be called Florence, changed in 1822 when a village in Oneida County established its earlier use of the name.[5]

78. Route 13 in 1960. Bisecting the Town of Newfield northeast to southwest, the highway follows some of the old New Town Road between Ithaca and Elmira. Newfield village is in the center, Pony Hollow in the valley beyond the village. Photograph by Ralph Baker, *Ithaca Journal.*

"Newfield" was the name chosen for the settlement and for the town itself, because of the large amount of land in the area remaining to be acquired. Eventually the settlement became the most populous hamlet in the town, and it is usually called a village, though it was incorporated as a formal village only between 1895 and 1925.

Richard Seabring, who had a command in the Revolutionary War, died in the town in 1821. His son Cornelius emigrated from Pennsylvania to Lansing in 1801 and in 1804 moved to Newfield, where land was cheaper. He is said to have brought his family and all his possessions on a wooden sled with a yoke of oxen and one horse over rough forest terrain, blazing trees as he went. They built on the west side of the valley, a section known as Seabring Settlement. Cornelius was the first postmaster in the town. Sebring Road and Sebring Cemetery recall the family today.

One history of Newfield relates that a typical early settler located land and set about felling trees with which to build a cabin. With oxen he uprooted tree stumps and plowed the soil to plant. Crops were mostly for home use and barter. Little was shipped to market because of poor roads. During the pioneering phase, neighbor helped neighbor, and families were largely self-sufficient, able to improve their situation primarily by clearing a few more acres of woodland each year.[6]

The story is told of one man, Abram Earl, who, in the early 1800s, walked to Lansing from Newfield and worked for a man named Judge Townley until he had earned a bushel and a half of wheat. Earl took his earnings to the only mill then in existence, on Cascadilla Creek in Ithaca, had it ground into flour and carried it home to his wife, having made a round trip on foot of thirty-six miles.

The names of early settlers are attached to roads and other landmarks in the town: David Linderman arrived in 1803; the years 1809–1815 were prolific in the arrival of new families, Smith, Gillett, and Kellogg from Lansing, and Dudley from New Jersey and Ithaca among them. William Hine of England became the first man to come directly from Europe to the town, when he set up a blacksmith shop in 1834. His wife, "Aunty Hine," lived to be a few weeks over one hundred years old.

Before too long, enterprising men set up mills and a tannery along the town's steep gorges. The first two mills to grind grain into flour went into use in 1804, and Eliakim Dean built the first sawmill in 1809. Major farm crops in the early 1800s were hay, wheat, corn, oats, and buckwheat.

A hotel was constructed where new arrivals could live until they had put up their own crude cabins. In 1815 Samuel Rogers built the town's first factory, for carding wool and manufacturing cloth. Later came a wagoner, and a cooper to make barrels.

Schools appeared very early, the first being built in 1804 or 1805 on Bank Street. Following passage of the 1812 state law to provide public schools, Newfield began building. By 1822 twelve schools in Newfield were enrolling 654 pupils. Average daily attendance was about half that number, and some years school was open for only three months. First through sixth or eighth grades often shared a single room and stove. Children walked to school. Some teachers boarded in homes, with the homeowner's school tax being waived in return.

Trails were crude, covered with ice and snow in winter, mud in the spring, and large potholes most other times of the year. Travel was not widespread, but when heavy snow made it necessary, landowners were responsible for clearing a way past or over their land, contributing a team or labor—a practice required until 1906. A pathmaster saw that the job was done, on occasion opening fences so a path could be made.[7]

Throughout its history the town has been governed by an elected council, headed by an elected supervisor. Until 1969 the supervisor also represented the town on the county Board of Supervisors. After 1969 a county Board of Representatives was made up of legislators elected independent of town office.

The population of the town had grown to 976 in an 1814 census. The next available census figure is 2,664 in 1830. The economy was growing.

Pre–Civil War Growth

After an unsettled period around 1820, which resulted in foreclosed mortgages, abandoned farms, and farms for sale, the population of the town increased. Between 1825 and 1850 the area's best lands were taken up.

Lumbering was important in the early years. Deerskins were exported. On warm days in the village in the 1830s, the tannery gave off a powerful stench. Tompkins County Mills went up in the village in 1830, later renamed Newfield Flouring Mills and using steam as well as waterpower. In an average year at midcentury the mills produced 65,000 bushels of flour. The miller was often paid with one of every ten of the bushels he ground.

Farm families no longer made their own clothes and furniture. The *Gazetteer of New York State* for 1836 listed 5 gristmills in the town, 21 sawmills, 2 fulling and 2 carding machines, 1 ashery, 1 tannery, 1 tavern, and 2 stores.

By 1850 such a list included 1 bootmaker, 2 harnessmakers, a tailor, a tinsmith, a cabinetmaker, and a building mover, 2 each coopers, blacksmiths, painters, and physicians, and 3 lawyers. The town also counted 3 grocery–dry goods stores, 2 hotels, 2 flourmills, 1 woolen factory, and 1 tannery, and had added a cigar manufacturer, a shingle mill, and a carriagemaker. The hotels and taverns suffered a setback in 1846 when the town voted to ban the sale of alcoholic beverages, 304 to 250, but the town went "wet" again the next year, 339 to 289.

School attendance continued to grow, swelling to 1,087 in 1844. Teachers taught for 75 cents to $1 per week in addition to their board.

Religion was well represented. Before churches were built, missionaries and traveling preachers brought the gospel. Sunday School classes began meeting in various homes around the town. The first Methodist Episcopal church organized in 1834 and put up a building a year later, on the site of the present church. Trustees had the family names Clark, Mead, Ferguson, Murray, Reynolds, Dudley, Seabring, and Swartwood. Baptists first organized in 1820 and built a church on Bank Street in the village in 1842. In the summer candidates for baptism were often immersed in a millpond near where the town library now stands. Presbyterians first met in the Yellow School House in 1820 and built a church on Shaffer Road in 1832.

Although in 1824 a turnpike was built through Newfield to Athens, Pennsylvania, access to outside markets remained difficult and transportation slow and inefficient. As late as 1850, two town residents made their living as drovers.[8] For some parts of Tompkins County, beef cattle were sent in droves to Philadelphia. Turkeys were driven on their own feet to New York City.

In 1849 Andrew Jackson Van Kirk of Newfield took his satchel, saddle, and dog and went from Ithaca to Cleveland by boat and then by four-horse stage to Chicago, which was at that time a swampy village. There he hired a man and bought a horse, and in Indiana bought 150 head of cattle for $20 a head and drove the cattle on foot, traveling about ten miles a day. It took him from November until February to get back to his farm in Newfield. (Grandson Lochary Van Kirk still occupied the farm in 1972.) In the spring Alexander drove the animals to Orange County in downstate New York for slaughter.

79. Residence of I. B. Palmer in Newfield village in 1879. Palmer owned the tannery in the village from 1840 to 1844. He married a Widow Poster in 1843 and they had seven children. Palmer held several town offices. Photograph from FCH, opposite 534.

In 1834 a stagecoach began to travel regularly between Ithaca and Elmira, stopping at Newfield village. Passengers rode for a quarter, and freight was carried for a price. In the spring holes were so bad coming up Newfield Hill from Ithaca that the stage would sink to its axle and the horses to their knees. Many times a four-horse team had to be sent to pull them to the top of the hill. A plank road was built between Ithaca and Newfield at a cost of $15,000 in 1852, and tolls brought in nearly $1,700 in its first year. For years, into the 1900s, a four-horse stage went from Newfield to Ithaca three days a week.

Midcentury Challenges

The economy of the town was tested in the middle of the ninteenth century. Wheat midge ruined the wheat crop in central New York in 1850, Newfield's overworked soil was showing signs of exhaustion, and most important western wheat was being shipped east over the Erie Canal, which had opened in 1825.

The Ohio territory had already passed through its pioneer stage and into agricultural surplus. Western wheat drove down prices, leaving Newfield farmers with three choices—stick to farming and diversify (many already had flocks of sheep), seek jobs in Ithaca where laborers were always needed, or move west.

The town's population rose from 2,664 in 1830 to 3,816 in 1850, but fell to an estimated 2,800 by 1855. A large part of that drop resulted from the annexation to Schuyler County of the western one-fourth of the town, including the hamlet of

Alpine and the eastern half of Cayuta Lake. But the number of families that worked small farms continued to drop steadily, and with them the town's population, well into the twentieth century.

The Civil War was an additional drain. Some 225 men from Newfield enlisted to fight in the Civil War. Twenty-eight died, thirty were disabled, and others chose not to return but to go on to western lands, where opportunities were new and land less expensive than in New York State.[9]

Former Newfield residents sent word back from Ohio, Illinois, and other states to the effect, "We can raise twice as much in half the time as you can on that hemlock land." Town historian Alan Chaffee has visited Ohio cemeteries and found headstones with the names of former Newfield residents, among them Ford, Wilcox, Rumsey, Kellogg, and Stewart.[10]

Many farms in the western, Connecticut Hill, portion of the town were abandoned as a result of the area's acid soil, poor drainage, and high elevation.[11] An estimated 240 homes once stood on the hill. One can still identify old house sites by caved-in cellars, lilacs, and old orchards. New residents have found raspberries, rhubarb, currants, roses, and the old-fashioned flower known as Golden Glow around these ruins.

Life went on in the town. The number of schools grew, to twenty-three by 1866. Congregations were now meeting in five churches.[12] And the town's famous covered bridge went up between 1851 and 1853. Labor and materials were inexpensive at the time. The bridge, 115 feet long and 16 wide, cost $800 to construct. The original structure had solid siding; later, diamond-shaped openings were cut to admit light. A complete restoration took place in 1972, at which time Newfield boasted the oldest covered bridge in daily use in New York State, and one of twenty-five authentic bridges left out of more than 250 that once stood around the state.

The Erie Canal was expected to help New York move its products to market, and railroads were expected to accomplish the same result. A Pennsylvania & Sodus Bay railroad company was chartered in 1870, to connect with an Ithaca & Athens Road at Spencer, and then go through Newfield to Seneca Falls. A competing line was chartered two weeks later. Both started building roadbed but the P&SB was abandoned before it laid any track. The town had to repay $52,000 in bonds it had purchased to finance construction. The Ithaca & Athens was completed in 1872 and became the first (and only) railroad through the town. A station was built at Nina, first called East Newfield and then Newfield. The railroad consolidated with the P&SB's original competitor in 1874 and was later acquired by the Lehigh Valley. Roadbed of the defunct P&SB can still be seen, including a stone abutment on Piper Road in Newfield and a cut near the Landstrom dump just over the county line to the south off Routes 34 and 96. The Lehigh Valley survives as Conrail. And the line comes from Sayre, Pennsylvania, through Spencer in Tioga County, to Ithaca.[13]

Residents banded together in increasing numbers. Farmers organized a Newfield grange in 1874, and sixteen men formed a masonic lodge in 1880. Oddfellows, Eastern Star, and Rebekah followed.

A major fire broke out in the village in June 1875. The town had no fire com-

80. Newfield Bridge, c. 1890. Spanning the Cayuga Inlet in Newfield village, this covered bridge is the oldest such bridge in daily use in the state. Bridges were enclosed because roofing a bridge every twenty years was cheaper than building a new one. Photograph courtesy of the Newfield Town Hall.

pany of its own. Ithaca equipment was shipped by railroad flatcar, but village residents failed to send horses to draw the equipment the mile uphill to the village. By the time equipment reached the scene, the fire had burned itself out, razing twenty buildings that housed a total of fifteen businesses and destroying the town's official records.

New buildings were constructed of brick. Four years later a history said of the village, "Phoenix-like it rose from its ashes."[14] It now boasted 3 general stores, 2 each hardware, millinery, and wagon shops, hotels, smithies, and gristmills, and 1 each drug, boot and shoe, harness, and furniture stores, meat market, sawmill, woolen factory, and tombstone maker.

Common School District no. 2 in the village voted in 1873 to become a union free school district, which meant it could teach beyond the eighth grade. Students still had to go by horse and buggy to Ithaca to take state Regents exams in high school subjects. In 1895 Newfield became eligible to give its own Regents, and in 1898 the school graduated its first class.

Teachers were paid $99 in 1897 for an eighteen-week school year. Besides classwork, they were responsible for the conduct of students at school and in the village, and were expected to prevent quarreling, swearing, fighting, vulgar language, and disrespect.

Hamlets around the town were still vital. One, Trumbull's Corners at the foot of Connecticut Hill in the northwest part of Newfield, had a post office in 1846 and was sometimes known as Rumsey Corners. The hamlet had 150 residents in

81. Main Street stores in Newfield village about 1870, looking generally north. The covered bridge is at the lower right, and the back side of the old Newfield Hotel appears in the background at right.

1878, 2 general stores, 2 wagon shops, 3 smithies, and other stores. Just south of the Corners on a branch of Enfield Creek were 4 mills, a slaughterhouse, and a milk-processing plant. Two churches flourished, later to combine. More than one thousand people attended the Old Home Day Celebration in 1931.

A New Century, a Modern World

Former president Theodore Roosevelt became possibly the most notable celebrity to visit Newfield when he spoke in the village on October 24, 1910. The automobile and the telephone arrived in Newfield in the first decade of the 1900s, Rural Free Delivery of mail in 1902, but electricity and the first radio did not come until the 1920s. For all these changes, a good number of residents continued to make their living on farms.

To replace those who had left Newfield for greener pastures, others found the land cheap and felt it might be made to produce. Around the turn of the century, families originally from Finland and Czechoslovakia settled in the southwestern part of the town. They wanted lives in the open country rather than to continue

82. Old Newfield Hotel, c. 1875. One of the village's two hotels, it was later called the Shirley House. The Baptist church built in 1947 now stands on the site. Photograph given by Hubert J. Fenner.

in city shops, factories, or mines. Land agents attracted them with advertisements in newspapers in their native languages.

Czech settlers began arriving in 1905, attracted by ads in Bohemian-American newspapers. They came from New York City, New Jersey, and North Dakota to Pony Hollow, long considered a "poor weedy hollow." They took pride in their work, insisting each crop be "just so." With lime, fertilizer, care, and hard work, Czech families made theirs some of the most productive land in the town. In 1918 they built Bohemian Hall, with 130 members, as a gathering place. Children were taught the native language in Sunday school; native dances continued to be held there until the latter part of the century. Among early family names were Krejca, Mazourek, Vyskocil, Korbel, Novak, Wopat, and Holub, joined later by Blovskys, Cudlins, Malkovskys, Stepans, and Bednars.

People of Finnish descent arrived about 1910 from New York City, Massachusetts, Pennsylvania, and the Midwest. They loved rural life, agriculture was a main interest, and their ability to work with wood enabled them to repair rundown farm buildings. Many came from work in copper, iron, and coal mines.

83. Nate Cook's drugstore in the village, late 1800s. Photograph courtesy of the Newfield Town Hall.

Their steam bathhouses, saunas, used for relaxation after a hard day's work, were characteristic.

The first arrivals bought farms on Shaffer Road and Seely, Barnes, and Irish hills, where fields were already cleared. In December 1913 about fifty families organized the Finnish Evangelical Lutheran church just across the county line in North Van Etten. Names familiar today appear in the minutes of that meeting: Lehtonen, Nurmi, Mattson, Knuutila, Olli, Lampila, and Lehto. Later came Pakkalas, Ruuspakkas, Huhtanens, Makis, Walls, Tuuris, and many others. Their descendents moved into professions and business as well as agriculture and many other vocations.

The town's population bottomed out around World War I, at 1,456 in the 1920 census, just under half the total in 1860. For all the grimness of the economic picture of the late 1800s, old residents recalled much farming activity. New varieties of wheat were thriving, rows of teams drew up to unload barrels of apples and potatoes at the railroad depot, mills processed carloads of wheat and corn, and a creamery operated for several years. Milk was taken from farms on Barnes and Irish hills every day to Ithaca and Cayuta.

Federal and state governments bought up thousands of acres of poor and abandoned farms in the 1930s, for reforestation and wildlife conservation. Much of the abandoned land has since been planted to trees, primarily pine, spruce, and larch.

84. Union Free School in 1906. Completed in 1871, with later additions, the school, *lower left*, was replaced by Newfield Central School in 1939. This view shows school outhouses in the foreground, the village center at the right.

New institutions appeared to ameliorate life. After the Baptist church burned, a fire department came into being in 1917, which over the years helped quell many minor fires and control major fires that occurred in 1925, 1926, 1959, and 1969.

Teams of horses were used by farmers until the 1930s, but tractors began to appear in the 1920s and cars as early as 1910. Early owners of cars included the McAllister, Cronkrite, McDaniels, Bush, and Dassance families. Macadam began to be used to surface roads in the second decade of the century. Steamshovels were used in construction.

Floods, war, and the Depression had their impact. A flood in 1905 knocked out bridges in the eastern part of the town and stranded passengers on a milk train for two days. In the flood of 1935 several bridges were damaged, making it necessary to go to Ithaca by way of Danby. Snow storms and hurricanes left their mark as well, notably snow in 1944–1945 and 1958 and Hurricane Hazel in 1974.

Thirty men from Newfield fought in World War I. Delmar D. Carpenter and Odus N. Everhart gave their lives.[15]

The Depression years, 1929–1933, did not seem to have a disastrous effect on residents. Many went to Ithaca to take their money out of the banks, but none of the Ithaca banks failed. Most farmers had all they needed right where they were, and as one said, "You weren't used to living very high on the hog anyway so it did

85. Newfield Old Home Day in 1921. Ice cream socials, musicals, oyster suppers, and lawn festivals were popular in the town around the turn of the century. Recent old home days have included a fair, parade, and art displays.

not seem to make much difference." Business did drop off in the village, and the value of goods and property fell.

Some 124 men from the town served in World War II, of whom five were killed: George H. Goff, Smith G. Griffin Jr., Donald H. Moon, Joseph H. Smith, and Herman Vollmuth.[16]

The Fourth Half Century

Railroad passenger service through the valley ended in 1959, but freight trains continued to ply the old Lehigh Valley line in the 1990s.[17] Buses provide passenger service between Ithaca and Elmira. New York State Route 13, the principal artery through the town, was rebuilt in 1959–1960.

The town acquired natural gas service in 1966 and formed a water district between 1966 and 1969. Residents of the village formed a district to light the streets, and the town government took over responsibility for lighting certain intersections elsewhere in the town.

A study around 1970 registered fifty-five active farms. Dairying was the principal enterprise, with 2,200 cows on these farms. About five thousand acres were producing hay, ensilage, corn, and grains.

Construction began to flourish as an occupation in the 1940s. The town's population grew gradually until by the 1960s it passed the post–Civil War fig-

86. Pierre L. Cronkrite's garage, 1925. The building formerly was Newfield's creamery. Out in front are, *left to right*, George L. Beach, Cronkrite, and Pierre L. Cronkrite Jr. driving his car. Photograph courtesy of Jeanette Beach.

ure of 2,984. Census figures show rapid growth between 1960, when the town counted 2,193 residents, and 1990, when the number reached 4,867.

Newfield's role as a bedroom community for a prosperous Ithaca became more evident after 1957, when George Vandermark started the first of many mobile home parks in the town, with 200 units. By 1990 the town had 842 trailers, second in number only to Dryden, and nine trailer parks, attracted by the absence of zoning.

The 1990 census found 71 percent of eligible adults in the labor force and employed (6 percent of these self-employed), 27 percent not in the labor force, and 2 percent unemployed. Education, defined broadly, was the biggest employer, of 26 percent of those working, followed closely by manufacturing and construction combined, retail and wholesale trade, and professional service.

The town had thirty-four businesses, many operated from home, in 1972, a number that would grow to ninety-eight by the mid-1990s. Several light industries located there: Omni, manufacturer of turbine and other precision parts; American Polysteel Forms, for the building industry; Palisade Corp., a software firm; Hot Rod Road Cases for musical instruments; Brown Cow Yogurt; and the veteran Landstrom Gravel Co. The community also had a weekly newspaper for the first time in a century, the *Newfield News*, published in Ithaca.[18]

The Newfield Fire Department had two pumpers, tank trucks, and rescue trucks, and one crash truck in 1996. About fifty active firefighters belong, ten or eleven of whom are available during the weekday.[19]

87. George Vandermark's Meadowbrook trailer park on West Danby Road. Begun in 1957, it was the first of many built in the town. Photograph by Douglas M. Payne, courtesy of the Newfield Town Hall.

New community organizations came into being and others ceased to meet in the 1900s. Among those that served for years but exist no longer are the Ladies Monday Club, a literary society and debating club, a dramatics club, the Women's Christian Temperance Union, the Newfield Cornet Band, and Grand Army Band. Among the newcomers are Lions, school boosters, and rod and gun clubs, and Senior Citizens.

The Newfield Public Library has been in existence since 1889, in one structure and another. In 1958 it joined the Finger Lakes Library System, from which it receives partial funding, and moved into the former Grange Hall in 1970.

The school system is the town's biggest employer, with 97 teachers and administrators and 74 other staff serving 1,100 pupils from pre-kindergarten to twelfth grade. A starting teacher earned $28,400 for ten months in 1996. The district's annual budget of nearly $7.8 million is made up of $4.9 million in aid from the state, $2.3 million in property taxes, and the remainder from tuition and other income.

As in many communities, town residents come together around their youth, expressed through the years in interest and pride shown in Newfield Central School. The present elementary and middle school building was constructed in 1939 at a cost of $220,000, shared by federal and state governments. New rooms were added in 1949, 1957, 1962, and 1967. A junior-senior high school of thirty-four rooms was built in 1975 at a cost of $3.2 million.[20] Course offerings have come a long way in 190 years, with strong academic and vocational programs now available.

The community's independence expresses itself periodically when the New York State Department of Education attempts to cajole Newfield into merging with one or another neighboring school system. Such efforts came in 1962, 1965, 1972, and again in 1995. In each instance Newfield chose to go its own way in spite of financial incentives to merge.

Making a living in Newfield has never been easy, but its citizens clearly enjoy being able to live their own way in rugged surroundings.

9 Town of Ulysses

S.K. List

Nearly 100 years have passed since the settlement of this piece, but the next century will not mark the changes of the past; the country has reached its limit of population, and the one who reads these lines in 1990 will see no great change in the general aspect of the village or country from that described here, only the names will be new.

> —A. P. Osborn, History of Trumansburg, 1890[1]

Nothing is more certain than that the Town is going to change. It has been changing before and since Sullivan's Revolutionary Army took the heart out of the Indian opposition in these parts. It probably is going to change faster in the future than in the past.

> —Edward A. Lutz, Letter to the Ulysses town supervisor, 1964[2]

The most unchanging feature in the Town of Ulysses is Taughannock Falls, along with the dramatic gorge its creek has carved and the lake in which its stories mingle with others from Cayuga country. Formed by the Ice Age, Taughannock is the very bones of this place and, in one way or another, all of the local past is marked on its walls. In every epoch, it has commanded awe.

Every year, some half-million visitors come to Taughannock Falls State Park. The park probably draws more people than any other spot in Tompkins County and far more than anywhere else in the Town of Ulysses or the nearby Village of Trumansburg.[3] The visitors come to swim, picnic, sail boats, and throw Frisbees. In the summer sunset they gather on the Great Lawn below Taughannock Farms Inn for free concerts. In winter they sled down Rice Hill, north of the falls. In spring smelters wade the creek waters at night, probing with lanterns and nets. Fair or frigid, almost every day finds someone fishing off the park's concrete piers.

It is likely that few park patrons realize they are passing their leisure under the eternal gaze of some of the area's earliest visitors. Just above the stately Victorian inn, in a small cemetery nestled amid towering trees on the shoulder of the gorge, a cluster of old gravestones marks the final resting place of white families that began the work of clearing the wilderness. Bearing belongings and babies, on foot or in crude wagons, they were non-natives, among the first who arrived in the midst of a nearly trackless forest, usually in the depths of winter to avoid the muddy season, and decided to stay. They claimed land newly signed out of the hands of Indians who were still in the vicinity. They left behind stories of streams

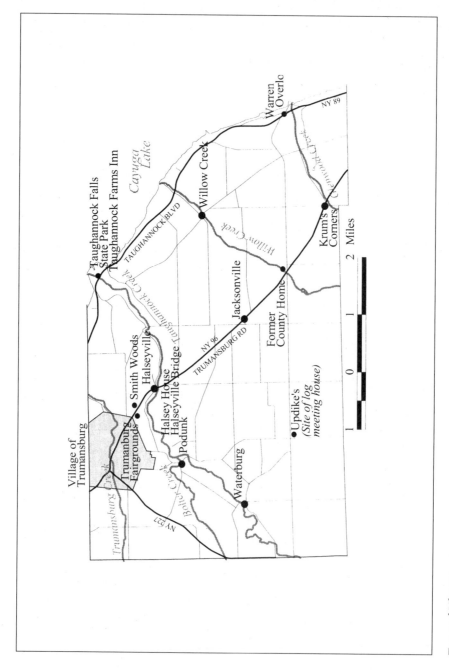

Town of Ulysses

88. Taughannock Giant, 1879 (from a stereograph). A quirky, original, and resilient nature has persistently characterized the Town of Ulysses. A homemade hoax resulted in this "prehistoric man."

teeming with fish and of encounters with wolves in the woods, panthers on the bluffs, and bear in the gorges.[4]

The old graveyard is mowed, but some of its stones are cracked and fallen, and one is all but swallowed up in the trunk of a tall tree. Time has blurred some inscriptions, but others are easy to read, citing lives that began before the Revolution and ended when the nineteenth century was still new. Among the names are Lee, Ganung, Frost, Smith, and Goodwin.

Early Settlements

A state historic marker names the first white settler along that stretch of Cayuga Lake as Samuel Weyburn, in 1790, but it was the brothers Richard and Benjamin Goodwin who established a lasting foothold on the lakeshore. Arriving in about 1794, Benjamin soon constructed a gristmill on the north side of Taughannock Creek and, for a time, the settlement known as Goodwin's Point grew faster than Trumansburg and was the largest in the Town of Ulysses.[5] For at least a century after its start, in fact, the settled area at the mouth of Taughannock Creek was known as Goodwin's Point. Tourists knew it as the staging point for an excursion to Taughannock Falls.

But as in other parts of the Europeans' "New World," these developments deliberately eclipsed the activities and culture of a host of native peoples, hereabouts the Cayuga and Seneca nations of the Iroquois confederacy. In 1677 a traveler out of Albany had visited the area and reported that "the Indians had built a small town and were growing corn, beans and potatoes on the rich flats."[6] Other early records mention "apple trees [there] of two and a half centuries' growth."[7] Those "rich flats" are easily recognizable as the wide delta—ten thousand years of sediment carried by Taughannock Creek[8]—that now forms the popular park.

Colonel Henry Dearborn with his contingent of Sullivan's troops reached Goodwin's Point on September 22, 1779; the *History of Tioga, Chemung, Tompkins and Schuyler Counties* (1879) reports—without explanation—that this native settlement, unlike others nearby, somehow escaped destruction. According to the *History,* a fortified village (memorialized in the name Indian Fort Road) in western Ulysses, the home of a large number of Cayugas and some Senecas, likewise survived, thanks to "its retired location."[9] Later study, including a 1979 archaeological dig, however indicates that the latter village had passed out of existence more than a century before Sullivan's men arrived.[10]

Abner Treman, traveling with his family and his wife's brother John McLallen, came to Samuel Weyburn's homestead in 1792. As he had while in Colonel Dearborn's detail, Abner followed an old Indian trail that led his little party north along the hillsides above western Cayuga Lake. He was coming to claim lot no. 2 in the Town of Ulysses of the Military Tract.[11] Little did he know that he would lend his name to Trumansburg village.

At that time, Ulysses encompassed the present towns of Ithaca, Dryden, and Enfield. The present Town of Ulysses was organized as of March 5, 1794;[12] the first town meeting took place on April 7, 1795.[13]

While the Goodwins were developing the lakeshore, Treman took to the hills, where he found abundant waterpower. He built a gristmill and dam, near where Trumansburg Creek now flows under central Main Street, but paid a heavy price. Traveling out of town in 1794 to purchase the mill machinery, he returned in a severe February snowstorm, reaching the Weyburns' home half-frozen. Eventually, his foot had to be amputated. Some accounts say one foot and part of the second were cut off by a physician; others, that the surgeon was simply a carpenter.[14] In any case, Treman survived. Using a wooden leg,[15] he thrived as an active

89. Abner Treman's house, January 1897. The first frame house in Trumansburg, this dwelling re-placed Treman's original log cabin in 1806. The supposed site is identified today by a state historical marker and a boulder and plaque.

participant in the growing community until he died at 61 in 1823.[16] The site where he had built a log cabin and later a house was marked by the state in the 1930s and, in 1972, by the village as it celebrated its centennial of incorporation.

Treman contributed his name to the fledgling community partly by chance. His brother-in-law John McLallen had established himself on the knoll north of Treman's mill by nailing up a chalked sign saying "Inn." Hence, some knew the young village as McLallen's Tavern. McLallen Street survives today, and the house at no. 22 is reportedly one of the village's oldest residences (some say *the* oldest), built of "unburned brick"—dried mud blocks—by John McLallen's son William.[17] DeWitt Clinton passed through in 1810 and made reference to dining at "Treman's Village." But Clinton is also credited with an oft-told story calling the place Shin Hollow, after a few drunks who banged their legs on the way home one night. (That name was still cropping up in the 1970s, when the Shin Hollow Tavern operated on Main Street.) Nevertheless, it was Abner's name that stuck. A post office was established for Treman's Village about 1811, but postal records soon listed it as "Trumansburgh," which it remained until the 1890s, when the U.S. Postal Service dropped the "h."[18]

As more pioneers arrived, other small population centers started up. Persisting now as little more than road names and clusters of houses are Halseyville, Waterburg and its suburb Podunk, Willow Creek, Krum's Corners, and Glenwood. Even further faded into time are the Quaker Settlement and Updike's.[19]

Like Goodwin's Point, Updike's Settlement, in the vicinity of the junction of Perry City and Podunk roads, initially outstripped Trumansburg in growth. About 1801, Burgoon Updike of New Jersey brought his family to Ulysses.[20] According to a genealogical record:

> There on Burgoon's farm they built the Log Meeting-house, and for fifty years their neighborhood was known as the Updike Settlement, so much did they prosper and multiply. But their later descendants have again sought broader fields further West, the Log Meeting-house has been taken down, and its graveyard, full of the tombstones of the early Updikes, is now the strongest remaining memento of their settlement in Ulysses.[21]

The old meetinghouse was the first building used for formalized worship in Ulysses.[22] Trumansburg's Presbyterian and Baptist congregations got their start there and, before the Ulysses rural schools consolidated in Trumansburg, District no. 15 was still sometimes known as Updike Corners.[23]

The Quaker Settlement two miles east is also marked by an old cemetery, where Perry City and Jacksonville roads meet. In fact, two graveyards are there. The large plot on the corner hill is known as "the Quaker Settlement cemetery" for the Quakers who made their homes in the area—but in many cases it is not their resting place. In a smaller plot behind the old meetinghouse, and not apparent from the road, lie bona fide members of the Hector Monthly Meeting (so called although it was in Ulysses). It is said that members of this community were abolitionists, active in the Underground Railroad.[24] Schism in an earlier group created the contingent of Friends in Ulysses, which held its first meeting in 1864.[25] The white Hector Monthly Meeting building and its cemetery are in current summer use by the Ithaca Friends Meeting, with an interment as recent as 1993; an old stone post at the driveway entrance shows the carved letters HMMSOF—Hector Monthly Meeting, Society of Friends.[26]

Just outside Trumansburg on Taughannock Creek, Halseyville was the site of many active mills. It is marked by a long, straight road from Enfield (following the grid of the Military Tract), and also by a state historical sign noting settler Nicoll Halsey and his substantial white house, c. 1829, which still stands.[27] Halsey arrived in 1793 and by 1808 had established his own family in Ulysses. At one time the Halseys owned the property encompassing Smith Woods and the Trumansburg fairgrounds, both significant Ulysses landmarks. In his lifetime Nicoll served as town supervisor, county sheriff, county judge, member of the state assembly, and member of Congress. In addition to being a "carpenter, miller, farmer and blacksmith," he was master of the local Masonic Lodge (as well as one of the "Twelve Apostles" who held fast to their fraternal bonds during widespread anti-Masonic fever) and a pivotal figure in the formation of the Ulysses Philomathic Library, Grove Cemetery, and the Tompkins County Home.[28]

An early Trumansburg settler remembered crossing a log bridge at Taughannock Creek in the winter of 1805.[29] By 1833 Dr. Lewis Halsey, a nephew of Nicoll's, had supervised the building of a covered bridge there. It stood until 1926 when, over local objection, it was torn down by New York State and replaced by a steel and concrete span which, for more than sixty-five summers, arched over swimmers in the creek below, until it too was replaced by the state.[30]

In 1936, within sight of the bridge, B. H. Duddleston, a graduate of agriculture programs at Purdue and Cornell, started Halsey Seed Farms, producers of hybrid seed corn. Still farming at 96 and living in Nicoll Halsey's house, Mr. Duddleston marked the firm's fiftieth anniversary in 1985.[31] He died in 1991, just days short of his 102d birthday. Generations of Trumansburg teenagers have found summer employment detasseling corn at Halsey Farms.

Upstream from Halseyville, where Taughannock Creek cuts through western Ulysses, is the hamlet of Waterburg. One early inhabitant was Captain Jonathan Owen, another soldier of the Revolution, who claimed a mile-square military lot and built two mills on the creek. Other early Waterburg settlers included the Scot Alexander Bower, who arrived in 1804. His son Alexander served three terms as Ulysses town supervisor, and in 1950 the original Alexander's great-great-grandson, Clifford Bower, took up the same office. The Bowers' lasting presence is marked by a very old fenced cemetery in the woods off Waterburg Road.

For a small place Waterburg ran through a surprising number of names—Slab Harbor, Middleburg, Middlebury, for a time Waterburgh, and occasionally Waterbury[32]—and by the mid-nineteenth century it was apparently a bustling community.[33] It held onto its own post office and some mills until 1902, and later, in the 1930s and 1940s, a grange hall kept things lively. Into the 1990s the impressive Greek Revival shell of the Methodist church was still standing.

Nearby, saddled with the archetypal hick-town moniker, Podunk lies in the lowland where Bolter Creek feeds into Taughannock Creek. Osborn's 1890 history mentions "the Glen Mills at Podunk," but a hundred years later the name fastens to the spot primarily because of the long, straight road that peters out there on its way from Enfield. Some sources say the name is a Native American word for "low place," others that it replicates the sound of a mill wheel.[34]

From Route 89, the old Taughannock Boulevard, two roads—Willow Creek Point Road and Willow Point Road—lead down to the lakeside cottage community of Willow Creek. Paralleling the roads, the creek itself spills over an impressive waterfall. In September 1779, the night before they reached Goodwin's Point, Colonel Dearborn's troops camped uphill from the creek, and the spot (where Krum's Corners Road ends at Duboise)[35] is marked by a boulder placed in 1911 by the Webster Success Club (see below).

The enduring pleasures of lakeside life have kept much of the Willow Creek Point land in family hands, including a long line of Vanns whose ancestor, mason Samuel Vann, settled thereabouts in 1812 and lived to be over 100.[36] Uphill, near the junction of Kraft, Duboise, and Willow Creek roads, was the Willow Creek train station, where the last train passed in 1961. Abandoned in 1962, the railroad bed is overgrown but the line is still visible. Heading north, it runs alongside Willow Creek Road, passing close to the junction with Agard Road. There, remodeled into apartments, stands the former Willow Creek School—District no.

90. "Always Do Right." Now consolidated in the Trumansburg Central District, the schools of Ulysses have served families since the establishment of the town. These students of Willow Creek School (District no. 11) at the turn of the century were honoring the Father of the Country.

11, which began across the road with a log structure in 1813. Originally one room, the building was remodeled to two in 1951 and, even though Trumansburg had a centralized district school by 1925, Willow Creek continued to serve area elementary pupils until 1964.[37]

Krum's Corners, at the intersection of its eponymous road and Route 96, was named for blacksmith Landon Krum who came there from Caroline. As a regular stage stop on the main road, it was a busy community and, until 1856, site of a post office bearing the name "Ulysses."[38] Into the 1990s the Smith Brothers Farm, on land cleared along Krum's Corners Road before 1800 by Platt Smith, was still family-managed, by Marguerite Smith of the fifth generation. Mrs. Smith confirmed that oxen had been used on her farm until 1936, and she remembered the Webster Success Club, founded in 1902, as a social club organized by farmers for debates and dinners—"for fun," she said, enjoyed by men, women, and young people alike. Some club meetings had been held in her house.[39]

The most going concern in Krum's Corners began in 1935, when Monroe C. Babcock founded Babcock Poultry Farms with borrowed funds.[40] His business took off quickly, and two years later he began the scientific poultry-breeding that became Babcock Industries. The firm eventually had nearly two hundred employees in its Ithaca-area locations, and a hundred more at branches in the United States and abroad. In 1981 its hatchery functions were sold to Institut de Séléc-

91. "Ice Cold Sodas Sold Here." Charles Rogers is shown in 1886 setting off from Krum's Corners on his rural grocery route. Mrs. Rogers stands in the doorway, holding her dog Greedy. For a time later on this site was occupied by Bishop's Restaurant.

tion Animale (ISA). Now based in France, ISA-Babcock also maintains a Trumansburg Road office.[41]

Although it never had a post office, Glenwood and the point of that name have long been a popular destination for Ithacans. Longtime home of the Ithaca Yacht Club, Glenwood once boasted "a picturesque waterfall, a towered hotel . . . , and a dance hall which lured the townspeople and college students."[42] For the past forty years, that same clientele has been drawn to the casual restaurant on Route 89 known as the Glenwood Pines, run since 1979 by the Hohwald family.

The Pines was originally a farmstand started by Dorothy Warren Evans, daughter of Ithaca physician Richard C. Warren,[43] and her husband, to sell products from their farm up the hill on Glenwood Heights. In 1934, during construction of Route 89, Dr. Warren had deeded a portion of his lakeshore property to Tompkins County for a public overlook; marked by a sign, it is just up from the Glenwood Pines. The road between Ithaca and Taughannock Point originally dipped much closer to the lakeshore there, following the hairpin path of Maplewood Road in order to cross the big stream gullies.[44]

Jacksonville, an officially recognized hamlet clustered around Route 96 and the namesake of another long road in the Revolutionary grid, has had a postal identity since before 1822. Once known as Harlow's Corners and VanCortlandtville, the locale was renamed in 1815, in honor of Andrew Jackson. Historian John Selkreg identified little manufacturing there. Nevertheless, a lead pipe factory was in place until about 1840, a potash factory until 1845, and, as of 1879, the village had a variety of civic institutions and businesses. Through 1915 farmers for miles around sent their milk to a Jacksonville creamery begun by the Mekeel family.

In the 1990s Jacksonville harbors a few small businesses, some in a set of old Babcock buildings dubbed Ulysses Square. The present church in the middle of the hamlet, the Jacksonville Community Church, was originally incorporated in 1826.

In 1845 James Monroe Mattison opened a nursery in Jacksonville and, via lake steamer and stagecoach, provided plant stock to central New York. He brought in many unusual species and is credited by some with early commercial introduction of the Tompkins County King apple.[45] Mattison left his mark on his community, in the rose window honoring him at the Jacksonville church and, more grandly, in the stone home he built in 1869, which still stands. He designed the eighteen-room house himself but in the end would live there for only two years, dying in 1871. The estate is named The Trees, for Mattison's nursery business.[46]

Summer 1877 saw the organization of Ulysses Grange no. 419 in Jacksonville, with thirty-two charter members. Like most of the county, Ulysses Grange benefited from proximity to Cornell University, recording the occasional participation of Dean Liberty Hyde Bailey as well as the "father of poultry science," Cornell professor and Trumansburg farmer James E. Rice, who was "a loyal and helpful member." Active through World War II, the grange worked to get a fire and recreation pond built in the early 1950s and, in 1961, deeded it to the Jacksonville Community Association. In 1958 the Waterburg Grange merged its dwindling membership with that of Ulysses Grange, and in 1975 the grange hall was sold to the Close family, who maintain its function as a community center.[47] Grangers met in the hall for a time after the sale, but the Ulysses Grange has since disbanded.

In the late 1970s eight Jacksonville residences near the gas station at the central crossroads were found to have contaminated water as a result of gasoline leaks. In March 1988 the Mobil Oil Corporation announced a buy-out offer for the homeowners but no plans to solve the contamination problem.[48] Owned by Mobil, some of the affected houses still stand empty.

Trumansburg Takes the Lead

Access to abundant waterpower, proximity to Taughannock, and a site on the main road between Ithaca and Geneva gave Trumansburg the edge over other communities in the town. For many years, in fact, it ranked second in the county in population and prosperity. Mills were established at every available spot along the creeks, so affecting the streams "that water for power purposes became an uncertain quantity, at least in summer."[49] This situation pressed local entrepreneurs to diversify, and the Village of Trumansburg grew to include dozens of businesses—retail (paint, crockery, clothing), service (doctors, lawyers, banks, butchers), and manufacturing (looking glasses, sleighs, cabinets).

Prominent figures left their names on streets and landmarks,[50] including Trumansburg native Herman M. Biggs (1859–1923), "the Father of Public Health," whose work with tuberculosis is memorialized by buildings in the county's hospital complex. One who cut a wide swath was Hermon Camp. Arriving on the scene in his late teens, he bought out the village's first merchant and proceeded to buy and sell almost everything else. Until the flood of 1935 took it down, his brick store stood at the heart of the village, where the creek crosses the main road. In time he himself was recognized as "the foremost merchant in all the country between the lakes."

Shrewd and aggressive, Camp was described by A. P. Osborn as "no saint" and "inflexible in purpose." Osborn wrote that Camp

> made more friends and more enemies than any man who has ever lived here; he never occupied a neutral position in business, public affairs or to individuals, he was always for or against, and as like begats like, the people with whom he was surrounded were either for or against him; but there is no doubt that for more than half a century he was the master spirit in all the affairs of this place.[51]

When Camp separated from his wife Lucinda in 1825, the entire village reportedly took sides in the matter, drawing divisions that stood for decades and infiltrated politics, juries, families, and friendships. However, the written history is sketchy.[52] In the mid-1930s, *Ithaca Journal* columnist Romeyn Berry commented that, during his life, Camp "came pretty close to being King of Trumansburg, Duke of Ulysses and Overlord of Tompkins County."[53]

In addition to his store, Camp ran a linseed oil mill and farm. He served as postmaster from 1813 to 1830, president of the village's first private academy, and first president of the Tompkins County Trust Company. He was a founder of the Ulysses Philomathic Library, which was housed in his store from 1811 to 1839; a cherry table now in the library came from the store.

But the real centerpiece of Camp's legacy—and of the architectural map of Trumansburg—is his 1845 Greek Revival mansion on Camp (once called Lawn) Street. Built almost entirely with local labor and materials, and situated on twelve acres of property including what were once formal gardens, the house has remained in the family since Camp's death in 1878.[54] Put on the market in the early 1990s, it prompted formation of a preservation committee to examine options for its use.

The rest of Trumansburg's physical appearance, particularly its business district, has been shaped by recurring catastrophe. For years every heavy rain brought flooding in the center of town; a severe flood in 1833 took out dams, machinery, mills, and bridges,[55] and a century later the village saw similar destruction. Because of this perennial problem, the grade level of Main Street where it crosses Trumansburg Creek has been repeatedly filled and raised.

Although the village still boasts many venerable buildings, two devastating fires, in 1864 and 1871, wiped out dozens of earlier wooden structures along Main Street. The first fire, intentionally set, burned every building on Union Street as well as everything along Main Street from the center of town to the Presbyterian

92. Camp House, 1847. Hermon Camp, in top hat, stands with family and friends (the boy on the fence is said to be William P. Biggs, later a business leader himself) in front of his grand Greek Revival house. Legend tells that his annoyance at the front gate's being left open brought on a fatal apoplectic fit.

church (dedicated in 1850, it still stands). Brick was the subsequent material of choice; witness the block of Main Street stores running south from opposite Elm Street corner to the Masonic Temple.

In Osborn's view, the 1871 conflagration caused even greater change than the earlier fire: "The area was not so great but . . . the buildings were for the most part better, and were all used for business purposes." Burning out in both directions from the center of the block, the second fire demolished stores from the creek north to the area of what is now the P&C, as well as others across the street and nearly up to the Baptist church. Although provision for fire fighting and prevention seems not to have been uppermost in the civic mind, the church was spared largely because, about halfway through this second big blaze, a rickety, moth-balled pumper was trundled into service against the flames.[56]

93. Village center, Trumansburg. The devastating flood of 1935 wrought widespread destruction to the area. The A&P, once a roller rink, spanned the creek here. This photograph, marked "Taken Tuesday" (July 9), was made by William Goodwin for the Spires Studio.

From these ashes rose the brick block of stores which still stands on the west side of Main, as well as the three-story Opera Block across the street (on today's site of the Tompkins County Trust Company), which itself burned in 1922. By 1912 the block could also boast the handsome Biggs Hardware building with three imposing floors, huge display windows, and the character of an urban department store. But an even more significant result of the fire was that villagers became convinced of the need for a real fire department, and their conviction helped catalyze Trumansburg's incorporation in 1872. For some time, several independent fire companies, functioning rather like clubs, flourished under supervision of the village board. They were consolidated in 1927.[57]

The cast-iron fronts and decorative grilles for most of the new brick buildings on the west side of Main were produced by the iron-working firm of Gregg and Co., one of the village's most notable businesses, and the company imprint can be seen at the foot of the buildings' Italianate facades.[58] Begun in 1847 in Farmer Village (now Interlaken), the Gregg company built a new Trumansburg shop on

94. Gregg and Co. workers. The men employed at the iron works gather for a photo sometime in the 1880s.

Hector Street (née Avenue) in 1865 and, until 1887, produced a wide variety of farm machinery.

In time the Gregg foundry building was occupied by the Morse brothers, who developed a high-quality bicycle chain and whose businesses grew into the Morse Chain Co. Morse operated on the Gregg site until 1906, when it moved to Ithaca. For a few years in the 1920s dresses were manufactured in the Gregg building, but in 1955 it was torn down.[59]

With encouragement from the local Business Men's Association, presided over by William P. Biggs, the Hartley Brothers, silk manufacturers, were persuaded to build a new mill on Hector Street in 1907. Producing taffeta and, during World War I, parachute silk, this factory employed as many as seventy-five workers and operated until 1931, when it became a casualty, at least in part, of the Depression. Used in the interim for boatbuilding and defense industries, the site was sold in 1946 to another pair of brothers, the Coopers, who opened a tannery to produce fine leather. Until they closed in 1964, the Coopers' success stemmed from a special formula which, some village residents maintain, eliminated the smell of imported hides as they were processed. Others, located close to the factory, remember its odors as distinctive.[60]

One of the most innovative concerns to do business in Trumansburg was the Robert A. Moog electronic synthesizer company. As the horizons of popular music and the arts expanded in the late 1960s, Moog's synthesizers drew the attention of a wide variety of composers and celebrities.[61] In fall 1969 the Trumansburg Area Development Corporation proposed to build Moog a warehouse, with room for a hundred employees, between Cayuga and Prospect streets. But this building never materialized, and in time the company was sold.[62]

Then and Now

In the 1880s nearly twice as many residents of the Town of Ulysses lived outside Trumansburg as lived within its boundaries. At that time "practically all of the people living outside the Village were farmers or members of farm families, and the people in the Village ran local businesses which served the farmers in the surrounding area."[63] The census for 1880 also marked the peak of population for Ulysses and for Trumansburg since the first white settlers had arrived. But ten years later, at the locale's hundred-year mark, population had begun to decline. Historian Osborn expressed concerns that the village has faced ever since. Consider this analysis:

> The tendency of the last half of a century has been toward centralization of capital; the growth of the country, its increasing needs and rapid development of all industries has stimulated inventive genius, machinery has to a great extent supplanted hand labor and today almost everything necessary to our comfort and convenience can be bought "ready made." . . . [This has] also been a death blow to small towns and villages, individual mechanics and small proprietors. . . . Before the factory system had absorbed all small manufacturers almost everything used in a community was built there.

Allowing that large-scale manufacturing cut costs and labor, as did large-scale production of food and clothing, he pointed out that "the small towns do not derive the benefit."

Nevertheless, Osborn observed, Trumansburg was faring better than many. As the twentieth century came on, the village patronized over a hundred businesses including two hotels; passenger trains stopped twice a day at two stations, and stores stayed open late on Saturday nights; the village supported five churches—Presbyterian, Baptist, Methodist, Episcopal, and Catholic—and its school focused on excellence. The community's farming identity was crystallized in the Union Agricultural and Horticultural Society of the Towns of Ulysses, Hector and Covert, and celebrated at that society's annual fair held on the community's venerable fairgrounds.

As the twentieth century waxed, however, local population waned and farms waned with it. As of the 1920 census, the head count was at a low of about a thousand in the village and just a few over that in the town. Ten years later, in 1930, "many houses were vacant in the village, and any one could be rented for $25 and less."[64] Accustomed to penny-pinching and producing food at home, some area farm families did not feel the Depression's hardest hits. Just over the

95. Trumansburg Fair, c. 1910. Photo finish or not, horse races were always a big draw at the annual event. Even today, harness contests are a feature at the fair.

line in Seneca County, though, the failure to raise enough money to put in a 1934 crop brought one farmer to such despair that he killed himself along with his three children.[65]

World War II helped revive the region. Until winter in 1941 Trumansburg students attended high school only until noon, because farmers needed the boys' help. With the building of the Sampson naval base near Geneva, "every available room in Trumansburg and everywhere else was rented."[66] In the 1940s Trumansburg was able to support three movie theaters: the Star, the Cayuga, and—named by the people's choice—the Burg.

Movies, like radio and automobiles, contributed to broader horizons and a yearning among many for more urbane attractions than Ulysses could offer. Eventually, in service to the automobile, Trumansburg's Main Street, which had evolved organically with the village through various stages—dust, dirt, mud, macadam, fire, flood, and yellow brick—was artificially and officially altered in 1962. Its new size and shape emphasized the importance of passing through, not of stopping.

Still, by 1950 the town population had returned to its 1880 peak; by 1960 it had passed that by nearly a thousand souls, with the greater growth outside Trumansburg. When A. P. Osborn looked ahead hopefully from 1890, he wrote that "our magnificent farming country must always support the village with a fair prospect of increase." But in the view of town resident Edward Lutz, in 1964, the modern growth was different:

> The number of farms has declined drastically. I am told that you can count the number of full-time farmers in the Town on the fingers of two mutilated hands. . . . In the countryside of the Town there are many more residents than there are farms. There are also gas stations, stores, an outdoor movie, junk piles, and so forth. The countryside of Ulysses is becoming more like a city, not in the sense that a lot of people live close together, but in the sense that people want to use land for many purposes besides farming.
>
> The Village of Trumansburg has also changed. Most of the people there and in the surrounding countryside do not depend upon Trumansburg for a living but upon Ithaca. . . . The future of the Town may be most attractive as a residential area for people working in or near Ithaca.[67]

Similar thoughts are voiced by Ulysses residents in the 1990s, and certainly the increased complexities of the world have left the town vulnerable. But some fertile and persistent combination of down-to-earth values, originality, and quirky character make Trumansburg and Ulysses resilient. This is the place where a few "scientific wags" successfully passed off a homemade version of the Cardiff Giant in 1878 (not ten years after the original), then celebrated making money off their hoax with a big picnic and a specially written ode hailing "Tauggy"—the Taughannock Giant.[68] It is the place where the library was closed for ninety-six years and reopened with coverage in the *New York Times*.[69]

In 1890 A. P. Osborn observed, "this is a reading and thinking community and will not be satisfied with mediocre talent. [It is] one of the most beautiful inland villages in the state; . . . its dwellings neat, tasty and homelike, surrounded by beautifully kept lawns and well cultivated gardens, its streets are bordered with elms and maples, its sidewalks are of blue flag stone."

In 1894 John H. Selkreg described Trumansburg as "pretty and progressive."

To Edward Lutz in 1964, the Town of Ulysses has been a "good place to live. . . . I believe the Town has bright prospects for growth."

And a 1990s Ithaca realtor said, "It's the one town I can send people to and say it has *good* prospects for the future. It's alive and vital. People go there to live a lifestyle that doesn't exist anymore, but it's not artificial or contrived. It's not nostalgic. It's really alive, some genuine mixture of past and present."[70]

Although fragile in the face of Ithaca competition and a village population of just 1,611, the Trumansburg area offers a diverse and relatively energetic business community.[71] Its durable restaurant-nightclub, the Rongovian Embassy to the U.S.A. has drawn national press. Of four doctors in town, three are women;[72] there are also three dentists and a chiropractor. The village's vibrant central school continues to stress excellence, with more than 75 percent of graduates pursuing higher education, and it remains a factor that binds together the entire community, through innovative academic programs, lively activities, and conscious involvement with students. Five churches have become eight, with a second Baptist church, a Mormon congregation, and an Assembly of God added.

96. Baptist church in Trumansburg, 1900–1910. Shown when it still sported a steeple, the 140-year-old building on Congress Street has been home to the Trumansburg Conservatory of Fine Arts since the 1980s.

Saved from the 1871 fire, the original Baptist church, a classic Greek Revival temple built in 1851, has metamorphosed into the Trumansburg Conservatory of Fine Arts. Providing music, dance, and art lessons as well as exhibitions and recitals, the nonprofit conservatory was born in 1982 from the determination of Calista Smith, its executive director and resident visionary.

Although the town's farming identity endures, it is threatened and growing scarce, but the Trumansburg Fair has lasted over 140 years, the charms of its head-spinning rides still sharing space with canned peaches, grange displays, horse races, and prize Jersey calves. For several years the fairground was used for the fall Woodcutters Fair, a fire department fundraiser, and in recent years it has hosted flea markets and provided space for a county recycling station. In July 1990 it became home to the first Grassroots Festival of Music and Dance, an increasingly well-attended annual event with an eclectic blend of internationally, nationally, and regionally significant performers. Devised as a fundraiser for AIDS Work of Tompkins County, with considerable volunteer effort, the festival is organized by a loose coalition of musicians and friends. It reflects a small but diverse, entrenched and offbeat artistic and musical community that calls Trumansburg and its environs home.

Following a severe 1989 windstorm, which brought down many trees in Smith Woods opposite the fairgrounds, Woods trustees hired a logger to "clean up" the acreage in spring 1990. Controversy ensued: arguments over the origins and meaning of the stipulation that Smith Woods be left "in its natural state" were voiced all over the media. The question was unresolved and the trustees stood by their decision, but they allowed that if there were a next time, they might engage ecologists earlier on.

Almost all the written history of Ulysses has been about white Protestants, because they have been most of the residents since the Sullivan campaign. A few Irish families, the foundation of St. James Catholic parish, arrived in the mid-nineteenth century to work on the railroads or in stone quarries. Many accounts mention Lloyd Dorsey, born a slave in Maryland, who followed the Underground Railroad north to Elmira and, ultimately, Trumansburg. The first black man in Tompkins County to vote, own property, and pay taxes, he married Nancy Hermans of Watkins Glen, settled on Dorsey Hill near the present waste-water treatment plant, and raised eight children.[73] Some of the Dorseys lie in Grove Cemetery. A memoir written in 1977 by Edna Wakeman Newell mentions Dorsey and his son Charles, who worked as the high school janitor around 1909. Newell also mentions Porter Johnson, another Trumansburg man of color, as "a fine barber and noted character."[74] The 1990 census numbers 4,759 whites in the town, 40 blacks, 8 American Indians, 49 individuals of Asian or Pacific Island origin, 45 Hispanics, and 5 others.

In 1890 Osborn wrote, "It is said that the last wild deer ever seen where the village now stands was on the bank of the creek opposite John McLallen's log tavern. He was shot at from the back door of this building, and altho wounded was not captured until he had led a chase of several miles." Other informants say that all the game, especially deer, disappeared until the 1930s. But nowadays the wild deer range placidly through flower beds and, in hard winters, even non-

97. Main Street in Trumansburg, before 1912. An 1890 description calls it one of the most beautiful villages in the state. Trumansburg still strikes many residents and visitors the same way today.

chalantly munch the shrubbery on Cayuga Street, in full view of passing cars. The McLallen's tavern precedent notwithstanding, in the 1990s shooting is prohibited in the village.

Out in the old named crossroads and hamlets of the town, little commercial presence exists anymore—the exceptions are in Jacksonville, some home businesses, a few country auto repair shops, and a couple of other businesses already noted. In 1987, when the county home on Perry City Road closed for good after 160 years, it was down to about twenty residents. The big brick buildings and clinging ranks of barns and sheds stand eerie and empty on the farmland set aside for them long ago—farmland where "the soil . . . is first-class, perhaps as good as can be found within the limits of the county."[75]

In that soil, some distance out in the fields behind the buildings, are said to be several old, unmarked cemeteries where many of the home's past residents were laid to rest in papier-mâché coffins. Little more than hummocky clearings and vague outlines, the lost paupers' graves were discovered, visited, and marked by the county on aerial maps in 1986 through the diligent efforts of a history buff who lives nearby.[76]

As the seasons wheel past, some fields are still plowed in patterned furrows, some lie fallow, some are for sale as building sites. Some of the town's 4,906 residents live in dignified old frame houses, some in new modular homes—a total of 1,446 detached dwellings. Some live in apartments, some live in trailers—over 150 throughout Ulysses.[77] Some work at home, some travel to Ithaca and beyond, some don't work at all. Some things change, others never do, but which is which can be confusing.

Photographs show that, sometime between 1888 and 1896, the apparently immutable outline at the lip of Taughannock Falls did change—from an angular projection outward into space to the sharp cut inward, toward the stream bed, which we know today.[78] Eternal as its gargantuan outline seems on every visit, the great bowl is worn, washed, changed in shape every day. Likewise, even as the words here were written, new pages have been added to change the story of the Town of Ulysses.

Notes

Full documentation for note references is provided in the bibliography. The following abbreviations have been used in the notes and bibliography.

CU   Division of Rare and Manuscript Collections, Cornell University Library.
DHS   DeWitt Historical Society of Tompkins County.
Dryden HS   Dryden Historical Society.
1866 *Atlas*   *New Topographical Atlas of Tompkins County, New York.*
Enfield   Historian's files, Town of Enfield.
"Enfield History"   Projected publication by the Enfield Commemorative Committee, Enfield, N.Y.
FCH   Four County History—*History of Tioga, Chemung, Tompkins, and Schuyler Counties, New York.*
French   French, J. H. *Gazetteer of the State of New York.*
IJ   Ithaca Journal.
IN   Ithaca's Neighborhoods: The Rhine, the Hill, and the Goose Pasture.
Lansing   Historian's archive, Town of Lansing.
Lee   Lee, Hardy Campbell. *A History of Railroads in Tompkins County.*
Norris, *Old Indian Trails*   Norris, W. Glenn. *Old Indian Trails in Tompkins County.*
Norris, *Place Names*   Norris, W. Glenn. *The Origin of Place Names in Tompkins County.*
SC   Seasons of Change: An Updated History of Tioga County, New York.
Selkreg   Selkreg, John H. *Landmarks of Tompkins County.*
SH   Dieckmann, Jane Marsh. A Short History of Tompkins County.
Spafford   Spafford, Horatio Gates. *A Gazetteer of the State of New-York.*

Overview

In addition to the individual contributors to this volume, who have shown great conscientiousness, dedication, and patience throughout, I am particularly grateful to county historian Gretchen Sachse for supplying countless pieces of essential information and invaluable assistance with the illustrations and to John Marcham for help on the revision of this first chapter and for immeasurable work behind the scenes on this publication.

  1. According to New York State law, cities are a separate political entity, on the level of the town. The City of Ithaca, though originally and geographically part of the Town of

Ithaca, is a separate governmental unit. The hamlet of Ithaca, named as the county seat in 1817, was incorporated as a village in 1821 and granted a charter as a city in June 1888. The development of the city is treated in *Ithaca's Neighborhoods (IN)*, companion volume to this book.

2. I thank John Chiment, paleobiologist and dean at Cornell University's College of Arts and Sciences, whose articles in the *Ithaca Journal* and other local publications have informed this account.

3. Erl A. Bates, who retired in 1961 as adviser in Indian Extension at Cornell, related this legend in his article "A Little Fishing Village Called Ne-ah-Dak-ne-at," *IJ*, The Journal's 150 Years, May 22, 1965, D 1. Named honorary chief of eighteen Indian tribes, Bates was known as the Little White Father of the Six Nations. Throughout his life he worked to help Indians through training in farming and the trades.

The early Indians moved from place to place in the county on established trails, many of which became routes for later settlers and ultimately the basis of modern roads. A map of these trails can be seen in Norris, *Old Indian Trails*, 24–25.

4. For more information on Simeon DeWitt and his role in Tompkins County history, see *SH*, 28–32, and *IN*, 2, 26–28.

5. Early county maps clearly show the difference in land origins; lots in the Military Tract are much larger than those in the Watkins and Flint Purchase.

6. David M. Ellis et al., *A History of New York State* (Ithaca: Cornell University Press, 1967), 186. The army mustered by Tompkins in the War of 1812 defended a New York City seriously menaced by a mighty and highly experienced British fleet. With private and personal funds he helped sustain the government by endorsing loans from New York banks, maintain the U.S. Military Academy at West Point, and keep recruiting offices open in the district.

Before serving as governor Tompkins had been delegate to the Constitutional Convention and judge of the State Supreme Court. He also founded The New-York Historical Society and served as chancellor of the state university. His life ended unhappily, however. Induced to run again for governor in 1820, he was defeated in a campaign during which his enemies accused him of default in his war accounts, charges found later to be largely without foundation. Never fully recovering from the shock, he died at 51.

7. Linda McCandless in her chapter on Danby briefly describes Indian life in the region.

8. Laura Case to Betsey Louisa and Luke Crittendon (her sister and brother-in-law), November 14, 1832, in *What They Wrote*, ed. Carol Kammen, 54.

9. Some of these farms were described by Elizabeth Rogers in her article "Descendants Still Working 10 Pioneer Farms," *IJ*, The Journal's 150 Years, D 1. The story was updated by Helen Mundell in the *IJ* special issue Ithaca's Centennial, April 8, 1988, 44–45. Both articles have been useful.

10. The church is described in *IN*, 88–90.

11. The Fugitive Slave Act required Northern states to aid in the return of fugitive slaves and granted legal sanction to Southern states to send slave catchers north after any runaways.

George Johnson (1835–1919) was a member of the Republican party. He served as doorkeeper at the state senate in 1872–1873. His 1915 letter to the *Ithaca Journal* (see Town of Ithaca chapter at note 3) was addressed from 121 East State Street, where he kept a barbershop until 1918. For more information on Johnson and the Underground Railroad, see *SH*, 153–55, and Vincent W. Howell, *History of St. James A.M.E. Zion Church*, brochure published for the 155 anniversary celebration, May 15–21, 1988, DHS.

12. The story of Dinah Ten Broeck is based on material supplied by Gretchen Sachse.

Dinah's Dutch name was attached to her mother, a slave of the Ten Broeck family. A slave usually did not have a surname and was given the owner's. For accounts of other black settlers, see the Simms family in the chapter on Danby, and Lloyd Dorsey and Porter Johnson in the chapter on Ulysses.

13. I thank S. K. List for information on the Haley Memorial. On the black community in Ithaca and its leaders, see *IN*, 99–105.

14. Pop's Place remained a Greek business; in 1949 it expanded into a restaurant, closing in 1977. Chacona Candy moved to 401 College Avenue in the 1920s. Many Greeks settled in the Collegetown area and opened businesses there.

15. Louise Bement in the chapter on Lansing tells of the Syrians who came to the county at the turn of the century to work at the salt plant.

16. In the flood's aftermath came serious discussions of flood control measures. Nonetheless, construction on the city's flood control channel did not begin until 1964. Major flooding has occurred in 1972, 1978, 1981, 1993, and 1995.

17. I am grateful to George Frantz, assistant town planner, and to Larry Fabbroni for essential information on Town of Ithaca government. In the summer of 1997, after lengthy discussion and serious consideration of moving outside the city, the town made the necessary arrangements to move their offices into a portion of the post office building on the corner of Buffalo and Tioga streets.

18. Or paupers, according to the Four County History. See FCH, 375–77, for a description of the poorhouse and the 1876 annual report of the State Board of Charities concerning the "inmates."

19. See the remarks of Armand L. Adams made at the dedication of the Old Courthouse, September 13, 1976, history file in the county clerk's office.

20. Information on the building scheme comes from Ferris Cronkhite, "How Can One Possibly Plan?" *DeWitt Historical Society Newsletter*, June 1976, 4–8; the article includes reproductions of the architectural plans. I thank Stuart Stein of the county board for supplying this article as well as other relevant information concerning the history of the county, its government, and public buildings.

21. Both post office and airport are in the Village of Lansing. For the airport's history see the Lansing chapter.

22. The elementary schools in the new consolidated district were Belle Sherman, Caroline, Cayuga Heights, Central, Danby, East Hill, Enfield, Fall Creek, Forest Home, Hayts Corner, Henry St. John, South Hill, West Hill, and Willow Creek. For further information on different school buildings in the district and their uses, see *IN*, 23, and 208n35.

Town of Ithaca

The County's Central Town

1. See Overview, n. 1. The companion to this present volume, *Ithaca's Neighborhoods*, treats the diverse neighborhoods of the city. For a general discussion of the city's history see that book's Overview and *SH*, 38–55. Cayuga Heights, Forest Home, and the Renwick community are treated later in this chapter.

2. The church book is in the DHS archive. A handwritten account of several pages tells of the organization of the congregation and lists its members. I have retained the original spelling.

3. This and the following quote come from a 1915 letter written by Johnson to the *Ithaca Journal* (see Overview and *SH*, 154).

4. Quoted from Hilda Butler Babcock's typed account of the Inlet Valley in 1922, DHS. Much of my information relies on her reminiscences; on David Barnett Jr., "Ithaca Firm,

36 Years Old, Adds Automatic Gravel Yard," *IJ*, September 20, 1957; and on a conversation in October 1996 with Margie Rumsey.

5. H. E. Babcock died in 1950, and in 1955 Hilda Babcock wrote her notes on the farm and the house. The newsletter of Historic Ithaca, winter 1977, reprinted some of her recollections, "Inlet Valley 1922 and Some Notes on Sunnygables Farm."

6. The development of the modern Ithaca College campus is described in *IN*, 85–87. For further information see John B. Harcourt, *The Ithaca College Story* (Ithaca: Ithaca College, 1983).

7. Material on the Pew family can be found in Barbara Black's column, *IJ*, November 8, 1969, and in a newspaper article of April 10, 1940, in the Pew file folder, DHS archives.

8. Elizabeth Rogers, "Descendants Still Working on 10 Pioneer Farms," *IJ*, The Journal's 150 Years, May 22, 1965, D 4.

9. For the story of Cornell Heights, see *IN*, 176–88.

Village of Cayuga Heights: Its Development by Newman and Blood

1. Portions of this section are drawn from my book, *Enterprising Families*, 97–121. I have also relied on the Newman Collection #2157, CU.

2. Drawing on the Cayuga Heights village minutes, John Marcham developed the following list of presidents, later mayors:

1915, 1916, 1917   C. T. Stagg
1918   William A. Stocking
1919   Stagg
1920, 1921, 1922   Stocking
1923   E. Dwight Sanderson (election at the Ithaca Country Clubhouse)
1924   Clyde H. Myers
1925   John Bentley Jr.
1926   Karl M. Wiegand
1927, 1928, 1929   Dr. Walter L. Williams (referred to as mayor)
1929   Wiegand
1930, 1931, 1932, 1933   Leonard A. Maynard
1934, 1935   Arthur J. Heinicke
1936, 1937, 1938, 1939   Hubert E. Baxter

3. Jared T. Newman to Mrs. Urquhart, October 16, 1919, Newman Collection #2157.

Village of Cayuga Heights: 1940 to the Present

In addition to interviews noted below, I have received assistance and information from John B. Rogers III, Gordon Wheeler, Julian Smith, John Marcham, and Gerald Clark, former principal of Cayuga Heights School.

1. Julian Smith, *Breaking Ninety*, 13–28.

2. Interview with Julian Smith, 1993.

3. Interview with Sal Indelicato Jr., January 1992.

4. Office of the Cayuga Heights Village Engineer, John B. Rogers III (Village Map).

5. Interview With Frederick Marcham, January 25, 1991.

6. Ibid.

7. Frederick Marcham, *Memories of Cayuga Heights, N.Y.*, pamphlet published in Ithaca, March 22, 1988, 5.

8. Ibid., 5–8.

9. Ibid., 13–14.

10. Ibid., 21–22.
11. Interview with William Tucker Dean, January 30, 1991.
12. John Marcham, "Notes on Cayuga Heights School," *Village Voices,* March 1993.

Renwick Heights

1. For more information see William Heidt, *The Blue-Eyed Lassie and the Renwicks in Ithaca.*
2. Henry Abt, *Ithaca,* 132.
3. A. K. Fletcher, "My Memories of Fall Creek" (1989).

Town of Caroline

Caroline has had several historians whose writings or collections have been used here.

Charles F. Mulks (1837–1907) haunted courthouses and libraries and interviewed countless old-timers to collect data. He was a major contributor to the Four County History of 1879, as well as to Selkreg. His papers, donated to Cornell in 1909, include 24 scrapbooks and 12 notebooks, and are cited below as CFM with notebook number.

Lyman H. Gallagher of Slaterville, who died in 1945, contributed many historical articles to the *Ithaca Journal.* Collected at the DeWitt Historical Society, they are cited as LHG, with date of publication.

Gertrude Conant, born and raised in Brooktondale, has collected photographs and information on Caroline. Her four scrapbooks of clippings are invaluable, although early clippings are not always dated; cited as Caroline I, II, III, IV.

Other sources include Will Osburn, Art Volbrecht, Chuck Mandeville, and Barbara Kone, town historian.

1. An undated map at the DeWitt Historical Society shows "Speedsville" as the only town between Lisle and Ithaca, with the distance between Lisle and Speedsville 25 miles. This Speedsville must be the post office established by J. J. Speed in 1806.

2. The piece known as Cantine's Little Location was about 2 miles long and 1 mile wide, along Six Mile Creek (FCH, 457). He also had 800 acres on Willseyville Creek in an area called The Location. Cantine's Great Location of 6,000 acres was in the Candor area (Norris, *Old Indian Trails,* 11–12).

3. A full history of the farm and house is given by Jane Vaughn, in "A Caroline Valley Farm: 1800–1976," typescript, Caroline History Room. A photo of the cabin, interior and exterior, is in the Catskill Turnpike scrapbook, DHS.

4. CFM, #84, 7.

5. CFM, #81, and LHG, June 30, 1925.

6. LHG, June 30, 1925. Road building began in 1804. In later days, this road was referred to as "the old 76 Road." The proper name is 76 Road. The eastern end of the original road is now called Boiceville Road. Boiceville Road becomes Central Chapel Road, which continues past the intersection where 76 Road is now considered to begin. Natives refer to the intersection as Guideboard Corners, after a sign that was there as late as 1963.

7. It was demoted to West Slaterville by the Four County History of 1879 and is signed that way today. Boiceville remains in the road name.

8. Black servants are said to have entered by a side door to sit in the balcony. Perhaps these servants are buried in the slave cemetery just off Ellis Hollow Road. LHG (July 25, 1935) refers to this cemetery as having Indian graves. There are no records or headstones. A photo in the Catskill Turnpike scrapbook at DHS shows Gallagher at

the site. Many churches of the period had balconies. Rev. Mandeville did not condone slavery.

9. CFM, #81.

10. Eunice D. Weber, ed., *A History of Caroline Township*, [38].

11. FCH, 457. Present-day Jenksville, south of Speedsville in the northwest corner of the town of Newark Valley (SC, 561), should not be confused with the early Jenksville.

12. CFM, #81. Mulks says he was known as "old Rawson" although only 54 years old. Norris in *Place Names*, 18, says he operated without a license, but CFM (#79) found that he had bought a license to sell spirits in 1814, 1818, 1819, and 1820.

13. *Ithaca Democrat*, December 29, 1881, in Caroline file, DHS.

14. Bob Edwards's shop was later bought out and then sold to the Ithaca Gun Company. Edwards worked at Ithaca Gun as a gun barrel specialist in 1880 (Ron Kellogg, quoted by Barbara Bell, *IJ*, April 11, 1970).

15. Carol Kammen, "The Dancing Academy of Leopold Leo," *IJ*, January 9, 1982.

16. Handbill in Caroline file, DHS. John Gee of Central Chapel went with three friends on the train to see the Chicago Exposition. After that, he went to every fair he could (Weber, 51).

17. A historic marker says that Dr. Gallagher sank the first artesian well in the valley. Since the whole village presently taps the artesian system, and since people were getting water before 1870, his was surely not the first. The year 1871 is also when the St. John fountain, now installed at Fountain Manor, was cast.

18. William Heidt, *Forests to Farms in Caroline*, 53. Gathering arbutus was very popular. George Jansen writes in his diary on April 22, 1917: "Jesse [Shurter] and I went & got trailing arbutus today" (see note 22 below). In April 1925 the *Newark Valley Herald* warned readers that "those who proudly wear a bunch of arbutus will be interested to know that they are quite likely liable to arrest" (SC, 564).

19. FCH, 457–58. The Ridgway Butter and Cheese Factory was also built here in 1873.

20. Rural sociologists from Cornell helped rural churches arrange mergers. Brooktondale and Morris Chapel and Slaterville churches joined to form the Tobey Larger Parish in 1929, with a federation achieved in 1935; Amy Atwater, *History of the Congregational Church*, 10. See also Carol Kammen, "A Caroline Church Reverses a Trend," *IJ*, January 30, 1988.

21. The section between Cooks Corners and Buffalo Road in Slaterville was finished in 1910; between Buffalo Road and Speed Hill, in 1914. In 1921 work proceeded as far as Level Green Road. As each section was completed, it became a state road. Water-bound macadam is a tamped surface achieved with layers of 6", 2", and ½" stone. Asphalt was not used until the late 1920s.

22. Six diaries in the Caroline file, DHS, cover 1908–1909, 1917–1918, 1922, 1923, 1923–1924, and 1925. Gertrude Conant has additional diaries.

23. Vaughn, 44–46. Rothschild's in Ithaca sold it as "Slaterville Glass." The ambering property of the spring at the old Mulks farm was discovered about 1889 but was not used until Ella Middaugh, who moved to the farm in 1905, recognized ambered glass as another source of income. (The Middaugh family regularly moved to the barn for the summer and "let rooms" in the house.) Other springs in the area can color glass; one writer thought that the Middaugh water worked faster (*IJ*, November 16, 1939, in Caroline file, DHS).

24. Vaughn, 52. The oxen were pictured in the *IJ* (May 18, 1937) as belonging to Homer Wool of Slaterville.

25. LHG, January 24, 1925. He adds, "the Poughkeepsie bridge will do even more for us."

26. Glenn A. Bakkum and Bruce L. Melvin, *Social Relationships of Slaterville Springs—*

Brooktondale Area, Tompkins County, New York, 10, gives a map of the Caroline study area, including some of Ellis Hollow, which shows the location of about 60 abandoned farm houses. One success story of this period is the Clark Seed Farm, centered in Richford but using 100 acres of hillside land on Blackman Hill in Caroline. Mr. Clark ignored the experts who said that the land was "sub-marginal" and fit only for reforestation. He was successful at scientific farming (including the use of DDT in 1946). The potatoes were kept in insulated storage at Richford.

27. Barbara Kone, *A History of the Town of Caroline*, 9, gives 6,821 acres. My calculation from DEC information is 6,972.44 acres. The federal land was originally leased to the state for state forests; later it was deeded to the state. State forests in Caroline are Shindagin Hollow, Hammond Hill, Potato Hill, and Blackman Hill.

28. Interview, Lillian Robbins, October 1994; group photo, Bill Sherwood and Clarence Lacey; interview, Clarence Lacey, April 8, 1995. Clarence Lacey worked here for $21 a month; he was happy to move on to a job at Wickwire's in Cortland for $19 a week.

29. Mildred English had a 46-trip school ticket dated May 1932; photocopy in Art Volbrecht's scrapbook.

30. White graduated in 1921. In "I'd Send My Son to Cornell" he wrote, "a New York boy still has the opportunity of changing at Owego to the spur line of the DL&W (the most romantic journey of my life) and rolling along with the late afternoon through Catatonk, Candor, Willseyville, Caroline, where September lies curled up asleep in every pasture."

31. Governor Al Smith promoted consolidation, which happened in other areas as early as 1900 (*SC*, 227, 262). E. R. Eastman, as editor of a farm paper, encouraged consolidation. He notes that the "Committee of Twenty-One" found poor districts paid 15 or 20 times as much as rich districts did. He also notes that the railroads paid hefty school taxes, which benefited the individual taxpayer in those districts (E. R. Eastman, "He Stopped the Train," Caroline II, 80; see also Caroline I, 111).

32. Louise Lounsbery and her siblings parked their car, lunches inside, next to Rothschild's. At noon, they sat on the store stairs or the balcony to eat (*IJ*, February 27, 1982).

33. Barbara Bell, *IJ*, June 1977, in Caroline IV, 114–16. In 1959–1960 other companies helped deliver students: Swarthout and Ferris had 18 drivers, the Ithaca District 14, Crispell 24.

34. The Interstate Commerce Commission grandfathered their right to operate in 15 states and the District of Columbia because they could prove they had been in business before trucking regulations began (Leslie Crispell Jr. in Kone, 55). The family's three enterprises were Crispell Brothers, Inc., Crispell Charter Services, Inc., and Crispell Automotive Service (Caroline II, 17).

35. Speedsville Superspeeders 4-H Club, *Places, People and Events of our Town—Speedsville*, (1979), with information from village historian Will Osburn. *The Pictorial History of Speedsville* (1995) compiled by Mary Jordan, expands on the 4-H booklet but does not have this information.

36. E. R. Eastman, *Journey to Day before Yesterday*, 37.

37. Gertrude Conant and Eloise Phinney, *Brooktondale, U.S.A.* The complete file of the *Brooktondale Bugler* is at DHS, accompanied by a brief history by Gertrude Conant.

38. W. A. Anderson, Olaf F. Larson, Fathalla A. S. Halloul, *Social Change in the Slaterville Springs–Brooktondale Area of Tompkins County, New York, 1926 to 1951*, 35.

39. Letter from Bob Albertson to Anne Blodgett, in *Brooktondale Community Newsletter*, June 1987. Art Wells in *Remembrances: Stories of a Pennsylvania Farm Boy*, 255, credits Bob Tucker with being "the father of the fire department." See also Caroline II, 23 and 46–47.

40. Eight more classrooms were added in 1965; in 1969 enrollment was 470. In 1990 the

cafeteria was enlarged and six more classrooms added; enrollment was 390. New teaching methods required more rooms for fewer students.

41. The club was named for two boys who were killed in an auto accident in 1954. A good first-hand account of Skip and Joe, the club, and the school purchase is in Wells, 256–62. He also tells (259) of a man who went to the auctions to buy up all the schools in Tompkins County.

42. Kone, 74–75.

43. *Syracuse Post Standard,* July 29, 1962, in Caroline II, 8; see also *IJ* photo follow-up by George Clay, Caroline II, 73–77.

44. Hazel Brampton has a file of papers relating to her father's association with the camp and with the N.Y.S. Division for Youth.

45. The Crispell, Hildebrant-Crispell, Snow-Taft, Yaple, Maynard, Whittaker, and Shaw-Mix properties have been farmed by members of the same family for more than one hundred years (Kone, 31).

Town of Danby

This chapter has been informed by personal conversations with Ken and Lois Travers (longtime residents), Onni Kaartinen (on the history of the Finns), George Peter, Jean Alve (Spencer historian), Bert Dean (longtime Danby farmer), Linda and Gene Getz, Ralph Bowles (fire chief), Augusta and Walter Chapman (longtime residents of West Danby), Milton Todd (farmer), Tony Ingraham (Finger Lakes State Park), Kathy Morris (one-time resident of Dawes Hill), Diane VandeBogart (former town historian), Elizabeth Melchen (longtime resident), Warren and Jan Schlesinger (on the Danby Dish), Dave Reardon (from the Department of Environmental Conservation on Danby State Forest), Paul Stearns (H&E Machinery), Roswitha and Fritz Daemen-Van Buren (Trakehner farm), Susan Beeners (town clerk), and Ed Kretsch (Empire Speech & Hearing Clinic).

This contribution would not have been possible without the able assistance of town historian Susan Hautala, who provided open access to her Danby files.

1. *American Agriculturalist Farm Directory of Yates, Schuyler, Tompkins and Seneca Counties,* 217; and *Demographic Profile of the Central Region,* vol. 2.

2. FCH, 11.

3. See Overview for information on the Iroquois League of Nations.

4. Nelson H. Genung, "A Tribute to South Danby," 6.

5. *IN,* 1–2.

6. Selkreg, 13.

7. See William Heidt Jr., *Lewis Beers, Danby's Pioneer Doctor,* 25–26.

8. *IJ,* July 11, 1970.

9. *Random Harvest,* December 1, 1982.

10. A driver of a wagon with two draught animals paid $0.125 and each additional animal cost $0.03. Drivers of carts with two draught animals paid $0.08 with $0.02 due for each additional draught animal. Sleigh drivers paid $0.06 for two draught animals, and $0.03 for each additional. A traveler on horseback paid $0.04. Cattle drivers paid $0.01 per cow; sheep herders paid $0.06 for 20 (*Random Harvest,* December 8, 1982).

11. Ibid.

12. Ibid.

13. Norris, *Place Names,* 26.

14. Selkreg, 297.

15. FCH, 468.

16. *Danby Area News,* May 1985.
17. FCH, 469.
18. *IJ,* July 25, 1970.
19. From conversations with Ric Dietrich, former Danby board member.
20. FCH, 469–70.
21. Tresa Cortright, *Danby Historical Sketches,* from old ledgers lent to her by Charlotte Eckert Hautala.
22. Genung, 3.
23. Quoted in *Danby Area News,* March 1987.
24. *Rails North,* 3.
25. Lee, 52, 26–28.
26. French, 654.
27. Jennings's diaries.
28. George A. McGonigal, "Finnish-American Immigrant Workers and Institutions."
29. *Syracuse Post Standard,* April 26, 1931.
30. Ralph W. Jones, "History of the Ithaca Summer Speech Clinic," 2.
31. Minutes of Danby Fire Company No. 1, 1947.
32. *IJ,* March 25, 1974.
33. *The Grapevine,* April 2–8, 1987.
34. Merrill N. Knapp, "The Todd Farm."
35. Lorraine Pakkala, *Yea-God!,* 11, 104, 176.

Town of Dryden

Sources for this chapter include the Dryden Historical Society, Gina Prentiss, and Joan Manning, Village of Freeville historian.

1. W. Franklin Moore, *Dryden: Being a Miscellaneous Dissertation upon That Beautiful Little Village of Central New York,* n.p.
2. George E. Goodrich, ed., *The Centennial History of the Town of Dryden, 1797–1897,* 14. Most of the early facts about the Town of Dryden come from this wonderful book. See also *History of Dryden—from 1797 to 1857, By the Old Man in the Clouds,* transcribed by Betsey L. Clark.
3. Seven lots were annexed by the Town of Caroline in 1887 because of their proximity to Slaterville.
4. Spafford, *Gazetteer,* 148.
5. Goodrich, 140.
6. Ibid., 92.
7. Albert Benjamin Genung, *Historical Sketch of the Village of Freeville, Tompkins County, New York.* Most information on pre-1942 Freeville comes from this book.
8. Other newspapers include *Rumsey's Companion,* 1856–1857; *The Dryden News,* 1857–1865; *Dryden Weekly Herald,* 1871–1881; *The Dryden Herald,* 1891–1919; *Dryden Echo,* 1889–1890; *The Dryden Rural News,* 1933–1983.
9. The village was reincorporated in 1865.
10. Goodrich, 96.
11. Genung, 25.
12. In 1994 the Town of Dryden received a $55,200 grant from the New York State Environmental Quality Bond Act to improve the park and trail system at Dryden Lake.
13. Genung, 43–45.

14. For more information about Nivison and the Dryden Springs Sanitarium, see Samuel A. Cloyes, *The Healer.*

15. "William R. George and the George Junior Republic Papers: 1895–1970," 10. The George Junior Republic has archival papers at the school and some materials in the Dryden HS.

16. The Octagonal or Eight-Square schoolhouse was sold by the Dryden School District in 1955 to the DHS through the efforts of Stan Warren, professor at Cornell, and A. B. Genung, DHS president at that time. For more information about Dryden's rural schools, see files, Dryden HS.

17. See the file "Disasters," Dryden HS.

18. The Goodrich book was an outcome of the Dryden centennial celebration in 1897. The Dryden bicentennial committee is preparing a volume that covers the second hundred years (1897–1997). In 1957 Dryden held a centennial celebration in honor of incorporation. Freeville has had two celebrations; a sesquicentennial celebration of the founding in 1948 and a centennial celebration of the incorporation in 1987.

19. See Dryden HS files for more information on Dryden clubs and organizations. See the paper by Dick Blackman on Freeville's baseball team in the history files at the Freeville Village Hall.

20. The Dryden HS has files on individuals associated with the town. Goodrich provides an extensive section of short biographies at the end of his book.

21. Spafford, 148.

22. Goodrich, 47.

23. Ibid., 186. There is an extensive file on the Dryden Fair, Dryden HS.

24. "Dryden: The Township, the Village," was created by the Dryden Business Association in 1951. Dryden has long been known for its farming and has several century farms in the town. See the agriculture files, Dryden HS. See also individual files on Griswold, Willard Downey, McClintock Barn, Carpenter family, Beck family, George Monroe.

25. The Dryden HS has files on the Pioneer Co-op, including a paper written by Harlan Carpenter, a technician for the cooperative for many years.

Town of Enfield

In addition to references given below, my sources have included M. C. (Jack) Hubbell, past town historian; Gary Fisher, head of the Enfield Commemorative Committee and Town Council member; Ellen Hobbie, committee member and "Enfield History" friend; Alice Laue, town clerk; and the members of my family.

1. The names are listed in a letter dated July 8–9, 1823, of which a copy was received from Carol Kammen. The original letter, written in Enfield by Benjamin Hadden Jr., is in the Westchester [N.Y.] Historical Society. Hadden had traveled from New York to Enfield to visit his friends throughout the area. He described people clearing acres for their new homes and farms and hunting black squirrels, pigeons, and deer.

2. Franklin B. Hough, *Census of the State of New York for 1865* (Albany: Charles Van Benthuysen, 1867), 370–77. See Gary Fisher, chapter 8, "Enfield History."

3. 1866 *Atlas.*

4. See Leah Carpenter's contribution on the Enfield Valley Grange in chapter 14, "Enfield History."

5. Maurice C. Bond, *Tompkins County Census Data.*

6. Ulysses Prentiss Hedrick, *A History of Agriculture in the State of New York.*

7. Timothy Dougherty, "Nine Tompkins County Farmers Accepted in Dairy Buyout Program," *IJ,* April 1, 1986.

8. Coverage of agriculture includes all operators of U.S. farms that sold or normally would have sold $1,000 worth of agricultural products during the census year.

9. *Boyds New York State Directory.*

10. Interview on July 23, 1990 with Warena Ramsey, Helena Schaber, and M. C. Hubbell, Enfield (hereafter designated as 1990 interview).

11. R. D. Jerome and H. W. Wisbery Jr., *Mark Twain in Elmira.*

12. Personal written and verbal communication between Eunice Beardsley and Ellen Hobbie of Enfield, Enfield.

13. 1990 interview.

14. On December 24, 1923, Louis C. Leonard became Louis F. L. Humphrey. Published in the *Ithaca Journal-News* on November 24, the change became official on December 24. He changed his name because there were too many Leonards in the area and, according to hearsay, he was quite taken with Humphrey Patent Medicine.

15. Neil A. Poppensiek's 1990 article, "Robert H. Treman State Park—The Hamlet of Enfield Falls," offers further information about the area.

16. 1990 interview.

17. Road and Road District Journal, Town of Enfield, 1825, Enfield.

18. Diary of Emma Rolfe, 1896, Enfield.

19. Conversation in March 1996 with lifetime Enfield resident Hilda Amberge regarding her father's diary.

20. Spafford, *Gazetteer*, 160.

21. This information was received from School Recollections Forms used during one-two school house reunions.

22. *SH*, 149.

23. Ellen Hobbie, chapter 6 on buildings in "Enfield History."

24. Informational notes written by Enfield resident Helen Smith for "Enfield History."

25. The WCTU organization was started in New York State in 1874 to promote moderation and complete abstinence in the use of intoxicating beverages.

26. WCTU minute books, Enfield.

27. See Roger Brown's 1992 article "Baseball," written for Enfield Town Historian Collection. Roger's baseball career ended in 1965.

28. See Wilma Fisher's contribution on the Mothers' Club in chapter 14, "Enfield History."

29. It is used each month by such groups as the Enfield Town Board, Boy Scouts, Girl Scouts, Teen Youth, Enfield Historical Society, and 4-H.

30. See Margaret Hamilton, chapter 4, "Enfield History."

31. The reference of 1858–1923 was given in the Tompkins County Board of Supervisors proceedings and related to the town's holding meetings and thus paying rent at this hotel. The hotel went under different ownership through the years, including the VanMarter, Harvey, and Teeter families.

32. M. C. Hubbell, chapter 1, "Enfield History." Documentation was based on official documents held by the Enfield town clerk.

33. Randolph Warden, chapter 11, "Enfield History."

34. R. G. Fowler, "Enfield Named for a Town in Connecticut," *IJ*, May 22, 1965.

35. Spafford, 160.

36. New York State Population 1790–1980.

37. *IN*, 9.

38. The Pennsylvania & Sodus Bay Railroad was to be built through Enfield in 1869 connecting to the Geneva, Ithaca & Athens Railroad. By 1872 the company ran out of money and the railroad was never built. Only an empty railroad grade goes north-south

through the town. The town had voted to pay for support of the P&SB with a bank bond for the amount of $25,000, which was not paid off until March 1, 1911.

39. Olaf F. Larson, *The People of New York State's Counties: Tompkins*, 4.
40. The park is located on the Mecklenburg Road, at Miller's Corners.

Town of Groton

1. M. M. Baldwin, *The Beginnings of Groton*, 8.
2. Ibid., 10.
3. Ibid., 13.
4. Quoted in ibid.
5. FCH, 209.
6. Norris, *Place Names*, 33–35.
7. Joseph P. Hester, *Boyhood in Pleasant Valley*.
8. "Expense Book of W. W. Williams, Agent, Groton Iron Bridge Co., 1887," Flora Williams French Collection, Account Books 1858–1926, box 315, CU.
9. *Groton, N.Y. and Vicinity*, 36.
10. Priscilla Stringham, "Groton—What Next?"
11. *General Development Plan, Town & Village of Groton, New York*.

Town of Lansing

In addition to sources given below, information has been supplied by Mike Walter.

1. Letter from Erl A. Bates, adviser in Indian Extension at Cornell University, to Mrs. Robert Conlon, 1961, Lansing.
2. W. Glenn Norris, *Early Explorers and Travelers in Tompkins County*, 49.
3. Florence Dates Worsell gave this information to Isabelle Parish in 1959.
4. Alice Adele Bristol, "The History of Ludlowville" (c. 1930), 6, 40, 47, 52, 55, Lansing.
5. Ibid., 13, 14.
6. Louise Bement, ed., *International Salt Memory Book*, 3.
7. Letha S. Henry, *North Lansing's Remembrance of Things Past*, 2, 3, 9. The Rose Inn is open today as a bed and breakfast establishment.
8. Louise Bement, *Town of Lansing, Its Beginning* (Lansing, 1984), 17, 18.
9. Nellie Tucker Minturn, *More Bits and Pieces of Lansingville History*, 2–5.
10. Isabelle H. Parish, *It Happened in Lansing*, 13, 14.
11. This information, in DHS's Town of Lansing Collection, V-16-1-4(B), is from a letter by Lloyd A. Bower to Mrs. Smelzer, librarian, DHS.
12. *International Salt Memory Book*, 3, 4, 25.
13. Newspaper clipping in Susan Howell Haring's scrapbook, Lansing.
14. Haring scrapbook, newspaper clipping.
15. Louise Bement, ed., *Portland Point Memory Book*, 16.
16. Isabelle H. Parish, *This, Too, Happened in Lansing*, 38.
17. Louise Bement, ed., *The Rock Salt Mine*, 4, 17, 18, 19.
18. Information from a 1990 phone call to personnel at Milliken Station.
19. Borg-Warner publication, *First 100 Years*.
20. Rita Smidt, "Origins of the Village of Lansing."
21. Norris, *Old Indian Trails*, 10–11.

22. Lee, 48–49.

23. May 22, 1965.

24. April 21, 1990.

25. Figures were supplied by Robert Nicholas, airport manager, January 14, 1997.

26. Isabelle H. Parish, *It Happened in Lansing*, 16.

27. Information from a booklet, printed by the Lansing Central School System, which informed Lansing residents about a proposed addition in 1950.

28. Information on the Lansing Residential Center was written for the author by director Linda Albrecht. Material on the Gossett Center came from a phone call with John Marcham, January 15, 1997.

29. From M. Crim, "All Saints Parish," manuscript.

30. *IJ*, February 18, 1961.

31. Information was written for the author by members of the Faith Baptist Church.

32. Quotation from Mrs. C. L. Buck, "History of the Groton and Lansing Church, 1804–1904"; recent information from Charlotte Scheffler of the West Groton–East Lansing Church.

33. *IJ*, October 12, 1963.

34. Jennie H. Conlon, *Silently They Stand*, 1–23.

35. "History of Asbury Church."

36. Information on the Lakeview church was supplied by Mike Walter.

37. William Heidt Jr., *Kingdom Farm and Gilead School*, 5–11.

38. Town of Lansing Directory (1991), which is the source for information on government as well.

39. Information from the Lansing town clerk, telephone call, January 14, 1997.

Town of Newfield

1. First settlement dates in *Newfield—150 Years (1822–1972)*; Norris, *Place Names*; and 1866 *Atlas*.

2. Nearly all material from 1972 and earlier is taken from *Newfield—150 Years*, except as indicated below. Population figures come from *Manual for the Use of the Legislature of the State of New York* (the Red and Blue Books) and from the Tompkins County Planning Office.

3. Selkreg, 16.

4. Norris, *Old Indian Trails*, 15, 27.

5. Norris, *Place Names*, 43.

6. *Newfield—150 Years*, 42.

7. Historian Gould Colman to the author, March 1, 1996.

8. *1850 Federal Census, Newfield* and Tompkins County Clerk's Office, Ithaca.

9. FCH, 531–33.

10. Transcript, "Newfield Town History," 19.

11. Colman to the author, March 1, 1996.

12. 1866 *Atlas*, 13.

13. Alan Chaffee to the author, February 29, 1996; and Lee, 53.

14. FCH, 253.

15. *Newfield—150 Years*, and *IJ*, November 11, 1919.

16. *Newfield—150 Years*, and *IJ*, November 10, 1945.

17. Lee, 51.

18. *Newfield Business Directory, 1993–1994* (Newfield: People for Newfield Committee, 1993); and Lois Minteer, Newfield town clerk.

19. Roy A. Trask Jr., and John W. Schulte Jr., of the Newfield Fire Department to the author, February 25, 26, 1996.

20. Catherine Shipos of the Newfield Central School District to the author, Feb. 23, 26, 1996.

Town of Ulysses

In addition to sources listed below, I have received assistance and information from Judy Barkee, librarian at the Ulysses Philomathic Library and former librarian at the Interlaken Library; Esther Northrup, town historian; Ruth Wolverton, Marion Hoffmire, and others in the Ulysses Historical Society; and neighbors Jack and Harriet McConnell.

1. A. P. Osborn, *History of Trumansburg;* from *Trumansburg Free Press.*

2. Edward Lutz, in 1964 letter to Clifford Bower, Ulysses town supervisor and chair of the town board, in files of Ulysses town historian.

3. Conversations with Don Oliver, park superintendent, and Todd Van Dusen, manager of Tompkins County Convention and Visitors Bureau, December 1994.

4. A panther attack is reported in the manuscript of Orlo Horton's 1876 address at Covert centennial, "Early Settlement of Trumansburg," 9; bear attack on Samuel Weyburn in Taughannock Gorge, comes from manuscript of Dr. Farrington's 1876 centennial address, "Historical Sketch," 3; bear in lake and wolves are found in manuscript in Early Settlers collection, 4–5 Interlaken Public Library and in Ulysses historian's files.

5. Goodwin's Point is described in 1903 newspaper reports reprinted in 1984 and 1995 newsletters of the Ulysses Historical Society.

6. The reference to an Indian village on the "rich flats" appears in Dr. Farrington's 1876 centennial address. [See note 7.]

7. Taken from FCH, 261; the reference to old apple trees is attributed to H. C. Goodwin (the Cortland County historian and a Goodwin descendant). Both this reference and the preceding one have been used and reused by nineteenth-century historians, usually with small variations in the wording (for example, in the 1868–1869 Tompkins County directory).

8. In caption for a photograph of the Taughannock Creek delta, O. D. von Engeln (*The Finger Lakes Region, Its Origin and Nature*) mentions the ten thousand years of outwash. He also writes (74) that it is "of quite the same origin as that at the mouth of the Nile, though of far smaller area."

9. On the survival of the Indian villages, the FCH (261) should be taken with a grain of salt.

10. Norris in *Old Indian Trails* (34) mentions that the Indian fort predated Sullivan. This was confirmed in a conversation with Sherene Baugher of Cornell University, who was on the 1979–1980 dig, although she said that Norris's contention that the Waterburg village was a "pre-contact" site was wrong.

11. According to FCH (262), Treman was granted 640 acres, but most other sources accept the wording of the grant itself, which says 600.

12. Formation of the county and township is described in Selkreg, 5–6.

13. Lydia Sears, *A History of Trumansburg, New York (1792–1967),* 6.

14. Carolyn A. Martin, *Trumansburg, New York: Incorporation Centennial 1872–1972,* sums up the various stories of Treman's amputation (13).

15. Carol Sisler, *Enterprising Families*, 12.

16. According to the 1890 *History* Treman died in 1828. But Sears and Sisler report 1823, the date carved on the monument in Grove Cemetery.

17. Oldest residence status of the "mud house" was reported in conversations with a Ulysses Historical Society member; its structure is described in Victoria Romanoff and Sarah Adams's "Architectural Sampler," in the *Free Press* Bicentennial issue. As for traces of McLallen, note that Frontenac Point, just over the Seneca County line and present site of the Boy Scouts' Camp Barton, was known for a time as "McLallen's Landing" (and, successively, as Port Deposit, Frog Point, and Trumansburg Landing).

18. Sisler, *Enterprising Families* (12), writes that Treman was the first postmaster; most other sources name O. C. Comstock.

19. Norris, *Place Names*, also mentions Mack Settlement (Macktown) and Pinckney's (52), both in the vicinity of Glenwood.

20. Papers of Carl Fischer, who did prodigious work on history and genealogy in Ulysses and surrounding areas and photocopied material from the Opdike (Holland) family genealogy (both in Interlaken library), differ on whether 1801 or 1802 was Burgoon's arrival date.

21. Taken from a photocopy of genealogical material for the Opdike (Holland) family; in file 14 of the Interlaken library.

22. According to Carl Fischer, *Some Cemeteries of the Between Lakes Country*, the log meetinghouse was "evidently not a church as such."

23. Brief information on this and an early twentieth-century photograph of the school is in Martin, *Trumansburg* (49).

24. Sears, *History*, mentions the Underground Railroad (47); it seems that most "stops" or "safe houses" were outside Ulysses.

25. First meeting mentioned in Fischer, *Some Cemeteries*, and Martin, *Trumansburg*.

26. Bill Tyler, clerk of Ithaca Friends Meeting, discussed current use of the Perry City Road property, December 1994.

27. The spellings of Nicoll Halsey's first name vary, as does the date for the Halsey house. A recopied letter from Joel Horton to the Syracuse *Post-Standard* (c. 1930) in the Interlaken library says 1835.

28. Martin, *Trumansburg* (95) describes Halsey's endeavors.

29. Sears, *History* (7).

30. Various stories are recorded about the first and last persons over the bridge. Norris, *Place Names* (50): "Foster Owen, . . . at 81, was the last person to drive across the bridge before it was torn down. . . . This honor was due him as a matter of family pride, for his grandfather, Aaron, was the first person to drive across the covered bridge when it was opened." According to transcribed information (August 5, 1935) in the Ulysses town collections at DHS and attributed directly to H. Foster Owen (who was descended from settler Jonathan Owen of Waterburg and was to turn 90 on August 31, 1935), he was "practically the last to cross." Columnist Frank Schaefer Jr. reported different information in the *Trumansburg Free Press*, September 15, 1993 (7).

31. A short article on Halsey Farms' fiftieth anniversary, with pictures, appears in *Finger Lakes Forum*, August 28, 1985.

32. Waterburg is called "Waterbury" in FCH (267), and on a map in the *Official Automobile Blue Book, vol. 1: New York State and Adjacent Canada* (1921) (756–57); Sears says the place was first called Glen Mills (7). Note Norris, *Place Names*, 51.

33. From *IJ* columnist Romeyn Berry, as quoted in Martin, *Trumansburg* (50).

34. Norris, *Place Names* (51), says flatly that Podunk is Algonkian for "a clean place."

35. The spelling of "Duboise" appears on the official 1972 Ulysses map, but differs from the modern road signs (Dubois). Local pronunciation favors the final "e."

36. The lasting family lines at Willow Creek are covered by Carol Sisler, *Cayuga Lake* (90) and by the author's conversations with residents.

37. See *IJ*, June 16, 1964, (7), as well as conversations with Elsie Vann and Trumansburg stone mason Steve Koski. Vann says that her daughter Joyce attended the school through sixth grade. The summer the 1951 addition was in progress, "a lot of the women went down to help," but Elsie couldn't because she was pregnant.

Koski says that the redrawing of district lines removed him from West Hill School in Ithaca, after two unhappy years, to take up third grade in 1959 in Willow Creek School. He studied under Miss Evans (first–third grade) and Mrs. Reynolds (fourth-sixth), and remembers riding his bike from his home on Garrett Road. "I won the bicycle contest two years," he says.

38. Norris, *Place Names* (51).

39. Conversation with Marguerite Smith, December 1994. According to Barbara Bell in the *IJ* (June 17, 1964), the Webster Success Club was among a number of such groups formed to back and promote *Success* magazine, brainchild of a New Hampshire editor, Orson Sweet Marsden. Apparently, the clubs met for general edification, as Smith remembers; the magazine was of good quality but designed to "advance the editor's financial position." Bell quoted the memories of founding member Mrs. Edward T. Wallenbeck, who remembered gatherings of the original 6 members growing to meetings of 50 or 60. "The club held meetings over a period of 20 years," wrote Wallenbeck. "What a lot of good it did our neighborhood!"

40. The history of Babcock Industries is discussed briefly in Martin, *Trumansburg* (45), and amplified by a printed advertisement on page 67.

41. ISA-Babcock update from conversation with general manager Ronald Myers, December 1994.

42. Sisler, *Cayuga Lake* (93).

43. Among the thousands of babies Dr. Warren delivered during his career was author Alex Haley, born in Ithaca in 1921; Warren's signature is on Haley's birth certificate.

44. Sisler, *Cayuga Lake* (93–94), mentions Route 89's construction in 1934. An engineer in the NYS Department of Transportation's Cortland office (which oversees Tompkins County) said the earliest set of plans he had for the road are marked 1932.

A retired DOT engineer, Ithaca resident Roger Yonkin said that Route 89 began as a turnpike. (The state of New York gave out permits for people to build roads, on which they could collect tolls, which got the roads built and gave people a little money too.) Around the turn of the century the pikes were rebuilt into what we know as modern roads. Sometime in the 1920s the state took over all roads, and Route 89 was rebuilt again in the 1930s. Yonkin said the original road from Ithaca to Taughannock went up and down the hillside, and he supplied the information about Maplewood.

The Ulysses town historian's files (in a folder marked "Railroads" and "Jim Rice") include an undated, unsigned, typescript of several pages which is a detailed argument for placing the "new, scenic route" where Route 89 now is rather than along the Route 96 line.

The 1921 *Automobile Blue Book* does not mention visiting Taughannock (perhaps at that time, most tourists arrived there by train) but, on a map that shows the recommended route from Ithaca to Trumansburg via what is now Route 96, it designates a route to the falls along what is now the line of Route 89 as "good road."

45. According to an undated *IJ* clipping (ca. 1930s; in files of Ulysses town historian) from columnist Romeyn Berry, Mattison's daughter claimed that the Tompkins County King apple originally came from a tree (grafted from an older tree in New Jersey) planted by egg-packer Cyrus H. Howe on his Jacksonville property. Her father developed thousands of scions, sending out 100,000 one year. With details from varied informants Berry concluded

that several pioneers must have brought the variety with them out of New Jersey, and that, once in the Finger Lakes, it flourished.

46. Information on "The Trees" came from a conversation with a realtor from the Audrey Edelman agency, December 1994.

47. A short, typed history of the Ulysses Grange was provided by an area grange member.

48. Steve Proctor, former editor of the *Trumansburg Free Press*, covered the gasoline contamination in an article, "Mobil Offers Buyout of 8 J-ville Homes," March 30, 1988.

49. Osborn, *History* (chap. 4). According to a mid-1830s post office report filed by James McLallen and cited by Sears, *History* (27), within eight miles of the village there were forty mills. What remained of these mills in the twentieth century was nearly all washed away by the 1935 flood.

50. Other prominent names, like that of blacksmith John Creque (pronounced "Creek" and, sometimes, "Creakey"), have faded or merged with those of other families; Creque's name, for example, became linked with that of the Wolvertons. An emigrant from New Jersey, Creque first moved to Updike's Settlement where he had family but eventually settled in Trumansburg. His life merited an extensive (and laudatory) description in Osborn, *History*, and he rests in an old section of Grove Cemetery. His gravestone stands within the remnants of an old fence which must have encircled the family plot; on one marble post is a scrolled piece of a handmade (by Creque himself? an employee? a descendant?) iron latch, testament to his profession.

51. Camp descriptions in Osborn, *History* (chap. 8).

52. Sears, *History*, quotes David McLallen's diary (16) to the effect that Lucinda's husband "hoped that God would forgive her," and alleges that "the lady, for she was indeed a lady, had been framed." A member of the Ulysses Historical Society claims that Camp wanted children and Lucinda was not producing, but Sears makes it sound more like she was accused of active, rather than passive, transgression. In any case, Camp married three more times before he died and fathered thirteen children.

53. Romeyn Berry, *IJ*, January 6, 13, 1936.

54. Sears, *History* (73), and Osborn, *History* (chap. 8), claim that Camp died in 1879; FCH says 1878, the date on Camp's imposing obelisk in Grove Cemetery. As reported by Wendy Skinner in the *Trumansburg Free Press*, December 22, 1992, "According to National Registry notes, Hermon Camp insisted the gate in [his front] fence be closed at all times. Legend has it that when he discovered the gate open one day, he 'kicked it shut in a fury and died in a fit of apoplexy.'"

55. Sears, *History* (25).

56. The old pumper is mentioned in Osborn, *History* (89, pamphlet version), and Martin, *Trumansburg* (25).

57. Martin, *Trumansburg*, covers the fire companies and incorporation in detail (27–29).

58. "Architectural Sampler," *Trumansburg Free Press*, July 1, 1992 (20).

59. Most information here on the Gregg/Morse building is from Sears, *History*.

60. Details on the silk mill/tannery drawn from Sears, *History*, plus conversations.

61. Although the synthesizer found its way into the music made by many big names, a lasting local rumor was that, taking a break during a visit to examine the new contraption, two of the Beatles sat down for lunch at the counter in Kostrub's Main Street restaurant one day. Former Moog worker John Weiss of Interlaken, however, handed down the word on this story: musician Keith Emerson (of Emerson, Lake and Palmer) came through, as did "space jazz" man Sun Ra, but "no Beatles."

62. Newspaper clippings, Ulysses town historian files.

63. Lutz 1964 letter.

64. Sears, *History* (133).

65. The up side of weathering the Depression comes from an interview with Ruth Wolverton *(Trumansburg Free Press,* July 1, 1992); the more sobering story is from a letter to the *Syracuse Post Standard* (June 21, 1934), quoted by George McGonigal, "'That Reserve Assigned to Us Will Be Overpowered by Strong Waters': Hector, New York and the Cayuga Indian Land Claim" (M.A. thesis, Cornell University, 1991).

66. Sears, *History* (143, 146).

67. Lutz letter.

68. Introduction to *The Cardiff Giant* (1949), a play by Cornell professor A. M. Drummond.

69. Photocopy of *New York Times* from microfilm. In describing the opening of the original library, Selkreg wrote, "It may be presumed that the pioneers of Trumansburgh were men *and women* [emphasis mine] of considerable culture and certainly possessed of a desire to improve their intellectual oportunities" (218).

The library still inhabits the small Masonic space where it reopened in 1935, serving a substantial clientele of all ages with its own holdings and those of the Finger Lakes Library System. It also houses the Ulysses Philomathic Costume Bureau (which also began in 1935, with just three items), a collection of vintage clothing, now winnowed down from thousands of pieces with which the community rather casually played dress-up, to more specific historic holdings with an eye toward preservation.

70. Conversation with Carol Bushberg of Christopher George real estate office, December 1994.

71. Population according to the 1990 census.

72. According to a typescript in the files of the Ulysses town historian, one early Ulysses doctor was a woman, Hulda Gould Smith, b. 1833 in Enfield, d. 1903 in Rochester, and buried in Grove Cemetery. She studied at Eclectic Medical College, New York, and practiced in New Jersey, then returned to her home on Iradell Road. "Patients came from New York and stayed at her home to be under her care. She also doctored many in the local area, travelling with her horse and buggy. It is said she wore men's clothes and wore a black top hat." Dr. Smith is listed in Selkreg, 86. Judging from first names in that listing, several other women born in Ulysses also became doctors.

73. Martin, *Trumansburg,* interviewed a living Dorsey descendant (47). Dorsey arrived very early (1813?). Selkreg (17) reports that the census of 1820 showed one female and two male slaves held in the Town of Ulysses "(then including the present towns of Ithaca and Enfield)," and eighteen "free colored persons."

74. Newell manuscript in Ulysses town historian files. Sears, *History* (125), says Porter A. Johnson died at 85 after fifty-two years of barbering without a vacation.

75. Selkreg, 50.

76. Conversations with Perry City Road resident Judy Cone, December 1994. Carl Burgess, staffer at the Tompkins County Health Department, said in December 1994 that although the cemeteries were marked on maps based on Cone's research and prompting, there was no official verification of their existence.

77. Population and housing figures are according to the 1990 census.

78. Engeln, *Finger Lakes,* 68–69.

Bibliography

Adams, Armand L. Remarks on the Occasion of the Dedication of the Old Courthouse. Typescript of speech made September 13, 1976. Tompkins County Board of Representatives history file.

Albertson, Helen. *Our Town.* Brooktondale, N.Y.: Brooktondale Community Center, 1970.

Alvarez, Lenore. "Freeville Centennial 1887–1987: Program and Self-Guided History Tour of Freeville." Brochure. Southworth Library in Dryden.

American Agriculturalist Farm Directory of Yates, Schuyler, Tompkins and Seneca Counties. New York: Orange Judd, 1914.

American Journal. Village of Ithaca, Tompkins County, New York. November 22, 1820– March 23, 1821.

Anderson, W. A., Olaf F. Larson, and Fathalla A. S. Halloul. "Social Change in the Slaterville Springs–Brooktondale Area of Tompkins County, New York, 1926–1951. Bulletin 920. Ithaca: Cornell University Agricultural Experiment Station, April 1956.

"Atlantic Woolen Mills: Incidents and Anecdotes of Dryden 1914–1917." Transcript of an audio tape by Alex Bernstein, 1985. DHS.

Atwater, Amy. "History of the Congregational Church, Brooktondale, New York." Updated by Erna Manchester, 1993. N.p. DHS.

Babcock, Hilda E. "Inlet Valley 1922 and Some Notes on Sunnygables Farm." Historic Ithaca newsletter, winter 1977.

Bakkum, Glenn A., and Bruce L. Melvin. "Social Relationships of Slaterville Springs– Brooktondale Area, Tompkins County, New York. Bulletin 501. Ithaca: Cornell University Agricultural Experiment Station, March 1930.

Baldwin, M. M. *The Beginnings of Groton.* Groton, N.Y.: Printed by the Journal and Courier, 1923. "Originally read Friday evening, April 10, 1868, at a meeting of the Groton Literary Association." DHS.

Balloting Book and Other Documents Relating to Military Bounty Lands in the State of New York. Rpt. Ovid, N.Y.: W. E. Morrison, 1983.

Beers, Aileen H. "Church of the Epiphany, Trumansburg, New York." Centennial Celebration (1871–1971). Brochure. DHS.

Bell, Barbara. Glance Backward columns. *IJ.* July 11, 25, 1970, and 1962–1977.

Bement, Louise. *Town of Lansing: Its Beginning.* Lansing, N.Y.: Published by the author, 1984.

——, ed. *International Salt Memory Book.* Prepared by Mrs. Bement's Fourth Grade. Lansing, N.Y.: Lansing Elementary School, 1978.

——, ed. *Portland Point Memory Book.* Prepared by Mrs. Bement's Fourth Grade. Lansing, N.Y.: Lansing Elementary School, 1976.

——, ed. *The Rock Salt Mine, 1916–1985.* Prepared by Mrs. Bement's Fourth Grade. Lansing, N.Y.: Lansing Elementary School, 1985.

Berry, Romeyn. State and Tioga column, *IJ,* 1935–1936. Clippings in historian's files, Town of Ulysses.

Bibliography on Land Utilization, 1918–1936. Edited by Louise O. Bercaw, Annie M. Hannay, and Mary G. Lacey. Washington, D.C.: U.S. Department of Agriculture, 1938.

Billard, Frederick L., comp. *McLean, 1796–1976—Through the Years.* McLean, N.Y.: McLean Bicentennial Committee, 1976.

Bond, Maurice C. *Tompkins County Census Data.* Agricultural Economics 907. Ithaca: Cornell University, 1953.

Boyds New York State Directory. Syracuse, various eds. 1864–1895.

Brooktondale Bugler. 1943–1946. File at DHS.

Buck, Mrs. C. L. "History of the Groton and Lansing Church, 1804–1904." Typescript, 1904. Lansing.

Carpenter, Harlan. "History of Artificial Breeding of Dairy Cattle in Tompkins County." Typescript. Dryden HS.

Celebration of the Bicentennial of the United States of America in the Town of Ulysses and the Village of Trumansburg. Sponsored by the Town and Village Boards and the Masons, 1976.

Centennial History of the Town of Dryden, 1797–1897. Compiled and edited by George E. Goodrich. Dryden, N.Y.: Dryden Herald Steam Printing House, 1898.

"Century of Farming in Tompkins County, A." Typescript for Historic Ithaca fall tour 1972. Dryden HS.

Chatterton, Leslie A. "Survey of Barns in Dryden, New York: June-September 1986." Typescript. Dryden HS.

"Clock System" Rural Index: Dryden Township. Tompkins County Farm Bureau, 1920. Dryden HS.

Cloyes, Samuel A. *Beyond the Footlights: Story of Dryden Opera House 1893–1936.* Ithaca: DHS, 1968.

——. *Healer, The: The Story of Dr. Samantha S. Nivison and Dryden Springs 1820–1915.* Ithaca: DHS, 1969.

Cody, Paul. "Farmer." *Cornell Magazine,* January/February 1994.

Collection of Historical Papers Concerning the Early Settlers of Trumansburg and Covert. Interlaken Public Library.

Cole, Mary, Nancy Zobel, and Nancy Siembor-Brown. "Enfield History." Chapter 13, Education.

Conant, Gertrude P., and Eloise Phinney. *Brooktondale, U.S.A.* Brooktondale, N.Y., 1944.

Conlon, Jennie H. *Silently They Stand.* Ithaca: DHS, 1966.

Cortright, Tresa. *Danby Historical Sketches.* Ithaca: DHS, 1968.

Court, Lavena, comp. "A Salute to Groton's Heritage, 1976: Sketches by Joey Jones." Typescript, 1976. DHS and Groton Public Library.

Danby Fire Company No. 1. Minutes, 1947–1994.

Danby Herald, vol. 1, no. 2. June 1881.

Day, Charles G. *Report of the Semi-Centennial Jubilee and Reunion of the 1/2 Century Club of Tompkins County, September 8, 1881.* Ithaca, N.Y.: Andrus and Church, 1881.

Demographic Profile of the Central Region, vol. 1. Research publication no. 4. Ithaca: New York State College of Human Ecology, Cornell University, 1974.

Development Strategies for the Village of Groton, New York. Cornell University Small Town Design Workshop, 1984. Groton Public Library.

Dieckmann, Jane Marsh. *A Short History of Tompkins County*. Ithaca: DHS, 1986. [*SH*]

"Dryden Mills." Interview with Ross Sherman, conducted by Ransom Blakeley, 1986. Typescript. Dryden HS.

"Early Federal Census Records of the Town of Dryden, N.Y. 1810–1820." Transcribed by Charles M. Sandwick. Southworth Library in Dryden.

Eastman, E[dward] R. *Journey to Day before Yesterday*. Englewood Cliffs, N.J.: Prentice-Hall, 1963.

Edelstein, Karen Leigh. "Changes in the Occurrences of Barns in Three Areas of the Town of Dryden, New York, 1853–1984." Typescript, 1988. Dryden HS.

Edwards, Charlotte. "Recollections of Forest Home in Early Days." Typescript, n.d. CU.

Edwards, Walter W. "Reminiscences of Forest Home." Typescript, 1947. CU.

"Eight-Square School, The: A History." Compiled by Frederick Billard et al. *Dryden Spirit '76*, July 1976.

"Enfield History." Projected publication by the Enfield Commemorative Committee, Enfield, N.Y. A reference copy is in the historian's files, Town of Enfield. ["Enfield History"]

"Enfield's First Highway Was in Use for 53 Years." *DeWitt Historical Society Bulletin*, vol. 10, no. 3. March 1962.

Engeln, O. D. von. *The Finger Lakes Region: Its Origin and Nature*. Ithaca: Cornell University Press, 1961. Rpt. 1988.

"55 Years of Service to Children with Disabilities at Lions Camp Badger 1939–1994." Program for Lions-Lioness-Leos Service Day, July 31, 1994.

Finger Lakes Region of Central New York, The. Ithaca: Ithaca Chamber of Commerce, Ithaca Automobile Club, 1929–1930.

"First National Bank of Groton, 1865–1965, The." Groton Public Library.

First 100 Years. A Graphic History of the Morse-Chain Division. Ithaca: Borg-Warner Corporation, 1982.

Fisher, Gary. "Enfield History." Chapter 8, Agriculture.

Fletcher, A. K. "Like Hell It's Fiction, It's the Real Thing." Typescript, 1986. Southworth Library in Dryden.

——. *My Memories of Fall Creek*. Groveland, Fla.: Published by the author, 1989.

Force, Albert W. "Free Hollow: The First One Hundred Years of Forest Home." Typescript, n.d. (c. 1954). CU.

——. "Oral History." Interview by Gould P. Colman, 1967. CU.

Freeman, Galpin W. *Central New York: An Inland Empire*. Vol. 1. New York: Lewis Historical Publishing Company, 1941.

French, Flora Williams, collector. Account Books, 1856–1926. CU.

French, J. H. *Gazetteer of the State of New York. A Complete History and Description of Every County, City, Town, Village, and Locality*. Syracuse: R. Pearsall Smith, 1860. [French]

"Future of the Land Is in Your Hands, The." *Farm Review & Forecast*, vol. 1, no. 4. November 20, 1974.

Gazetteer and Business Directory of Tompkins County, N.Y. for 1868. Compiled by Hamilton Child. Syracuse: Journal Office, 1868.

General Development Plan, Town & Village of Groton, New York. Prepared by Egner & Niederkorn, 1972. Groton Public Library.

Genung, Albert Benjamin. "Historical Sketch of the Village of Freeville, Tompkins County New York." Edited by R. D. Savage. Dryden, N.Y.: Dryden HS, 1987.

Genung, Nelson Howard. "A Tribute to South Danby." Typescript, 1934. DHS.

Groton, New York [bird's eye view]. Published and drawn by L. R. Burleigh, Troy, N.Y. Milwaukee: Beck & Pauli Lithograph, [1885]. DHS.

Groton, N.Y. and Vicinity. Albany: "Grip's" Valley Gazette, vol. 7, no. 10. Historical Souvenir Series, no. 6, 1899.

Groton Township "Clock System" Rural Index. Ithaca: American Rural Index Corporation, 1920.

Hardison, Lewis M. "The Story of Frank L. Clark: His Farm Operations and Clark Seed Farms of Richford NY." Typescript. Dryden HS.

Hautala, Susan. *Danby Area News.* Various issues, September 1983–February 1991.

Hedrick, Ulysses Prentiss. *A History of Agriculture in the State of New York.* Albany: J. B. Lyon, 1933.

Heidt, William, Jr. *The Blue-Eyed Lassie and the Renwicks in Ithaca.* Pamphlet. Ithaca: DHS, 1970.

——. *Forests to Farms in Caroline.* Ithaca: DHS, 1965.

——. *Kingdom Farm and Gilead School.* Ithaca: DHS, 1971.

——. *Lewis Beers, Danby's Pioneer Doctor.* Ithaca: DHS, 1967.

Henry, Florence J. "Silo Saga." Typescript, 1967. History room, Town of Caroline.

Henry, Letha S., ed. *North Lansing's Remembrance of Things Past.* North Lansing, N.Y.: North Lansing Auxiliary, 1982.

Hester, Joseph. *Boyhood in Pleasant Valley.* Groton, N.Y.: Published by the author, n.d. (c. 1970).

Historic Preservation in Tompkins County. Comprehensive Plan Studies prepared by the Tompkins County Department of Planning. Ithaca, June 1977.

"Historical Sketch of the Settlement of Trumansburg and Vicinity." Read at the Centennial Meeting of the Trumansburg M.E. Church on Sunday, September 24, 1876, by John M. Farrington M.D. Published in the Trumansburg *Sentinel*, December 21, 1876. Interlaken Public Library.

History of Dryden: From 1797 to 1857 by the Old Man in the Clouds. Transcribed by Betsey L. Clark. Ithaca: DHS, 1961.

"History of Halseyville, N.Y." Letter to the Syracuse *Post Standard*, c. 1930, attributed to Joel Horton. Interlaken Public Library.

History of St. James the Apostle R. C. Church, 1872–1972, A. N.p., [1972].

History of Tioga, Chemung, Tompkins, and Schuyler Counties, New York. By H. B. Peirce and D. Hamilton Hurd. Philadelphia: Everts & Ensign, 1879. Rpt. Ovid, N.Y.: W. E. Morrison, 1976. [FCH]

History of Trumansburg. [By A. P. Osborn.] Pamphlet. Trumansburg, N.Y., 1890. Interlaken Public Library.

Hobbie, Ellen. "Enfield History." Chapter 6, Buildings.

Holmes, Gerald P. *The West Danby Baptist Church (1810–1963).* Ithaca: DHS, 1963.

Horton, Orlo. "Early Settlement of Trumansburg" and "Historical Address Delivered . . . at the Centennial Celebration at Covert, N.Y. July 4, 1876." Interlaken Public Library.

Hubbell, M. Clyde. Interviews with the town historian, 1993. Enfield.

——. "Military Townships and Lots in Numerical Order # 136. Typescript, 1989. Enfield.

——. "Time Line." Typescript. Enfield.

Hunter, William C. "John Miller: First Governor of North Dakota." *North Dakota History*, vol. 33, no. 5.

Hurd, Thomas Norman. "An Analysis of Local Government in Tompkins County, New York." Ph.D. thesis, Cornell University, 1936.

Ithaca Board of Health. Investigation of the Sanitary Conditions of the Public Water Supply of the City of Ithaca, New York. 1904.

Ithaca's Neighborhoods: The Rhine, the Hill, and the Goose Pasture. Edited by Carol Sisler, Margaret Hobbie, and Jane Marsh Dieckmann. Ithaca: DHS, 1988. [*IN*]

Jacobs, Lawrence. *Early Boyhood Days in Ithaca.* Ithaca: DHS, 1970.

Jansen, George. Diaries for 1908–1909, 1917–1918, 1922, 1923, 1923–1924, 1925. DHS.

Jansen, Harold. *This Way to Podunk: Tales from "Far Above Cayuga's Waters."* New York: Vantage Press, 1954.

Jennings, Benjamin. Personal papers and diaries, 1903–1935. Historian's files, Town of Danby.

Jerome, R. D., and H. W. Wisbery Jr. *Mark Twain in Elmira.* Elmira, N.Y.: Mark Twain Society, 1977.

Jones, Ralph W. "History of the Ithaca Summer Speech Clinic." Manuscript, February 1969. DHS.

Jordan, Mary, compiler. *The Pictorial History of Speedsville.* 1995.

Kammen, Carol. *The Peopling of Tompkins County: A Social History.* Interlaken, N.Y.: Heart of the Lakes Publishing, 1985.

——, ed., *Studies in a Small Community, Past and Present.* Vol. 2. Ithaca: Ithaca High School, 1974.

Kemp, Russell A. "H. Emilie Cady: Physian & Metaphysician." *Unity Magazine,* August–September 1975.

Kensler, Gladys M., and Bruce L. Melvine, "A Partial Sociological Study of Dryden, New York." Bulletin 504. Ithaca: Cornell University Agricultural Experiment Station, 1930.

Knapp, Merrill N. "The Todd Farm." Written on the occasion of the Todd Farm's being named Century Farm, on January 13, 1960, by the New York Agricultural Society. DHS.

Know, Helen M. "Early Facts about Forest Home." Manuscript, n.d. CU.

Kone, Barbara Mix, ed. *A History of the Town of Caroline.* Slaterville Springs, N.Y.: Town of Caroline Bicentennial Committee, 1994.

Kopelson, Evan. "Forest Home's Industrial Age: An Historical Reconstruction from Mill-Era Remnants." Senior thesis, Cornell University, 1994. DHS.

Ladenheim, Melissa. *The Sauna in Central New York.* Ithaca: DHS, 1986.

Lansing Directory, 1979, 1991. Lansing.

Lant, M. W. *Lant's Directory of Ithaca and Owego, Containing a List of the Names and Residences of Families.* Lancaster, Pa.: H. G. Smith, 1867.

Larson, Olaf F. *The People of New York State's Counties: Tompkins.* Ithaca: Cornell University, 1970.

Lee, Hardy Campbell. *A History of Railroads in Tompkins County.* 1947. Revised and enlarged by Winton Rossiter. Ithaca: DHS, 1977. [Lee]

Livermore, K. C. "Butterfly Kisses." *Cornell Alumni News,* June 1984.

Lutes, Phyllis. *A Continuing History of Trumansburg, New York, 1968–1981.* Published by the author, 1982.

McGonigal, George A. "Finnish-American Immigrant Workers & Institutions: An Overview (1890–1925) and a Case Study (1918–1953)." Paper submitted for History Seminar 409, Cornell University, spring 1985. DHS.

McGurk, John L. "Farm Management Adjustments in Tompkins County 1907–1947." Ph.D. thesis, Cornell University, 1951.

McKinney, Mary E. "Brief History of Forest Home," 1916. CU.

Malone, Harry R. *History of Central New York . . .* Indianapolis: Historical Publishing, 1932.

Manual for the Use of the Legislature of the State of New York (the Red & Blue books) for 1852 and other years through 1972. Albany: By several publishers.

Marcham, Frederick. *Memories of Cayuga Heights, N.Y.* Pamphlet. Ithaca, 1988.

Marks and Strays. Town of Enfield Record Book. Manuscript, recorded by town clerk Samuel Rolfe, 1821. Enfield.

Martin, Carolyn A. *Trumansburg, New York: Incorporation Centennial 1872–1972.* Trumansburg, N.Y.: Trumansburg Centennial Association, 1972.

Mayer, Virginia W. *Ithaca Past and Present.* Ithaca: Art Craft of Ithaca, 1956.

Minturn, Nellie Tucker. *More Bits and Pieces of Lansingville History.* Ithaca: DHS, 1971.

Moore, W. Franklin. "Dryden: Being a Miscellaneous Dissertation upon That Beautiful Little Village of Central New York." Dryden, N.Y.: Business Men's Association, 1911.

Moran, E. G. *And They Touched Me: Friends of the Groton Community.* Groton, N.Y.: Published by the author, 1987.

———. *Early Groton Area Military Grant Lot No. 75: The Start.* Groton, N.Y.: Published by the author, 1993.

Morgan, Almyra H. "The Catskill Turnpike." Bound manuscript with photos, 1971. DHS.

Morgan, Barbara. "A Sociological Study of the Village of Dryden, N.Y." Typescript, 1961. DHS.

Muir, William A. "The Turnpike That Made Tioga County." *Random Harvest,* December 1 and 8, 1982.

Mulks, Charles Freer. Collection of papers, 1837–1907, #2157. CU.

New Topographical Atlas of Tompkins County, New York. Philadelphia: Stone and Stewart, 1866. [1866 *Atlas*]

New York. A Guide to the Empire State. American Guide Series. New York State Historical Association. New York: Oxford University Press, 1955.

New York State Population 1790–1980: A Compilation of Federal Census Data. Compiled by B. Shupe, J. Steins, and J. Pandit, 1987. DHS.

Newfield—150 Years (1822–1972). Compiled by George M. Finley, Francis Winch, Andrew Andersen, Robin Andersen, and Alan Chaffee. Ithaca: Artcraft of Ithaca, 1972.

"Newfield Town History." Interview of town historian Alan Chaffee by Janice Albright Sturm, January 1996. DHS.

Newman, Jared T. Collection of papers #2157. CU.

Norris, W. Glenn. *Early Explorers and Travelers in Tompkins County.* Ithaca: DHS, 1961.

———. *Old Indian Trails in Tompkins County.* 1944. Rev. ed. Ithaca: DHS, 1969. [Norris, *Indian Trails*]

———. *Origin of Place Names in Tompkins County, The.* 1951. Rev. ed., 3d printing. Ithaca: DHS, 1984. [Norris, *Place Names*]

O'Connor, Lois. Crossroads Comment columns. *IJ,* 1951, 1953.

———. *Finger Lakes Odyssey, A.* Lakemont, N.Y.: North Country Books, 1975.

Official Automobile Blue Book, 1921. Vol. 1: *New York State and Adjacent Canada.* New York and Chicago: Automobile Blue Book Publishing, 1921.

Pakkala, Lorraine. *Yea-God!* Trumansburg, N.Y.: Crossing Press, 1980.

Palmer, Richard F. "Ithaca-Auburn Short Line." Unpaged. DHS.

———. *"Old Line Mail": Stagecoach Days in Upstate New York.* Lakemont, N.Y.: North Country Books, 1977.

Parish, Isabelle H. *It Happened in Lansing.* Ithaca: DHS, 1964.

———. *This, Too, Happened in Lansing.* Ithaca: DHS, 1967.

Penrose, Barbara. "History of the Ulysses Philomathic Library." Typescript, 1985. Historian's files, Town of Ulysses.

Poppensiek, Neil A. "Robert H. Treman State Park—The Hamlet of Enfield Falls." Typescript, 1990. DHS.

Rails North. [Richard Palmer]. Marcellus, N.Y.: Central New York Chapter, National Railway Historical Society, 1971.

Road and Road District Journal. Compiled by Caleb L. Homel, David Brown, and John Applegate. Manuscript, 1825. Enfield.

Roehl, Harvey N. *Cornell & Ithaca in Postcards.* Vestal, N.Y.: Vestal Press, 1986.

Rolfe, Emma. Diary of Emma Rolfe, an Enfield resident, 1896. Enfield.

Roseberry, Cecil R. *Before Cayuga.* Ithaca: Ithaca Journal, 1950.

Sachse, Gretchen. "Around & about Etna." Typescript, 1974. DHS.

Sears, Lydia. *A History of Trumansburg, New York 1792–1967.* Trumansburg, N.Y.: Privately published, 1968.

Seasons of Change: An Updated History of Tioga County, New York. Edited by Thomas C. McEnteer. Owego, N.Y.: Tioga County Legislature, 1990. [SC]

Selkreg, John H., ed. *Landmarks of Tompkins County, New York.* Syracuse: D. Mason, 1894. [Selkreg]

Sexton, John L. *Outline History of Tioga and Bradford Counties in Pennsylvania; Chemung, Steuben, Tioga, Tompkins, and Schuyler in New York, An.* Elmira, N.Y.: Gazette Company, 1885.

Sisler, Carol U. *Cayuga Lake: Past, Present, and Future.* Ithaca: Enterprise Publishing, 1989.

———. *Enterprising Families, Ithaca, New York: Their Houses and Businesses.* Ithaca: Enterprise Publishing, 1986.

Smidt, Rita. "Origins of the Village of Lansing." Typescript, 1990. DHS.

Smith, Julian C. *Breaking Ninety: A History of the Country Club of Ithaca 1900–1989.* Ithaca: Country Club of Ithaca, 1990.

Smith, Clayton W. *History of Religion in the Danby Highlands 1806–1990.* Danby, N.Y.: Danby Federated Church, 1990.

Snodderly, Daniel R. *Ithaca and Its Past.* Rev. ed. Ithaca: DHS, 1984.

Soil Survey of Tompkins County, N.Y. Compiled by F. B. Howe, H. O. Buckman, and H. G. Lewis. Washington: U.S. Department of Agriculture, 1924.

Soil Survey: Tompkins County, New York. Washington: U.S. Department of Agriculture, 1965.

Some Cemeteries of the Between Lakes Country . . . Edited and and compiled by Carl W. Fischer, with Harriet Jackson Swick. 3 vols. Trumansburg, N.Y.: Sponsored by the Trumansburg chapter of the Daughters of the American Revolution, 1974.

Spafford, Horatio Gates. *Gazetteer of the State of New-York.* Albany: H. C. Southwick, 1813. Rpt. Interlaken, N.Y.: Heart of the Lakes Publishing, 1981. [Spafford]

"Speedsville Superspeeders 4-H Club: People, Places and Events of Our Town." Typescript, 1979. DHS.

Spirit of Enterprise, The: Nineteenth Century in Tompkins County. By Gretchen Sachse, Janet Mara, and Gretel Leed. Ithaca: Hinckley Foundation Museum, 1976.

Streeter, N. R. *Gems from an Old Drummer's Grip.* Groton, N.Y.: Published by the author, 1889.

Stringham, Priscilla. "Groton—What Next?" Typescript from course at Cornell University, 1935. Groton Public Library.

They Were Not Well to Do People But Having a Piano Was Important. Interviews with Hungarian immigrants by Eniko Farkas and Betty Whipple. Brochure, 1987. DHS.

Thompson, Sue. "156 Years in Enfield." Typescript, 1976. Enfield.

Thurber, Pamela. "A Study of the Groton Iron Bridge Company: The Preservation of America's Historic Metal Truss Bridges." M.A. thesis, Cornell University, 1984.

Tompkins County Board of Supervisors, proceedings, 1858–1993. DHS.

Tompkins County, New York, Rural Index and Compass System Map with Localized Almanac. Ithaca: Published yearly by Rural Directories.

"Tour of the Village of Danby, October 28, 1978." With Diane VandeBogart, Danby town historian. Pamphlet. DHS.

Treman family collection scrapbooks, XXIV, XXX. CU.

Trumansburg Conservatory of Fine Arts. Brochure.

Trumansburg Free Press. Trumansburg Bicentennial Commemorative Issue, July 1, 1992.

"Twentieth Anniversary—Artificial Breeding in NY State: 1938–1958." Brochure published by Pioneer Cooperative Dairy Cattle Breeding Association, December 1958. Dryden HS.

Ulysses Historical Society, newsletter. January and April 1984.

Ulysses town historian Esther Northrup, files of. Clipping from *Finger Lakes Forum*, August 28, 1985. "Hulda Gould Smith" typescript. Letter to Honorable Clifford Bower from Edward Lutz, May 13, 1964.

"Ulysses Grange #419 History." Typescript. Ulysses Philomathic Library in Trumansburg.

"Unpretty Labels Once Identified Local Villages." *DeWitt Historical Society Bulletin*, vol. 13, no. 2. December 1964.

U.S. Department of Commerce, Bureau of the Census, Decennial Census, 1990.

Van Astine, Jean B. "Festival '76. Dryden New York: The Way It Was 1797–1975." Pamphlet. DHS.

Vaughn, Jane. "A Caroline Valley Farm: 1800–1976." Typescript, [1976]. History room, Town of Caroline.

Warden, Randolph. "Enfield History." Chapter 11, Government.

Warren, S. W. and J. L. McGurk. *Rural Holdings in Dryden.* Ithaca: Cornell University Department of Agricultural Economics, 1949. Dryden HS.

Weber, Eunice D., ed. *A History of Caroline Township in Tompkins County.* [Caroline, N.Y.: Historical Association of Caroline Township, 1976].

Wells, Arthur J. *Remembrances: Stories of a Pennsylvania Farm Boy.* Edited by Lisa Montagne. Interlaken: Heart of the Lakes Publishing, 1992.

Wells, Elizabeth B., and Liese Price Bronfenbrenner. *Albert Force 1897–1970. Free Hollow to Forest Home.* Ithaca: Published by the Albert Force Memorial Fund, 1974.

What They Wrote: 19th Century Documents from Tompkins County, New York. Edited by Carol Kammen. Ithaca: Cornell University Department of Manuscripts and University Archives, 1978.

"William R. George and George Junior Republic Papers: 1807–1967." Edited by Douglas A. Bakken. Ithaca: Cornell University, 1970.

Wilson, Robert J. *The History of the First Baptist Church, Groton, New York, 1806–1856.* Groton, 1956.

Chronology

1600   Iroquois Confederacy is formed from the Mohawk, Oneida, Onondaga, Cayuga, and Seneca nations.

1683   The original New York county of Albany is formed.

1794   Ulysses, comprising the present towns of Ithaca, Dryden, and Enfield, is organized as a town.

1779   Major General John Sullivan's campaign of devastation begins against the Iroquois Confederacy; two troop contingents are sent through the county, destroying Indian settlements.

1789   The Cayuga nation surrenders lands to New York State.

1790   Survey of the Military Tract begins under the direction of Simeon DeWitt.

1794   Watkins and Flint patent is issued.

1801   The state legislature passes a series of acts regulating local government.

1803   Dryden organizes as a town and is set off from Ulysses by an act of the state legislature. A post office is established in 1811.

1804   A charter is granted for the Catskill Turnpike.

1807   A charter is granted to build the Ithaca-Owego Turnpike.

1811   The towns of Caroline, Danby, and Cayuta are organized as part of Tioga County and annexed to Tompkins County on March 22, 1822. Cayuta is renamed Newfield one week later.

1812   War begins between the United States and England, bringing increased commercial activity in the county.

       A New York State law creates a public school system throughout the state, providing for a school within walking distance of every child. Townships receive funding for education in 1813.

1817   Tompkins County is created on April 7 by act of the state legislature. The hamlet of Ithaca is designated as the county seat.

       Town of Division is set off from the Town of Locke and becomes one of the six original towns of Tompkins County. In 1818 the name Division is changed to Groton.

       Town of Lansing is set off from the Town of Genoa.

1818   The original county courthouse is erected in Ithaca.

1820   The earliest state census on record is made.

1821   Towns of Ithaca and Enfield are taken off from Ulysses and created on March 16. Ithaca is incorporated as a village on April 2.

1823   The law annexing Caroline, Danby, and Newfield to Tompkins County becomes official.

1825   Erie Canal opens along its entire length of 363 miles, linking New York City with the Great Lakes.

1826   The Baptist church in Danby is built. In 1896 it becomes the Danby Town Hall.

1827   New York State grants freedom to black slaves.

        The Eight-Square School House is built in the Town of Dryden.

1830   Central Exchange Hotel is constructed in South Lansing (then Libertyville). It soon is renamed Rogues Harbor.

1831   Village of Ithaca sets up its first board of health.

1834   Ithaca & Owego railroad opens officially.

1849   Groton Iron Works is founded.

1850   Congress passes the Fugitive Slave Act.

1851/3 Covered bridge in Newfield is constructed. It is completely restored in 1972.

1852   Elegant farmhouse called Sunnygables is built in the Town of Ithaca.

1854   Old Tompkins County Courthouse is built and used as a courthouse until 1932. Renovated in 1976, it provides county offices and courtrooms today.

        Rose Inn, Italianate-style residence with notable circular staircase, is constructed in North Lansing.

1856   Dryden Agricultural Society is organized and sponsors the Dryden Fair for 62 years.

1857   Village of Dryden becomes the first incorporated village in the Town of Dryden.

1860   Hamlet of Groton Hollow is incorporated as the Village of Groton.

1861   The Civil War begins with firing on Fort Sumter on April 12. It ends four years later with Lee's surrender at Appomattox.

1863   Work begins on the Cornell Public Library, inaugurated in 1866. The building is razed in 1960.

1864,   Major fires devastate the center of Trumansburg.
1871

1865   Gregg and Co. builds its foundry in Trumansburg.

1866   A major fire burns a portion of Dryden's Main Street.

1868   Cornell University opens.

1870   Pennsylvania & Sodus Bay railroad company is chartered.

1871   Geneva, Ithaca & Athens railway runs first train through West Danby. Lines through Newfield are completed in 1872.

1872   Cayuga Lake Railroad opens, with service along the eastern shore of the lake.

1874   Public School Act establishes a system of graded public schools throughout the state, consolidating schools into districts.

        Women's Christian Temperance Union is established in the state.

1875   The major fire devastates the center of Newfield, destroying the town's official records.

        Wooden trestle railroad bridge is built at Motts Corners (later Brookton). Removed in 1889, it is replaced by a steel bridge.

        Ithaca High School opens as a public school.

1876   Catskill Turnpike is abandoned.

        Free Hollow acquires a post office and receives the official name of Forest Home.

        East Ithaca depot opens.

        Groton Carriage Works is formed, remaining in business until 1908.

1877   Groton Iron Bridge Company is formed. In 1887 it reorganizes as the Groton Bridge & Manufacturing Company.

1884   Elmira Cortland & Northern railroad is organized. The Lehigh Valley assumes control of it in 1896.

1887   Freeville is incorporated as a village.

1888   The incorporated Village of Ithaca is chartered as a city.

1890   Ithaca Conservatory of Music is founded by W. Grant Egbert. It becomes Ithaca College in 1931 and builds its campus on South Hill between 1960 and 1965.

1893   Dryden Opera House is built on Library Street.

1894   Renwick Park opens at southeastern end of Cayuga Lake. Purchased by the city, it is renamed Stewart Park in 1921.

        Southworth Library on Dryden's Main Street is completed.

1895   Newfield is incorporated as a village; the charter is dissolved in 1925.

        William R. George founds George Junior Republic in Freeville.

1896   L. C. Smith typewriter company is formed and merges with the Corona Company in 1926 to found L. C. Smith and Corona Typewriters, Inc. The firm becomes Smith-Corona-Marchant in 1958.

1897   Triphammer Bridge is constructed over Fall Creek.

1900   Cayuga Lake Cement Company (formerly Portland Point Cement Company) is founded. The plant closes in 1947.

1901   Newman and Blood purchase land from Franklin Cornell, which will become the Village of Cayuga Heights.

1902   Rural Free Delivery of mail is inaugurated in the county.

1903   Cornell Heights is annexed by the City of Ithaca.

        Outbreak of typhoid fever in Ithaca brings board of health investigation of pollution of Six Mile Creek.

1904   International Salt Company is consolidated.

1905   Borden Milk Plant is built in Dryden.

1912   Ithaca City Hospital is established and is named Ithaca Memorial Hospital in 1926. It becomes a county facility in 1948.

1914   World War I begins and the United States declare war on Germany in 1917. The armistice is signed in November 1918.

1915   Cayuga Heights is incorporated as a village.

Forest Home Chapel is constructed.

1920   Robert H. and Laura Treman give a tract of land to the state containing Enfield Glen. It becomes part of the Finger Lakes Park Commission in 1923 under the name Robert H. Treman State Park.

Forest Home Improvement Association is founded.

1921   Elementary school in Forest Home is constructed. The district becomes part of Ithaca City School District, and the school closes in 1964.

Cayuga Rock Salt Company is formed. In 1970 the facility is purchased by Cargill and modernized.

1924   Robert H. and Laura Treman give land to the state, part of Buttermilk Falls State Park.

1927   Hitchcock Hall, original building of Cayuga Heights School, is erected. In 1956 the school becomes part of Ithaca City School district, and the building is replaced in 1968.

1928   Temple Beth-El, the only Jewish synogogue in the county, is built in downtown Ithaca.

Trumansburg forms its school district.

1929   Stock market crash on October 29 is forerunner of the Great Depression.

1933   Much of Roosevelt's New Deal legislation is passed; the Civilian Conservation Corps and the Resettlement and Land Administration are established.

1935   An enormous flood in early July devastates the county, with lives lost and great damage along all the creeks. The center of Trumansburg is wiped out.

Herman M. Biggs Memorial Hospital opens as county tuberculosis facility. It becomes Tompkins County Hospital in 1948.

Babcock Poultry Farms is founded.

1936   Town of Dryden establishes its school district.

1937   Town of Ithaca's first planning board is appointed.

1939   Town of Newfield forms its school district.

1941   United States enter World War II following the Japanese bombing of Pearl Harbor; the war is over in 1945.

1946   Tompkins County Health Department is inaugurated.

1947   Lakeland Homes apartment complex in Cayuga Heights is constructed.

1948   Lansing schools are centralized, and the town forms its school district.

1953   Ellis Hollow holds its fair for the first time.

1955   Milliken Station of NYSE&G is opened.

1956   Tompkins County Airport opens as a county facility.

Frederick G. Marcham, village trustee since 1954, is elected mayor of Cayuga Heights, serving until 1988.

Schools in Caroline are consolidated into the Ithaca City School District. A new Caroline elementary school is built in 1960.

1961   Cornell University erects a radio telescope in Danby.

1962   Austin MacCormick Center is built as a youth recreation camp.

1964   Brooktondale Community Center is dedicated.

1968   Tompkins County Community College opens in Groton. It moves to its Dryden campus in 1974.

        South Lansing School for Girls opens; it is turned over to the New York State Division for Youth in 1974.

1969   Tompkins County undergoes reapportionment and adopts a charter and code for county government. A county Board of Representatives is set up.

        Tompkins County Public Library is built in downtown Ithaca.

1974   The Village of Lansing is incorporated.

1976   The newly completed Bolton Point water treatment plant starts delivery of water.

1982   Trumansburg Conservatory of Fine Arts is established and locates in the former Baptist church.

1987   Tompkins County administrative complex, housing the sheriff's department and county jail, opens on Warren Road in Lansing.

1990   First Grassroots Festival of Music and Dance is held at the Trumansburg fairgrounds.

1993   Memorial in Ithaca to Alex Haley, author of *Roots*, is dedicated.

1994   A new terminal building and enlarged facilities are opened at the Tompkins County Airport in Lansing.

        A tornado rips through Dryden, taking off the roof of the Empire Livestock Pavilion.

1995   The Tompkins Community Hospital, formerly Tompkins County Hospital, is named Cayuga Medical Center.

        Kendal at Ithaca opens and is formally dedicated in June 1996.

1996   EcoVillage on Ithaca's West Hall opens its first units.

Contributors

Molly Adams has been a resident of Brooktondale since 1963. She has been active in the Brooktondale Community Center and the Ithaca School District PTA and is a longtime member of both Historic Ithaca and the DeWitt Historical Society. Most recently she has served on the Town of Caroline Bicentennial Committee.

Louise Bement has been town historian of Lansing since 1981. A resident of the town since 1969, she taught fourth grade in the Lansing Central School system for nineteen years, and her classes have researched and published four local history booklets. After her retirement from teaching in 1988 she has continued her research and writing on local history and has organized the Lansing Historical Association.

Bruce Brittain was born in Forest Home and has lived most of his life there. He has held several positions with the Forest Home Improvement Association and has served on the board of the DeWitt Historical Society. He is a member of Historic Ithaca, the National Trust for Historic Preservation, the Society for the Preservation of Old Mills, and the Timber Framers Guild.

Jane Marsh Dieckmann has lived in Ithaca since 1966. She is the author of *A Short History of Tompkins County* (1986) and *Wells College: A History* (1995) and was a contributing editor of *Ithaca's Neighborhoods* (1988). Former board member of the DeWitt Historical Society, she continues to be an active volunteer. The author of five cookbooks, she also writes features on music, literature, food, and local history and works as an indexer and copyeditor.

Rachel Dickinson, born and raised in Freeville, is an eighth-generation resident of Tompkins County. She has served as director of the Cortland County Historical Society and as administrative director of Cornell University's Telluride Association. She is currently working as a freelance writer.

Margaret Hobbie is a longtime resident of Tompkins County and a 1972 graduate of Cornell University. From 1983 to 1994 she served as director of the DeWitt

Historical Society and as Tompkins County historian. In 1995 she joined Audrey Edelman real estate where she is currently an associate broker.

S.K. List, a native of New York State, has lived in the Trumansburg area for more than twenty years. She is a former editor at the *Ithaca Times* and contributes to local, regional, and national publications from the *Ithaca Journal* to the *New York Times.* She is co-publisher and editor of *Ithaca Child, the Paper for Parents.*

Linda McCandless is a much-published local writer who has been exploring the Finger Lakes region since coming to Cornell in 1970. She has lived on a small farm in Spencer, near South Danby, since 1979. A former editor of the *Grapevine Weekly* and *Finger Lakes Magazine,* she is currently director of communications at the New York State Agricultural Experiment Station in Geneva.

John Marcham, former city editor of the *Ithaca Journal,* is the retired editor of the *Cornell Alumni News* and has edited the histories of Cornell's athletics, hotel school, and Willard Straight Hall, as well as *Sol Goldberg's Ithaca.* For ten years he served on the Tompkins County Board of Representatives and has been both a trustee and president of the board of the DeWitt Historical Society.

Pamela Monk lives with her family in Renwick Heights. She is a veteran middle school teacher, freelance feature writer, and playwright.

John Munschauer, a Buffalo native and 1940 graduate of Cornell University, retired in 1984 as director of the Career Center after thirty-eight years of service with the university. His *Jobs for English Majors and Other Smart People,* first published in 1982, is still in print. His memoir, *World War II Cavalcade,* came out in 1996.

Carol U. Sisler has lived in Ithaca since 1958. A journalist-historian, she served as executive director of Historic Ithaca from 1973 to 1983. She has researched, written, and published three books on local history and was a contributing editor of *Ithaca's Neighborhoods.* A former board member and president of the DeWitt Historical Society, she currently serves as adviser and active volunteer.

Susan Thompson, a resident of Enfield since 1974, started the Enfield Historical Society with Ellen C. Hobbie in 1992 and became town historian in 1995. Aside from building and maintaining the town's history collection, she participates in community sharing and education projects. She is general editor of the projected Enfield History book.

Index

Page numbers in boldface type refer to illustrations and captions.